The Persian Gulf and United States Policy

# GUIDES TO CONTEMPORARY ISSUES
Richard Dean Burns, Editor

This series has been developed, in part, in cooperation with the Center for the Study of Armament and Disarmament, California State University, Los Angeles.

# THE PERSIAN GULF AND UNITED STATES POLICY:

## A Guide to Issues and References

Bruce R. Kuniholm

Regina Books
Claremont, California

Library of Congress Cataloging in Publication Data

Kunniholm, Bruce Robellet, 1942—
  The Persian Gulf and United States Policy

  (Guides to contemporary issues; #3)
  Bibliography: p.
  Includes index.
  1. Persian Gulf Region — Politics and government. 2. Persian Gulf Region — Politics and government — Bibliography. 3. Persian Gulf Region — Foreign relations — United States. 4. Persian Gulf Region — Foreign relations — United States — Bibliography. 5. United States — Foreign relations — Persian Gulf Region. 6. United States — Foreign relations — Persian Gulf Region — Bibliography. I. Title. II. Series.

DS326.K83    1984          327.73053          84-9853
ISBN 0-941690-12-1
ISBN 0-941690-11-3 pbk

Cover Design by Clinton Wade Graphic Design

Regina Books
P.O. Box 380
Claremont, CA 94711
Manufactured in the United States of America

To Liz

## ACKNOWLEDGEMENTS

Research for this book was conducted in part at the Woodrow Wilson Center for International Scholars in Washington, D.C., where I was a Guest Scholar in 1982. I would like to thank the Wilson Center, Duke University, the Centro Studi sull Difesa, the Lyman L. Lemnitzer Center for NATO Studies, and the United States government, all of whom made it possible to write about and travel extensively throughout the Persian Gulf region in 1983.

# Contents

# PART I

# THE PERSIAN GULF REGION
# AND THE GREAT POWERS

The influence of the great powers on the peoples and political systems of the Persian Gulf has been longstanding and profound. Chapter 1 examines the interplay between external and internal forces in the region, focusing in particular on the rise and decline of Britain's Trucial system. The chapter also delineates how the historical rivalry between Britain and Russia in the Persian Gulf and Southwest Asia* provided the context—just as the gradual decline of the British Empire set the stage—for the emergence of the United States as an important factor in the Middle East.

Chapter 2 traces the process by which the United States gradually took over Britain's role in maintaining the balance of power along the empire's old lifeline. It also underscores the continuity of geopolitical considerations among the great powers. For the West, oil may have replaced trade and empire as a rationale for commitments, but the object of deterrence was still Russia and the lines that were drawn between East and West were more or less the same as those that existed during the imperial rivalries of the past.

The Persian Gulf, meanwhile, played only a marginal role in U.S. strategic thinking. In spite of American oil interests in Saudi Arabia, the Gulf assumed importance in U.S. policy councils only in the late 1960s when, as in the 1940s and 1950s, Britain's continuing withdrawal from the Middle East forced another reassessment of U.S. interests. Reassessment, in turn, precipitated the search for a policy that would allow the United States once again to fill the vacuum created by Britain's departure. The historical forces explored in Chapter 1, conditioned by the changing international circumstances of the 1970s, provide a framework within which to view the events of the last decade. American involvement in the Gulf during this time also provides an instructive lesson on the interplay between external and internal forces in the Gulf for those concerned about U.S. security interests in the region in the 1980s.

---

* Use of the term "Persian Gulf" is best explained by Hermann Eilts:

"The Arab-Iranian nomenclature controversy over the Gulf, which was so bitter in the late 50s and early 60s, was a by-product of the late President

"On his march eastwards from the conquest of Egypt, early in the autumn of 331 B.C. Alexander the Great, having reached the banks of the Euphrates at Thapsacus, and been permitted by the Persian army to cross unopposed, went on to victory at Arbela over Darius Codomanus. Darius, who is reported to have mobilized an army of more than a million men, had awaited Alexander on a plain near the ruins of Nineveh, because he was relying for victory upon his cavalry. Two thousand years later, classically educated Englishmen, remembering his defeat, compared it to the defeat of Crassus by the Parthians at Carrhae. They were ander on the march, and to stop him from crossing the Euphrates.'If the passage of the Euphrates had been properly guarded,' the resident of Baghdad told the British government in 1802, Darius might have been saved.' Over the history of British India these two battles cast long shadows. Bonaparte and Nicholas I were not to be allowed to copy Alexander."
Edward Ingram, *The Beginning of the Great Game in Asia: 1828-1834* (Oxford, 1979), p.143.

Nasser of Egypt's brand of Arab nationalism. It has in recent years been abated by quiet usage of the neutral term 'Gulf' both inside and outside of the Middle East area. Though reluctant to become involved in the dispute, the United States as early as 1960 formally opted for the use of the term 'Persian Gulf' on grounds of long established global usage and without any hegemonial connotation. 'Arabian Gulf' is in fact a recent Arab appellation for that body of water. Some Arab charts of the late 18th-early 19 century refer to it as the 'Gulf of Basra,' a designation drawn from the Arab (Iraqi) port on the Shatt Al-Arab at the head of the Gulf. The term 'Arab Gulf' (not Arabian) was used by the late 18th-early 19th century English and American ship masters to designate the southern reaches of the Red Sea, roughly from Jidda southwards to the Bab Al-Mandab." "Security Considerations in the Persian Gulf," *International Security* 5:2 (1980), p. 79.

The term "Southwest Asia" has been used within the U.S. government since 1979 when, according to former Assistant Secretary of State for Near Eastern and South Asian Affairs Harold Saunders, "it was no longer possible to allow continued use of 'the Middle East problem' as synonymous with 'the Arab-Israeli problem.' 'Southwest Asia' was introduced to broaden the focus to include the problems of the Persian Gulf and those stemming from the Soviet thrust into Afghanistan." Saunders observes that no sharp lines can be drawn and that relations of the states in the region with neighbors such as Turkey and India are on occasion important parts of the picture. *The Middle East Problem in the 1980s* (Washington, D.C.: American Enterprise Institute for Public Policy Research, 1981), p. 83.

# 1

## Great Power Rivalry
## and the British Imperium

### HISTORICAL BACKGROUND

The policies and imperial aspirations of the world's great powers in the Persian Gulf and Southwest Asia have been repeatedly influenced over the centuries by geopolitical considerations. In the sixth century B.C., Cyrus the Great and his successors subjected the civilizations along the region's great river systems—the Tigris, the Euphrates, and the Indus—to the dominion of a Persian Empire that stretched across the Near East from Greece to the frontier of India. Two centuries later the Achaemenid dynasty was conquered by Alexander the Great, who in turn extended his empire from the Balkans to the Indus Valley.

As kingdoms and empires vied for hegemony, indigenous cultures adapted to and in turn were transformed by the various influences to which they were subjected. After Alexander's conquests, the Near East was exposed to Greek and subsequently Roman influence, while the brilliant Sassanid dynasty emerged from its Iranian homeland to overthrow its Parthian overlords and extend its rule to the Arabian Peninsula and the Indus Valley.

Throughout, the Persian Gulf served as a line of communications and a natural channel for trade between the Mediterranean and East Asia. Its mercantile cities rose and fell, contesting among themselves for supremacy in the Gulf, competing with others on the littoral of the Red Sea for trade between East and West, and with them serving as the western termini for trade originating in the Far East.[1]

*The Advent of Islam.* In the seventh century A.D., the Prophet Muhammad and his followers united the Arabian Peninsula. Within a century, Islam radiated westward across the northern shores of Africa to the Iberian Peninsula, and eastward across Persia, which Arab armies defeated at the battles of Qaddissya and Nahavand. Islam eventually

---

1. George Hourani, *Arab Seafaring in the Indian Ocean in Ancient and Medieval Times* (Princeton: Princeton University Press, 1951), p. 4; and Roger Savory, "The History of the Persian Gulf: The Ancient Period," in Alvin Cottrell *et al.*, eds., *The Persian Gulf States: A General Survey* (Baltimore: Johns Hopkins University Press, 1980), pp. 3-13.

reached Central Asia and the subcontinent, where Turks, Afghans, and then Mongols swept through the northwest passes previously traversed by Alexander, carrying a new faith and dominating India. By the early 18th century, the Mughul empire, founded two centuries earlier by Babur, a descendant of Genghis Khan and Timur (Tamerlane), encompassed all but some coastal enclaves and the southern tip of the Indian subcontinent.

Islamic civilization, meanwhile, centered first in Damascus and then in Baghdad, flourished under the Umayyad and Abbasid dynasties. After the accession of the Abbasids to the Caliphate in 750 and the removal of the capital from Damascus to Baghdad, commerce flourished between the Persian Gulf and China, and the sea route between them became the longest in regular use by mankind before European expansion began. By following the monsoons, one could make the round trip in a year and a half.[2]

The Abbasid dynasty gave way, in time, to invaders from the north: first Seljuks; then Mongols under Hulagu, the grandson of Genghis Khan, who captured Baghdad in 1258; and finally the Seljuks' successors, the Ottomans, whose forces, converted to Islam, captured Constantinople in 1453 and brought about the fall of the Byzantine Empire. By the 17th century, the Ottoman Empire extended from North Africa and Eastern Europe to the western shores of the Persian Gulf, while the Gulf's eastern shores came under the jurisdiction of the Safavid dynasty, the founders of modern Iran, whose subjects, weathering both Arab and Mongol invasions, had preserved their separate identity. From this time until the present century, the states of greatest significance to the great powers in the Middle East would be Turkey and Iran.[3]

*The Coming of the Europeans.* The Portuguese, meanwhile, embarking on the voyages of discovery and conquest, rounded the Cape of Good Hope and established trading settlements along the western coast of the Mughul empire in South Asia. With the capture in 1515 of Hormuz, the chief commercial emporium in the Persian Gulf, they inaugurated a century of Portuguese supremacy in the Indian Ocean. Through control of the Red Sea, the Persian Gulf, and the Straits of Malacca, the Portuguese hoped to outflank their competitors and force European trade with the Indies to route itself via the Cape of Good Hope, where they could levy customs and port dues and harass the shipping of rival powers.[4]

---

2. Hourani, pp. 53, 61, 64, 70-75.
3. Savory, pp. 3-13; and Bernard Lewis, ed., *Islam and the Arab World: Faith, People, Culture* (New York: A. Knopf, 1976), p. 16.
4. Savory, "The History of the Persian Gulf: A.D. 600-1800," in Cottrell *et al.*, pp. 14-40.

Within a century, however, the British acquired increasing confidence in their maritime power and successfully contested the Portuguese monopoly in the region. The result was the establishment of the English East India Company in 1600, and the capture of Hormuz in 1622. Surviving a fierce challenge for mercantile supremacy by the Dutch, and subsequently the French, the British by 1765 had become the dominant European power in India and the East India Company a territorial power whose transformation had important implications for the Gulf.[5]

In 1798 the East India Company negotiated an agreement with Sayyid Sultan, head of the Al Bu Said dynasty and ruler of Muscat (Oman). It was the first of an elaborate web of treaties and agreements with the principalities of the Arabian Peninsula littoral that in time would define British hegemony over the first major Gulf system in modern times.[6] The agreement followed Napoleon's occupation of Egypt and resulted from British fear of a French assault on India—launched either from the Suez isthmus with ships from the Ile de France (Mauritius) and the Red Sea; or from the Eastern Mediterranean, overland to the head of the Gulf and then along the coast to India. Complementing the treaty with Oman was another with Persia in 1801 that had two objectives: to threaten the western frontier of Afghanistan, so restraining Zaman Shah, the amir of Kabul, who had invaded India several times; and to create an Iranian buffer against the possibility of an overland attack by Napoleon.[7]

*The "Great Game" and its Consequences for the Gulf.* While these threats had disappeared by the time the treaties were concluded, they raised for the first time the problem of how to ensure the security of British India.[8] After French operations in the Indian Ocean were brought to an end by the capture of the Ile de France in 1810, and following Napoleon's defeat at Waterloo in 1815, perceptions of the threat posed by France gradually gave way to that posed by Russia. The latter was expanding eastward by land as Europe's maritime states had by sea. By 1818 the British had destroyed the power of the principal Indian states, replaced the Mughul empire as the paramount power in India, and secured a continuous land frontier.[9] But when Russia acquired

---

5. Malcolm Yapp, "The History of the Persian Gulf: British Policy in the Persian Gulf," in Cottrell *et al.*, p.71.
6. Rouhollah Ramazani, *The Persian Gulf and the Strait of Hormuz* (Alphen aan den Rijn, The Netherlands: Sijthoff & Noordhoff, 1979), p. 25.
7. J.B. Kelly, *Britain and the Persian Gulf, 1795-1880* (Oxford: Clarendon Press, 1968), pp. 62-68, 96; and Yapp, pp. 72-73.
8. Edward Ingram, *The Beginning of the Great Game in Asia, 1828-1834* (Oxford: Clarendon Press, 1979), p. 4; Kelly, p.73.
9. Malcolm Yapp, *Strategies of British India: Britain, Iran and Afghanistan, 1798-1850* (Oxford: Clarendon Press, 1980), p. 584; Kelly, pp.73, 96-97.

valuable land from northwest Persia and eastern Turkey in the Treaties of Turkmanchay and Adrianople (1828 and 1829), the British became anxious about their new frontiers. Having failed to create protectorates in either Persia or Turkey, they sought to devise a counterweight to Russian influence. Thus began the so-called "Great Game" in Asia, derived from both geography and politics: the British had a frontier to defend and they could find no one to defend it for them. Lacking a geographical equivalent of the English channel, they looked for a political equivalent. Eventually they attempted to construct a zone of buffer states from Turkey through Persia to Khiva and Bokhara—recognized by both Russia and Britain as independent, possessing recognized boundaries, and preserved by equal British and Russian pressures.[10]

While the Great Game was in its infancy, the imperatives of territorial dominion in India were leading the British to obtain and hold command of the Gulf.[11] Implicit in their thinking was the notion that British seapower in the Gulf and Eastern Mediterranean could balance that of Russia in the Black Sea and the Caspian. The immediate target of British seapower, the Qawasim of Ras al-Khaimah and Sharjah, controlled several ports on both sides of the Gulf and were renown for their sailing skills. Deprived of considerable trade by the Cape passage and possessing few natural resources (oil was not discovered until the twentieth century), the tribal chiefs of the Gulf's small city-states were locked in a fierce maritime rivalry with the Al Bu Said dynasty of Muscat (which was also embroiled in a civil war with the conservative religious leaders of Oman's interior) over what little the Gulf itself had to offer: pearl fisheries and trade with India and Africa.[12]

---

10. Ingram, pp. 5, 13, 14, 17, 50, 328, 337-339. David Fromkin points out that tsarist expansion against the Islamic Asian regimes on the Russian frontier was not undertaken for the purpose of thwarting Britain: "It had begun before the British came to Asia, and would have continued whether the British had arrived or not." In this sense, he observes, it was similar to U.S. expansion westward in the nineteenth century, which was regarded as a national destiny that seemed manifest. Fromkin argues that Russian expansion, while not directed against Britain, without British opposition might have led to the incorporation of Persia, and so would have endangered Britain's internationsl interests. British expansion, therefore, was directed at Russia, for whom the British threat was equally real. As a result, he concludes, the Great Game in Asia "was played for real stakes, and not merely imaginary ones — the unjustified fears and mutual misunderstandings upon which historians tend to focus." David Fromkin, "The Great Game in Asia," *Foreign Affairs* 58:4 (1980), pp. 936-951. See also Chapter 5, n. 9.

11. Kelly, pp. 1-2.

12. Ingram, p. 326. For a brief discussion of trade in the Gulf, see Donald Hawley, *The Trucial States* (London: Allen & Unwin, 1970), pp. 118-120. While the feuding between these tribes is too complicated by and intertwined

The Qasimi naval confederacy, which was much larger than the 80-100 dhows of its Qawasim core, boasted a fleet of 63 large and 810 small vessels, many of which were faster and more easily handled than European ships. The largest, used for both trading and raiding, were between 200 and 500 tons, had crews of 150 men, and carried enormous sails—one British observer considered them equal to a 36-gun frigate. The Saidi opponents of the Qawasim had three brigs and 15 ships of between 400 and 700 tons, in addition to a smaller fleet of 100 sea-going vessels. Although the British were suspicious of Muscat's links with the French on Mauritius, developing ties with the Al Bu Said were reinforced by a desire to prevent Napoleon's acquisition of a base in the Gulf, and resulted in assistance to the Al Bu Said in their war with the Qawasim.[13]

While the Qawasim did not usually harm European crews, they were nonetheless responsible for numerous attacks on British vessels. They also attacked Indian merchant ships flying British colors, whose crews they sometimes put to death. As the war with the Al Bu Said continued, the Qawasim, encouraged in their actions by a moral imperative to proclaim *jihad* (holy war) which derived from the Wahhabi religious revival in the heartland of the Arabian Peninsula, were emboldened to step up their attacks on merchant vessels—twenty in November 1808 alone—and demand tribute for safe passage.

Britain, its imperial consciousness stimulated by a petition from the merchants of Bombay, in 1809 launched an expeditionary force to rid

with tribal migrations and splits to go into here, suffice it to observe that the Al Bu Said were descended from the Hinawiyah, a southwest Arabian stock (also designated as Qahtani or Yemeni) originating in Yemen and generally considered to be among the first wave of settlers on the Gulf littoral in the first millenium B.C. The Qawasim were descended from or allied with the Ghafiriyah (also designated as Adnani or Nizari), who originated in central and eastern Arabia and migrated to the Omani hinterland and the Trucial Coast in the fourth and fifth centuries A.D. In the eighteenth century, tribes in the area from the Trucial Coast to Oman aligned themselves with one or another tribal faction. Tribes in the interior of Oman tended to align themselves with the Ghafiri faction, the Al Bu Said with the Hinawi faction. Along the Trucial Coast, the Qawasim in Ras al-Khaimah and Sharjah aligned themselves with the Ghafiri faction (against the Al Bu Said) while their rivals the Bani Yas (in Abu Dhabi and Dubai) aligned themselves with the Hinawi. For insight into the tribal alignments in the Arabian Peninsula, see Robert G. Landen, *Oman Since 1856: Disruptive Modernization in a Traditional Arab Society* (Princeton: Princeton University Press, 1967), pp. 34-37, 58-60; Christine Helms, *The Cohesion of Saudi Arabia: Evolution of Political Identity* (Baltimore: Johns Hopkins University Press, 1981), pp. 51-60; Hawley, pp. 42-43, 80-84, 97, 147, 150, 179; J.B. Kelly, *Arabia, the Gulf and the West: A Critical View of the Arabs and their Oil Policy* (New York: Basic Books, 1980),pp. 107-108.

the Gulf of "piracy." Piracy, as one historian has observed, like treason, is a relative term; but, however one characterizes the maritime war among the Gulf states, and between the Qawasim and the British, it is clear that Britain intended to look out for its interests in Oman and preserve its prestige at sea. A brief occupation of Ras al-Khaimah coupled with the destruction there and across the Gulf of some 70 dhows allowed for a respite that was only temporary since most of the Qasimi fleet escaped.

Within a few years, East India Company vessels again were attacked. As the small city-states around the Gulf joined in, convoys of merchant ships from India were forced to run a gauntlet of Qasimi dhows in the Strait of Hormuz. Making use of a growing sea power to enforce their will, the British in 1819 mounted another expedition to the Gulf to break the power of the Qawasim. With 11 ships carrying 200 guns, and a force of 1,453 Europeans, 2,094 Indian sepoys, and 600 Omanis, the British expeditionary force destroyed fortifications, vessels and military stores at Ras al-Khaimah and 11 other sites on both sides of the Gulf, forcing the leading sheiks of the Pirate Coast (subsequently the Trucial Coast) to submit to the British commander and proffer friendship.[14]

## BRITAIN'S TRUCIAL SYSTEM, 1820-1971

Judging that peace would depend on cooperation within the Gulf as well as on the vigilance of Britain's naval and military forces, the British commander opted against a punitive settlement. The General Treaty for the Cessation of Plunder and Piracy by Land and Sea, signed by the sheikhs of the Trucial Coast and Bahrain between January and March 1820, ended coastal attacks against British shipping and served as the cornerstone of British policy in the Gulf for the next 151 years. Although the treaty avoided harsh treatment of the sheikhdoms and protected British shipping, it did not prevent maritime war between the tribes. A subsequent treaty in 1835 established a maritime truce during the six month pearling season and was renewed periodically until the Perpetual Maritime Truce in 1853 made permanent a complete cessation of hostilities at sea.[15]

---

13. Hawley, pp. 90-102, 121-122; Kelly, *Britain and the Persian Gulf,* pp. 109-111, 134.

14. Kelly, *Britain and the Persian Gulf,* pp. 65-66, 99-154; Hawley, pp. 90, 102-129. See Kelly, p. 363 n., for the origins of the term "Trucial Coast."

15. Kelly, *Britain and the Persian Gulf,* p. 159; Hawley, pp. 126-141, 314-318; Rosemarie Said Zahlan, *The Origins of the United Arab Emirates: A Political and*

In 1879 another agreement provided for the maritime extradition of debtors. It was also crucial to the stability of the pearling business, which by the 1870's employed a considerable number of Gulf workers—including 1,500 vessels and 42,000 men from Oman, and 713 vessels and 13,500 men from Bahrain. Other agreements attempted to prohibit the slave trade, which annually brought 10-15,000 slaves into the Gulf in the first half of the 19th century. The slave trade was reduced to a trickle by the 1870's, but because it provided divers for the pearling industry, it continued well into the twentieth century, ending only after the Gulf pearl industry foundered in the face of competition from the cultured pearl industry in Japan. Further agreements with the British addressed communications issues and prohibition of the importation of arms.[16]

As the 19th century wore on, Britain, in addition to initiating the complex of treaties and agreements described above, assumed increasing responsibility for the defense of the sheikhdoms. In 1892, it consolidated previous arrangements in the Exclusive Agreement, under which the coastal states promised not to enter into any agreement or correspondence with any power other than Great Britain. Britain, in turn, agreed to provide for the external defense of the Trucial states and look after their foreign relations. By the end of World War I, in spite of challenges—both real and perceived—from France, Turkey, Russia, and Germany, Britain clearly was the dominant power in the Gulf. Germany, Russia, and the Ottoman Empire had been defeated; Iran and Iraq, apparently, were at Britain's mercy; while Bahrain and Qatar had been brought into the Trucial system, and Kuwait guaranteed independence under a British protectorate.[17]

---

*Social History of the Trucial States* (New York: St. Martin's, 1978), p. xii. In 1839 the British occupation of Aden blocked Mehmet Ali's army in Yemen and precluded his obtaining command over passage through the Red Sea and the "overland" route to the East. British intervention in Syria also helped to deny him command of the "direct" route from the Eastern Mediterranean to the head of the Persian Gulf in 1840. J.B. Kelly notes the similarity between Mehmet Ali's tactics and those of Nasser in the 1960s. J.B. Kelly, *Arabia, the Gulf and the West*, pp. 240-241.

16. Hawley, pp. 316-321; Kelly, *Britain and the Persian Gulf*, pp. 414-417, 831, 834; Zahlan, pp. 8, 180.

17. Briton Cooper Busch, *Britain and the Persian Gulf, 1894-1914* (Berkeley: University of California Press, 1967), pp. 384-386; Kelly, *Britain and the Persian Gulf*, pp. 407-409; Hawley, pp. 138, 159, 181, 320-321; Zahlan, p. 17; Malcolm Yapp, "The History of the Persian Gulf: The Nineteenth and Twentieth Centuries," in Alvin Cottrell *et al.*, p. 59.

# RUSSIAN AND BRITISH EXPANSION IN ASIA 1801-1907

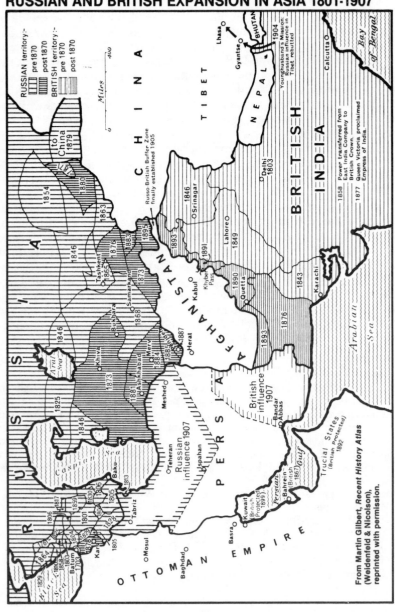

From Martin Gilbert, *Recent History Atlas* (Weidenfeld & Nicolson), reprinted with permission.

British policy toward the Gulf throughout this period does not seem to have been consistently informed by any one strategic theme except, perhaps, a general belief, held since 1798, that India's defense must be as far away from India and as cheap as possible. A corollary was that bases in the Gulf must be denied to other foreign powers and that a foreign presence in the Gulf could excite unrest in India. While the defense of India, the maintenance of lines of communication, and economic interest all played a part in British attitudes toward the Gulf, these objectives rationalized a general and more fundamental perception that peace in the Gulf was required. Since regional powers had failed to keep the peace, Britain assumed the responsibility. British policy, whether formulated primarily by the East India Company, the Government of Bombay (after 1858), the British India Government (after 1878), or the Foreign Office in London (which after the British withdrawal from India in 1947 had sole jurisdiction), was carried out through an economy of force: a political resident in Bushire (in Bahrain after World War II); a few agents in various towns; a British squadron of six cruisers that patrolled the Gulf; and the Indian army—meant not to fight but to exist and overawe. As with British India, "judicious coercion," in conjunction with the appearance of unassailable British power was expected to effect British ends. In the Gulf this meant preservation of the status quo—as long as the effort did not become too costly.[18]

*The Era of British "Predominance".* A British historian, writing of the Persian Gulf during the 19th and 20th centuries, has characterized its history as a product of the relationships among the geographically isolated local powers of the Gulf coast; regional powers centered in Baghdad, Riyadh and Teheran; and international powers such as the Ottoman Empire, Egypt, France, Germany, Russia, the United States and Britain.[19] Central to an understanding of the dynamics of these relationships is the fact that British predominance, more limited than many supposed, was confined generally to the lesser powers of the Lower Gulf. Regional powers such as Iran, Iraq, and Saudi Arabia had sufficient geographical advantages, resources, and energies to avoid complete domination. But until these countries were able to assert themselves, as they did later in the 20th century, they were otherwise preoccupied: first with the problem of survival; and subsequently with the need to provide security for their oil, as well as with the difficulties that accompanied internal modernization. Under these circumstances,

---

18. Yapp, "British Policy in the Persian Gulf," p. 98; *Strategies of British India,* pp. 13, 585; Ingram, pp. 332, 334; Zahlan, pp. xiii, 21; Hawley, pp. 164-166.
19. Yapp, "The Nineteenth and Twentieth Centuries," pp. 41-42.

the status quo prevailed and the illusion of British supremacy was perpetuated by the framework of consent within which the British exercised their influence.[20]

On the local level, the stability created by British control reinforced the paternalistic and authoritarian leadership of the coastal states. It also helped to preserve the region's traditional socio-political organization, which was characterized by a complicated and delicate balance of power among tribal dynasties. Saidi and Qasimi commercial activities, meanwhile, declined with the loss of their respective advantages in controlling the Gulf's trade routes. The Bani Yas tribal confederation of Abu Dhabi and Dubai correspondingly benefited from its relatively greater power on land; by the 1870s the ruling sheikh of Abu Dhabi was the most powerful sheikh in the region, and Dubai had begun to rival Sharjah as the principal port on the coast. Regardless of relative losses and benefits, the ruling factions of the small city states were protected by the British from absorption by their neighbors and collectively enhanced their prestige. While engaged in a confusing complex of feuds, intrigues, raids and wars, the tribal chiefs, most of whom in the early 19th century could hardly be called rulers, gradually came to acquire the authority sufficient to merit the title.[21]

Following World War I and the break-up of the Ottoman Empire, although most peoples of the Middle East gradually achieved independence, the Trucial states, under British protection, remained isolated from events in the region. Oil had been discovered in commercial quantities in Persia in 1908, and the British Government in 1914 had acquired a controlling interest in the Anglo-Persian Oil Company. These events presaged the development of the region's oil resources and pointed to the Gulf's new strategic significance, but they did not immediately affect the smaller Gulf states. With the exception of Bahrain (1932) and Kuwait (1938), oil was not discovered in commercial quantities in the smaller Gulf states until after World War II. As a result, the evolution of the sheikhdoms continued at a slow pace until the 1960s.[22]

---

20. Yapp, "The Nineteenth and Twentieth Centuries," pp. 58-61; "British Policy in the Persian Gulf," pp. 82, 88-89, 98; Zahlan, pp. 19, 21.

21. John Duke Anthony, *Arab States of the Lower Gulf: People, Politics, Petroleum* (Washington, D.C.: The Middle East Institute, 1975), p. 4; Hawley, pp. 142-146; Zahlan, pp. xi-xiii, 1, 9-11, 196-199; Yapp, "The Nineteenth and Twentieth Centuries," p. 66.

22. Zahlan, pp. 18, 190-204; Anthony, p. 4; Hawley, p. 146; Keith McLachlan, "Oil in the Persian Gulf," in Cottrell *et al.*, pp. 202-205.

*Gradual Demise of the Trucial System.* British withdrawal from India in 1947, meanwhile, eliminated the basis of Britain's responsibility as an imperial power and transferred responsibility for British policy from the government in India to the Foreign Office. Although the Gulf provided 85% of Britain's crude petroleum imports by the end of the decade, and protection of the Gulf oilfields had begun to emerge as an important concern, Whitehall was preoccupied with events elsewhere. As a result, Britain's unchallenged position in the Gulf left its purposes east of Suez undefined and its military presence unquestioned. In place of an integrated strategic doctrine, Whitehall simply assumed that Britain could remain in a position to influence developments in the Indian Ocean.[23]

Britain's decision in 1954 to withdraw its 80,000 troops from Egypt and the Suez crisis in 1956, however, challenged this assumption and significantly affected the Foreign Office's strategic thinking. The Suez crisis, like the Iranian crisis for the United States a quarter of a century later, provided a reference point for those advocating improvements in Britain's military capabilities: increased airlift capabilities, larger strategic reserves, and development of amphibious forces. More important, however, was the fact that restrictions on staging and overflight rights during the 1956 crisis called into question the reliability of any air route passing over the Middle East. As a consequence, military strategists began to focus on the desirability of stationing reserve elements on foreign bases in order to avoid dependence on precarious sea and air links. In the interim, public clamour for defense retrenchment and concommitant pressures to reduce manpower were resolved by a decision to abolish National Service (discussed below), an increased emphasis on smaller, better-equipped, more mobile conventional forces, and a greater reliance on nuclear deterrence.

The result of these developments was the creation of a more elaborate defense establishment "East of Suez." The British increased expenditures on their three major bases in Kenya, Singapore, and Aden; they also undertook smaller expansion projects, creating permanent accommodations for British troops and forward facilities for operations at

---

23. Phillip Darby, *British Defense Policy East of Suez, 1947-1968* (London: Oxford University Press, 1973), pp. 5, 22-26; Hawley, p. 168. Kelly notes the "considerable difference in outlook between the British foreign and colonial services, the guiding spirit of the one being accommodation [diplomacy and reconcilation of opposing interests], and that of the other, consolidation [a sense of responsibility and a habit of authority]." Kelly argues that when the Foreign Office assumed the duties of the India Office, it inherited neither the spirit nor the outlook of the Indian Civil Service. Kelly, *Arabia, the Gulf and the West*, pp. 37, 97-99.

Bahrain and Sharjah. In addition, the British established elements of a strategic reserve in Kenya and Singapore, and based a balanced fleet at Singapore. They prepositioned heavy equipment and supplies at selected points and they stationed an Amphibious Warfare Squadron at Aden, which became headquarters of a separate integrated command, responsible directly to London. By 1964 the Middle East Command had 8,000 members of the British armed forces, not counting dependents, in its garrison.[24]

Behind the arguments about commitments, alliances, peacekeeping and economic interest that explained Britain's role east of Suez, two considerations appear to have been central: British troops were already in the region and the Foreign Office continued to think of Britain as a world power. The armed services were also committed to this line of thinking, and as they were continually engaged in military campaigns east of Suez, they were not inclined to question it. As a result, Britain supported the independence of the oil-producing states during renewed violence and unrest in 1958; it also supported Kuwait (from which it received half of its oil needs in the late 1950s) against Iraqi threats in 1961. The 45 ships Britain deployed in the Gulf on ten days notice, whether or not they were crucial in deterring Iraqi designs, appeared to justify the overseas deployment of British power.[25]

By this time, however, doubts about overseas bases in an era of decolonization had begun to surface. As Britain's military burdens in Malaysia, Indonesia, and Aden became more costly, severe strains within the defense establishment provided evidence that those burdens would overtake the resources available. To make matters worse, the rising tide of nationalist opposition, initially thought to be decades away, proved closer than many had realized. The Labor Party, determined not to relinquish Britain's peacekeeping role and committed to cuts in defense spending, began to discover after its return to office in October 1964 that the two were incompatible. Throughout the next four years British defense policy east of Suez was driven by economic issues. The military demands and political ineffectiveness of United States involvement in Vietnam, together with a growing conviction within the British government that Britain's interests were primarily European, encouraged a reassessment of Britain's overseas role. The catalyst was Britain's deteriorating balance of payments position and the government's consequent determination to reduce overseas defense expenditures.[26]

24. Darby, pp. 94-95, 101-108, 118-126, 175, 280-281; R. J. Gavin, *Aden Under British Rule, 1839-1967* (London: Hurst, 1975), p. 344.
25. Darby, pp. 154-156, 219-221, 331.
26. Darby, pp. 209-216, 241-242, 283-284, 309, 317, 328-329. For a critical

A decision in 1957 to abolish National Service—implemented in 1962—resulted in a 50% reduction in manpower in the army. The growing cost of new weapons systems was compounded by a growing reluctance in the country to bear the burden of empire. Britain's increasing loss of influence over the Gulf's regional powers in the 1950s, while not paralleled in its relations with the smaller Gulf states, indicated a trend in Britain's relations with the world "East of Suez." In 1961 the British gave up their protectorate in Kuwait, and their control in the Gulf was reduced to Bahrain, Qatar, Oman, and the Trucial states. As well-armed guerrillas in the Yemen rendered old methods of control increasingly ineffective, and the base in Aden increasingly provoked the unrest it was intended to prevent, the government decided to withdraw from Aden. By this time a retreat from a world role had become an accepted aim within the British government; debate focused not on whether withdrawal should occur, but on how it should take place and at what rate. On November 29, 1967, the last British troops departed from Aden, and the stage was set for the end of the last important vestige of the nineteenth century's *Pax Britannica*.[27]

*Britain's Departure from the Gulf.* On January 16, 1968 ("Black Tuesday" to the British Ministry of Defense), Prime Minister Harold Wilson announced that British forces would be withdrawn from East of Suez before the end of 1971. Thereafter, he noted, Britain would retain no special forces for use in the area, relying instead on a general capability, based in Europe, to be deployed overseas as circumstances required.[28]

The political maneuvering that took place over the next three years was intense and deserves brief attention if only to convey a sense of the complex interplay between external and internal forces in the Gulf.[29]

---

account of the Labor Party's perceptions and political judgments of South Arabia, see Kelly, *Arabia, the Gulf and the West*, pp. 1-46.

27. Darby, pp. 103-108, 115-116, 162, 201, 297-298, 309, 328-330; Gavin, pp. 347-348; David Holden, *Farewell to Arabia* (London: Faber & Faber, 1966), pp. 17-68; Yapp, "British Policy in the Persian Gulf," pp. 95-98; David Holden, "The Persian Gulf: After the British Raj," *Foreign Affairs* 49:4 (1971), p.721.

28. Darby, p. 325.

29. The family and tribal feuding that is characteristic of the Gulf as a whole (personalities are more important than abstract ideas) has been aptly characterized by John Duke Anthony who notes that characteristically, owing to their territorial claims, the rulers of the sheikhdoms "have had poor relations with their immediate neighbors and good relations with the Ruler just beyond. This leapfrog pattern of good and bad relations has resulted in a sense of mutual animosity permeating both sides of nearly every frontier" within the emirates. Anthony, *Arab States of the Lower Gulf*, pp. 109, 111. See also David Long, *The Persian Gulf*, pp. 45-46.

While the smaller oil-producing sheikhdoms under British protection (Qatar, Bahrain, Abu Dhabi, and Dubai) wanted Britain to stay and were willing to pay the $35-40 million annual cost of retaining British forces in the Gulf, the Gulf's major powers (Iran, Iraq, and Saudi Arabia) insisted that Britain honor its commitment to withdraw. The Conservative Party in Britain, meanwhile, hoped to put a stop to the decision, and after its return to power in June 1970 attempted to see if it was either practicable or desirable to reverse Labor policy. In the interim, the Foreign Office suggested that the Gulf rulers form a federation to insure at least a measure of mutual protection. As a result, the rulers of Bahrain, Qatar, and the Trucial states in February 1968 duly signed an agreement to establish a Federation of Arab Emirates.[30]

Negotiations toward federation, however, were impeded by several factors. The Shah opposed the move because he saw it as a guise for the retention of British influence; he also claimed sovereignty over Bahrain (primarily as a bargaining chip for other interests in the Gulf) and saw British influence as an impediment to realization of his ambitions.[31] The Trucial states and Qatar, in turn, were unwilling to put themselves in a position of having to support Bahrain against Iranian claims; hence, they were wary of any federation that included Bahrain. They were also concerned that Bahrain's relatively large population (200,000) and thriving economy would dominate the federation. To make matters worse, the Al Thani dynasty of Qatar had a longstanding territorial dispute with the ruling Al Khalifa of Bahrain over the Hawar Islands and Zubarah (a village on the northwest coast of the Qatari peninsula).

Qatar and Bahrain, on the other hand, had good relations with Saudi Arabia; Bahrain in particular counted on Saudi support against Iran. Since federation with Abu Dhabi (the wealthiest of the Trucial states) would put Qatar and Bahrain in the position of having to support Abu Dhabi in an ongoing territorial dispute with Saudi Arabia, the sheikhdoms were reluctant to join. The Saudis, for their part, insisted on satisfaction of territorial claims in eastern Arabia before acquiescing in the creation of the federation. There were other complications, but these give a fair sample of the difficulties involved.

---

30. David Holden, "The Persian Gulf: After the British Raj," pp. 721-735; J.B. Kelly, *Arabia, the Gulf and the West,* p. 53.

31. Rouhollah Ramazani notes that Iran used the claim to Bahrain from the very start as a bargaining chip for Abu Musa and the Tunbs. Rouhollah Ramazani, *Iran's Foreign Policy: 1941-1973: A Study of Foreign Policy in Modernizing Nations* (Charlottesville: University Press of Virginia, 1975), p. 411. The Shah pursued a strategy of accommodation with as many Middle Eastern states as possible to avoid condemnation for anticipated acquisition of Abu Musa and the Tunbs, pp. 421-427.

Conservative opposition to Labor policies in Britain, meanwhile, gave hope to the rulers of the smaller Gulf states that they might yet retain British protection. This hope, given new life by Conservative support for the palace coup in Oman in July 1970, caused the rulers to drag their feet in negotiations toward federation. The British-supported coup in Oman, however, was intended primarily to stabilize the unravelling political situation there prior to Britain's departure from the region. Ultimately, the Conservatives realized that the decision to depart from the Gulf could not be reversed. As the eminent journalist David Holden noted at the time, "to retain British forces in the Gulf once their withdrawal had been promised would have done more than any other single thing to promote the disorder which their continued presence would have been designed to prevent."[32]

With British encouragement Abu Dhabi eventually was induced to concede some of the Saudi claims. Iranian claims were a more difficult matter. The Shah, in return for giving up his claim to Bahrain, insisted on sovereignty over three small islands in the Gulf—Abu Musa (administered by Sharjah) and the Greater and Lesser Tunbs (administered by Ras al-Khaimah). He coveted these islands because they were strategically located and would increase Iran's share of oil exploration rights on the continental shelf. As a consequence, the Iranian government informed Britain that it would not recognize the proposed federation of smaller Arab states unless its demands for the islands were met. After indications that the ruler of Sharjah would accommodate the Shah and a compromise on Abu Musa could be reached, the way was paved for the creation of the United Arab Emirates (UAE), which was proclaimed on July 17, 1971 (albeit without the participation of Ras al-Khaimah, which would not compromise on the Tunbs). Bahrain, which refused to be part of the federation, declared its independence on August 14, and Qatar followed suit on September 1, 1971.[33]

A tacit agreement between Iran and Britain, meanwhile, provided that Britain would not oppose Iranian occupation of Abu Musa and the Tunbs, and that Iran would not attempt to occupy the islands until December 1, 1971 — *after* the British treaties with the Trucial states were abrogated and Britain's obligations to protect them had ceased.

---

32. Kelly, *Arabia, the Gulf and the West*, pp. 53-59, 81-82, 141-42; Holden, pp. 724-730. Another factor complicating agreement among the rulers had to do with perceived caste differences. See the discussion of these differences by Anthony, *Arab States of the Lower Gulf*, p. 69. On the subject of withdrawal, Holden, p. 729, notes that the value of British troops had proved illusory.

33. Kelly, *Arabia, the Gulf and the West*, pp. 87-94; and Long, *The Persian Gulf*, pp. 48-49.

The UAE, scheduled to be inaugurated on December 2, would have no obligation to support Ras al-Khaimah's claims on the Tunbs because the latter was not part of the federation. As it turned out, Iran occupied the three islands on November 30, 1971, while British protection was still in force, but it made no difference. Aside from a few casualties among a police detachment from Ras al-Khaimah (which eventually joined the UAE in February 1972) and rhetorical protests from most of the Arab states, the main consequences were Libya's nationalization of the British Petroleum Company's assets and concessions, and Iraq's break in relations with Britain and Iran (to which Iraq expelled 60,000 Iranians). With the departure of Britain's 6,000 ground troops from Bahrain and Sharjah, and the emergence of the Gulf sheikhdoms as states, the question that now posed itself was how the Gulf's pluralistic power system would work and what system of security would replace the apparent vacuum in the Gulf.[34]

---

34. Kelly, *Arabia, the Gulf and the West*, pp. 95-103; and Ramazani, *The Persian Gulf and the Strait of Hormuz*, pp. 26, 28.

# 2

## The American Experience

The administration of President Lyndon B. Johnson took strong exception to Britain's decision to withdraw from the Gulf, although not necessarily for the reasons that many suppose. Secretary of Defense Robert McNamara opposed a U.S. presence in the Indian Ocean on the grounds that the United States Navy did not need commitments in another ocean. Secretary of State Dean Rusk wanted Britain to maintain its presence in the Gulf because he believed the United States needed a major ally in carrying out its global responsibilities. The Gulf itself, however, played a relatively insignificant role in U.S. strategic thinking up to that time. In January 1968, it appeared that the United States was seeking to *avoid* having to fill the "vacuum" created by Britain's departure. Instead it contemplated a security arrangement among the region's larger states (i.e., Iran, Turkey, Pakistan, Saudi Arabia and Kuwait).[1] By 1971, when the British withdrawal took place, the states among which a security arrangement was contemplated had been narrowed to Iran and Saudi Arabia.

### HISTORICAL BACKGROUND

*The Truman Doctrine.* From World War II, when the Persian Corridor played an important part in the supply of lend-lease goods to Russia, to 1971, when the British withdrew from the Gulf, the United States generally regarded the Persian Gulf (with the important exception of Saudi Arabia) as primarily a British preserve. Nevertheless, the steady decline of Britain's position in the Middle East gradually led the United States to assume Britain's role in maintaining the balance of power along the empire's old lifeline. Thus, in the 1940s, as Britain was forced to contemplate withdrawal from its empire, including Palestine, India, and Burma, Whitehall's decision to cease supporting Greece and Turkey led President Truman to enunciate the Truman Doctrine. In doing so, he implicitly commited the United States to maintaining the

---

1. Darby, 294-95, 325; Ramazani, *Iran's Foreign Policy,* p. 409. For a contemporary examination of the possibility that serious conflict would result from Britain's 1971 military withdrawal from the Gulf, see *The Gulf: Implications of British Withdrawal*, Special Report Series: No. 8 (Washington, D.C.: Georgetown, Feb. 1969).

balance of power in a region that previously had been virtually outside its cognizance and within the British empire's sphere of influence. By the early 1950s, the United States government had come to view the balance of power in the Near East as directly related to the balance of power in Europe and saw Turkey as the linchpin. As a result, President Truman supported incorporation of Greece and Turkey into the NATO alliance.[2]

*The Eisenhower Doctrine.* In the 1950s, Britain's decision to leave Egypt and to look instead to Iraq as a secure alternative for maintaining a political-military presence in the Middle East, led Secretary of State John Foster Dulles to encourage development of a regional defense arrangement in the Middle East's "Northern Tier" states. While Turkey, Iraq, Pakistan, Iran, and Britain became members of the Baghdad Pact in 1955, the United States did not. To do so, it was felt, might have limited U.S. influence with Arab states other than Iraq; it also would have allied the United States with Iraq, which was officially at war with Israel. Following the debacle over Suez in 1956, President Eisenhower promulgated the Eisenhower Doctrine to fill the void created by Britain's withdrawal and to serve notice that the United States would defend the Middle East against a perceived Soviet threat.

The Eisenhower Doctrine extended the containment policy from the Northern Tier states to the Middle East in general, and Congress subsequently authorized use of armed force to assist non-Communist Middle Eastern nations threatened by armed aggression from any country controlled by international communism. Rooted in a misperception of regional problems and a mistaken assumption of the preeminence of the Communist threat, the Eisenhower Doctrine ultimately foundered: instabilities in the region were neither caused by the Soviet Union nor capable of being deterred by the application of power. This was brought home by the revolution in Iraq in 1958 and Iraq's formal withdrawal from the Baghdad Pact in 1959. The American response was to restructure the Northern Tier concept of buffer states by negotiating executive agreements with Turkey, Pakistan, and Iran in what was now called the Central Treaty Organization (CENTO). U.S. obligations were to take such action, including the use of armed forces, as was mutually agreed upon—and as was envisaged in the Eisenhower Doctrine. Although not constituting a formal guarantee of their security, the bilateral agreements effectively institutionalized American military support to the CENTO countries.[3]

2. See Bruce Kuniholm, *The Near East Connection: Greece and Turkey in the Reconstruction and Security of Europe, 1946-1952* (Brookline, MA.: Hellenic Press, 1984).

3. See Kennett Love, *Suez: The Twice Fought War* (New York: McGraw-Hill,

However ineffective American commitments to the Middle East were in the 1950s, they presented few problems relative to those posed by the British decision to leave the area East of Suez a decade later. By then, global commitments and the war in progress in Vietnam precluded the kind of substantial American commitment that had been possible in the past. United States presence in the region at the time was minimal. The deployment of MIDEASTFOR (a flagship and two destroyers operating out of Bahrain) in the Persian Gulf was acknowledged to be symbolic. The U.S. lease of an airfield in Dhahran, Saudi Arabia, had been terminated in the early 1960s by mutual agreement. Aside from oil, which was selling for less than $1.50 a barrel when President Nixon took office, the primary United States interest seems to have been the communications and intelligence gathering sites that were established in the late 1950s. The Navy, however, had been seeking military facilities in the Indian Ocean at least since 1960, and this objective gained currency after India requested emergency air defense assistance during its brief war with China in 1962. The end result was an Executive Agreement between Britain and the United States in December 1966 that made the islands in the British Indian Ocean Territory available for joint defense. U.S. interest in the island of Diego Garcia stems from this period. However, according to one official familiar with U.S. policy during this time, U.S. interests in and strategic plans for the region were perceived by commentators as more expansive than they were in fact.[4]

## THE NIXON DOCTRINE AND THE TWIN-PILLAR POLICY, 1969-1979

Shortly after taking office, the administration of President Richard M. Nixon, burdened by the war in Vietnam, initiated a major review of U.S. policy in the Gulf. The focus of the review was the question of how the Nixon Doctrine, first enunciated in June 1969, could best be applied to the region. As subsequently elaborated, the Nixon Doctrine specified that the United States would furnish military and economic assistance to nations whose freedom was threatened, but would look to

1969); Townsend Hoopes, *The Devil and John Foster Dulles* (Boston: Little, Brown, 1973); and Stephen J. Genco, "The Eisenhower Doctrine: Deterrence in the Middle East, 1957-1958," in Alexander George and Richard Smoke, *Deterrence in American Foreign Policy: Theory and Practice* (New York: Columbia University Press, 1974), pp. 309-362.

4. Gary Sick, "The Evolution of U.S. Strategy toward the Indian Ocean and Persian Gulf Regions," n.d., in the author's possession. Gary Sick served on the NSC staff during the Carter and part of the Reagan administrations.

those nations to assume primary responsibility for their own defense.[5] The result of the policy review was the president's endorsement in November 1970 of what became the "twin-pillar" policy. Its rationale was that the United States had strategic interests in Iran and Saudi Arabia, which meant that support for either would alienate the other. Despite their mutual distrust, cooperation between the two was felt to be essential in the face of growing Arab radicalism, most recently evidenced during the Jordan crisis two months before. Britain, U.S. officials believed, would retain much of its political presence and influence in the Gulf. As a result, there would not be a power vacuum per se, but realignments of the region's power balance were expected to occur. The United States, for its part, could ensure stability through cooperation with Iran (which American officials recognized as the region's predominate power) and Saudi Arabia. MIDEASTFOR, of course, would be maintained. The United States could not withdraw when the British were departing; the Russians, moreover, had begun to deploy military forces in the region and might get the wrong signal. U.S. diplomatic representation in the Gulf, meanwhile, would be expanded and an austere communications station, along with an 8,000-foot supporting runway, would be built on Diego Garcia. The Lower Gulf states, however, would be encouraged to look to Britain for their security needs.[6]

This framework, in conjunction with the Nixon administration's increasing emphasis on the Iranian "pillar," served as the basis for U.S. policy until 1979, when the Iranian revolution and the Soviet invasion of Afghanistan forced the United States, once again, to reexamine its priorities and reformulate its policies. Until then, evolution of the twin-pillar policy was most affected by several important factors: the Shah's world view; the Nixon administration's decision in May 1972 to leave decisions over the acquisition of military equipment to the Iranian government; and the consequences of the oil embargo that followed the 1973 Arab-Israeli war.

---

5. Henry Kissinger, *White House Years* (Boston: Little, Brown, 1979), pp. 223-225.
6. Sick, "The Evolution of U.S. Strategy toward the Indian Ocean and the Persian Gulf Regions"; Barry Rubin, *Paved with Good Intentions: The American Experience and Iran* (New York: Oxford, 1980), pp. 125-126; U.S. Congress, House, Committee on Foreign Affairs, *New Perspectives on the Persian Gulf*, Hearings before the Subcommittee on the Near East and South Asia, Washington, D.C., G.P.O., 1973; and *U.S. Interests in and Policy Toward the Persian Gulf*, Hearings before the Subcommittee on the Near East, Washington, D.C., G.P.O., 1972. For Soviet naval deployments in the Indian Ocean see Bruce Watson, *Red Navy at Sea: Soviet Naval Operations on the High Seas, 1956-1980* (Boulder: Westview, 1982).

*The Shah's View of the World.* Iran's emergence as a key pillar in U.S. policy was due as much to the Shah's vision of Iran's role in the world as it was to circumstance. His goal was to transform Iran into the region's paramount power in order to protect Iran's resources and acquire the military capability to counter threats to the regional status quo.[7] Informing his vision, and his longstanding desire to obtain a security commitment from the United States, was the history of his own weakness—dating back to World War II, the Azerbaijan crisis in 1945-46, and the nationalization crisis in the early 1950s when, with U.S. and British assistance, the Mossadeq government was overthrown and Pahlavi rule restored. U.S. policies during the Indo-Pakistani wars of 1965 and 1970-71, however, led the Shah to conclude that allies and their security commitments were unreliable and to dismiss the value of CENTO as having "never been really serious." The Indo-Pakistani wars also reinforced a desire for self-reliance and confirmed the Shah's belief that military might was its most important component.[8]

The Shah's unlimited appetite for weapons and his overruling concern for security were fed by a myriad of threats to the regional status quo. These threats had been accentuated, in his view, by the revolution in Iraq in 1958. They were made more dangerous after 1968 when a new regime in Baghdad challenged Iranian interests in the Shatt al-Arab and Khuzestan (which a conference of Arab journalists in 1964 had declared to be "an integral part of the Arab homeland"). And that was not all. Following Britain's withdrawal from Aden in 1967, a Marxist-oriented government had been formed in the People's Democratic Republic of Yemen (PDRY). The PDRY and Iraq were supporting an on-going rebellion in Oman's Dhofar province; Iraq was also supporting Kurdish and Baluch movements for autonomy in Kurdistan (which includes the western part of northwest Iran) and Baluchistan (which includes the eastern part of southeast Iran). Saudi Arabia, finally, had suffered a coup attempt by Air Force officers in 1969. These developments, in conjunction with the changing balance of power in the region, made the Nixon administration receptive to the Shah's concerns; they also led the United States and Britain to underwrite a $1 billion Iranian defense program before Britain's military forces had withdrawn from the Gulf.[9]

---

7. Amin Saikal, *The Rise and Fall of the Shah* (Princeton: Princeton University Press, 1980), pp. 137-147.
8. Rouhollah Ramazani, *The United States and Iran: The Patterns of Influence* (New York: Praeger, 1982), pp. 39-41; Alvin Rubinstein, *Soviet Policy Toward Turkey, Iran, and Afghanistan: The Dynamics of Influence* (New York: Praeger, 1982), p. 74.
9. Rubin, pp. 142, 204-205; Ramazani, *Iran's Foreign Policy*, pp. 405, 416-418, 428; Selig Harrison, *In Afghanistan's Shadow: Baluch Nationalism and Soviet*

*The May 1972 Agreement.* By the time that President Richard M. Nixon and his National Security Advisor Henry Kissinger arrived in Teheran in May 1972 (on their return from the Moscow summit), Britain's forces had departed from the Gulf. Kissinger now judged that the balance of power in the region was in grave jeopardy. Syria had invaded Jordan in 1970, and Syria's relationship with the Soviet Union was well established. Egypt had signed a friendship treaty with the Soviets in 1971, and over 15,000 Soviet troops were still in Egypt. The Soviets had concluded a similar treaty with Iraq only seven weeks before the Nixon visit, and two days after the ceremony a squadron of Soviet warships had arrived at the Iraqi port of Umm Qasr. The Soviets had then begun massive deliveries of advanced modern weapons to Iraq. Britain's military forces had been gone from the Gulf for less than half a year and already the situation appeared to be getting worse. In Kissinger's view, it was imperative that the regional balance of power be maintained. Iraq would achieve hegemony unless local forces were strengthened or American power built up. Neither Congress nor the American public, however, would support the deployment of American forces in the region.[10]

Since Iran was willing to fill the vacuum left by Britain and was willing to pay for the necessary equipment out of its own revenues, the president acquiesced in the Shah's desire to obtain advanced American aircraft and insisted that future Iranian requests not be second-guessed. In short, the decision on what military equipment Iran could acquire would be left to Iran and review procedures would be eliminated. The controversy over whether this U.S. commitment was "open-ended" or not began after the policy was called into question by Secretary of Defense James Schlesinger in August 1975, and continued in the aftermath of the Iranian revolution when critics cited it as one of the revolution's causes. Henry Kissinger argues that the commitment was not open ended and that the substantial quantities of arms that were sold were needed to maintain the balance of power.[11] In retrospect, it seems

*Temptations* (Washington, D.C.: Carnegie Endowment for International Peace, 1981), pp. 35, 106-108; Kelly, *Arabia, the Gulf and the West*, p. 134.

10. Henry Kissinger, *White House Years*, pp. 1258-1265; *Years of Upheaval* (Boston: Little, Brown, 1982), p. 669; see also Ramazani, *The Persian Gulf*, p. 46, for the visit of the Soviet squadron.

11. Kissinger, *White House Years*, pp. 1258-1265; *Years of Upheaval*, pp. 668-670; U.S. Congress, Senate, Committee on Foreign Relations, *U.S. Military Sales to Iran*, A Staff Report to the Subommittee on Foreign Assistance, Washington, D.C., G.P.O., 1976; Ramazani, *The United States and Iran*, pp. 44-45; Rubin, pp. 162, 170-71. For Kissinger's deflection of Schlesinger's concern over arms sales to the Shah, see Rubin, pp. 170-171.

clear that expenditures on high-tech equipment were excessive and that the exposed profile of the many technical and advisory personnel necessary to make sophisticated equipment operational were a fundamental part of the Shah's burgeoning domestic problems.[12] "In Iranian eyes," Barry Rubin observes, "it was the arms-sale program, more than any other aspect of the alliance between the United States and Iran, that compromised the Shah's image with Iranians and led them to believe that the Shah was America's 'man.' "[13]

*The 1973 Arab-Israeli War and its Consequences.* The effect of the 1973 Arab-Israeli war on U.S. policy in the Persian Gulf and Indian Ocean was profound. U.S. and Western economic vulnerability to the oil embargo underscored the strategic importance of the region, which was recognized as vital. A comprehensive reevaluation of U.S. strategy in the Indian Ocean, moreover, concluded that the United States could not place heavy emphasis on allied support. This judgment, along with heightened suspicions of a growing Soviet military presence in the region (reinforced by a Soviet treaty of friendship with Somalia in July 1974), had two important consequences: the U.S. Pacific Fleet's periodic deployment in the Indian Ocean as a contingency naval presence; and, after considerable debate, the expansion of Diego Garcia from a communications station to a naval facility capable of supporting major air and naval deployments.[14]

From Kissinger's perspective, the 1973 war also underscored the value of Iran as an ally. It was the only country bordering the Soviet Union that did not permit the Soviets to use its air space. The Shah refueled U.S. fleets, did not use his oil to bring political pressure on the United States, and absorbed the energies of his radical neighbors (i.e.,

---

12. Robert Graham, *Iran: The Illusion of Power* (New York: St. Martin's, 1979), pp. 168-189.

13. Rubin, *Paved With Good Intentions*, p. 260.

14. Sick, "The Evolution of U.S. Strategy." See also David Long, "The United States and the Persian Gulf," *Current History* (January 1979), pp. 27-30, 37-38, esp. p. 29. Maxwell Johnson notes that the Pentagon first realized the significance of Diego Garcia after the contingency deployment of a carrier strike force to the Indian Ocean during the 1971 Indo-Pakistani war. *The Military as an Instrument of U.S. Policy in Southwest Asia: The Rapid Deployment Joint Task Force, 1979-1982* (Boulder: Westview, 1983), p. 31. Kissinger's response to a question as to whether he would consider using military action against oil prices set off a furor. "I am not saying that there is no circumstance where we would not use force," he observed. "But it is one thing to use it in the case of a dispute over price, it's another whether there is some actual strangulation of the industrialized world." *Business Week*, January 1975. The issue of the use of force is discussed in Part II.

Iraq), thus preventing them from threatening the region's moderate regimes. Nixon's encouragement of the Shah's support for the Kurds in Iraq also prevented Iraq from making more than one division available to participate in the 1973 war.[15]

The Shah's ability and inclination to make large weapons purchases, meanwhile, increased greatly following the war. Iran had ceased receiving direct economic assistance from the United States in 1967, partly because of changing realities in the international petroleum market and partly because of massive U.S. expenditures in Vietnam. Now, following the 1973 Arab-Israeli war, the Shah's already fast-increasing revenues quadrupled. The difference in earnings that increased oil production and higher prices made in the space of a decade is extraordinary: where 1.7 million barrels a day (MBD) brought in $482 million in 1964, 6 MBD brought in $21.4 billion in 1974. As a consequence, the level of expenditures on arms increased exponentially. Where the value of purchase agreements between 1950 and 1972 amounted to slightly over $1.6 billion, purchase agreements in the next four years totalled over $11.6 billion. The value of arms transactions in 1974 alone ($3.9 billion) was twice the value of *all* arms contracted during the 22 years prior to the Arab oil embargo.[16]

It is not possible here to examine in detail the effects of modernization on Iran or the consequences for Iranian stability of Iran's massive expenditures on military equipment and economic development. It may be useful, however, to suggest the magnitude of Iran's absorptive and management problems by illustrating the extent to which the Iranian economy was out of control by 1975, and why, as one astute observer noted, less and less was being achieved at greater and greater cost:

> The development of the ports illustrates the point. The boom in expenditure stimulated imports and put even greater pressure on the already strained port infrastructure: in 1974 the volume of imports increased 39 per cent.
> Port handling equipment was insufficent and poorly maintained. . . . The southern ports handled over 80 per cent of all maritime imports with insufficient berthing space and very limited warehousing. All this was compounded by an elephantine bureaucracy which could require up to 28 signatures to clear goods from customs. . . .
> At Khorramshahr, the principal port, over 200 ships were waiting to unload their cargoes by mid-1975: ships were having to wait 160 days and more before entering harbor. At one point more than 1 million tons of goods were being kept in ships' holds awaiting the opportunity to unload. . . . Once the offloading of goods was speeded up,

15. Kissinger, *White House Years,* pp. 1262, 1265.
16. Rubin, *Paved With Good Intentions,* p. 130; Ramazani, *The United States and Iran*, pp. 40-42, 47-48.

many goods lay around unwarehoused. At Khorramshahr 12,000 tons were being unloaded per day but only 9,000 tons were being removed per day. At the most congested point in September/October 1975, there were over 1 million tons of goods piled up on the jetties and around the port.

Goods were cleared slowly for two main reasons. First, almost 50 per cent of the imports were governmental purchases, and Ministries took sometimes up to six months—and more—to clear them. Second, there were not enough trucks. A special emergency government purchase of 2,000 trucks and 6,000 trailers proved no remedy in itself. The trucks needed drivers and 2,000 more Iranian drivers were not available. As a further emergency measure it was decided to "import" 800 South Korean and Pakistani truck drivers. . . . They quickly became disenchanted . . . . when they discovered that Iranian drivers were being paid higher wages. By July 1975 most of these drivers had left after less than six months. Finally, the government was forced to consider what it should have done in the first place—a crash course for Iranian drivers. This only filled the gap slowly, and a large number of unused trucks rotted in the hostile climate. Even in 1977 it was still possible to see rows of trucks, neatly parked at Bandar Abbas, that had been awaiting drivers for three years.

The delays in the ports were quickly transferred to the construction sites and other projects. There was a built-in delay of six months on the start up of virtually every project, added to which much of the goods suffered in poor handling, causing further delay. The cost is difficult to quantify. The only readily identifiable costs were demurrage charges for keeping ships waiting at anchor. In 1974/5 these cost Iran over $1 billion, almost 5 per cent of total foreign exchange earnings.[17]

*The Iranian "Pillar" Crumbles.* The Shah's massive expenditures, coupled with Iran's lack of a developed infrastructure and its shortage of trained manpower, magnified the opportunities for and disposition toward corruption, waste, and inefficiency.[18] Fluctuations in the international oil market, meanwhile, wreaked havoc with Iran's overheated economy, loosened the existential underpinnings of its burgeoning urban population, and contributed to a contempt for authority that was accentuated by the progressive breakdown of the economic and social system. In the absence of any meaningful structures for political participation in Iran, the only person who could be held accountable when things went badly was the one who took the credit when things went well: the Shah. His inability to reach out to his people, or to mobilize

---

17. Graham, *Iran: The Illusion of Power*, pp. 87-88.
18. Jack Miklos, *The Iranian Revolution and Modernization: Way Stations to Anarchy* (Washington, D.C.: National Defense University Press, 1983), pp. 61-62, and Robert Graham, *Iran: The Illusion of Power*, pp. 15-125.

their energies, and his association with foreign and un-Islamic forces became a serious liability.

If there is a consensus among the scholars who have investigated the Iranian revolution's complex causes, it is that support for the Ayatollah Khomeini derived less from what he stood for than from what he opposed: the Pahlavi regime, the monarchy itself, foreign control and cultural domination. Thanks to Khomeini, the dislocations and identity concerns that accompanied Iran's uneven development were given a focus; economic grievances, existential need, and political frustration among the lower and middle classes coalesced into a common opposition to the Shah. Beyond that, none of the sociopolitical groups who supported the revolution could agree on even basic conceptions of legitimacy and authority. The Shia religious establishment, meanwhile, which was independent of the state, provided a framework (if not the motive) for the revolutionary movement as a whole. After the revolution, this framework, in conjunction with the charismatic figure of Khomeini, would facilitate the ulama's control of the government.[19]

The causes of the Iranian revolution and an analysis of U.S. policy toward Iran during the hostage crisis are beyond the scope of this study. What is pertinent is that the revolution undermined the two-pillar policy that had been followed with little change by both the Ford and Carter administrations, and raised serious questions about its central premise (i.e., that regional states could assume primary responsibility for their own defense). A Marxist coup in Afghanistan in April 1978 had been followed by a Soviet-Ethiopian treaty in November 1978; by early 1979 the PDRY was creating problems in the Yemen, and in March, following the crumbling of the Iranian "pillar" and the reorientation of Iran's geopolitical posture, Turkey and Pakistan withdrew from CENTO. In the course of these adverse regional developments,

---

19. Nikki Keddie, "The Iranian Revolution in Comparative Perspective," *American Historical Review* 88:3 (1983), pp. 579-598; Ramazani, *The United States and Iran*, pp. 122-123; James Bill and Carl Leider, *Politics in the Middle East*, 2nd ed. (Boston: Little, Brown, 1984), p. 382; Edward Mortimer, *Faith and Power: The Politics of Islam* (New York: Vintage, 1982), pp. 296-376, esp. 300-303; and Rubin, *Paved With Good Intentions*, pp. 252-272, who discusses over twenty factors that contribute to an explanation of the Iranian revolution.

A number of former American officials such as Henry Kissinger (*Years of Upheaval*, pp. 672-673) and Jack Miklos (*The Iranian Revolution and Modernization*, p. 64) question the argument that broader political participation would have made a difference in the situation in Iran or that anyone has a coherent idea of how to channel the forces let loose by the process of development. While the problem clearly deserves much more extensive examination, the Shah's record on the issue was abysmal and deserves most of the criticism that has been heaped on it.

American officials were left without a strategic conception of how to protect their regional interests.[20]

In this conceptual vacuum, President Jimmy Carter's National Security Advisor Zbigniew Brzezinski first broached the concept of a security framework for the region. He proceeded to develop this idea in interagency discussions throughout the rest of 1979. The essence of the concept, as it developed, was an increased naval presence in the region, an improved capability to introduce rapidly deployed forces into the area, and access to facilities in the area (as well as coordination with NATO allies) in order to support an expanded presence and broadened contingency capability. The hostage crisis that began in November 1979, meanwhile, pointed to the limitations on U.S. ability to project military power into the region.[21]

## THE SOVIET INVASION OF AFGHANISTAN AND THE CARTER DOCTRINE

The Soviet invasion of Afghanistan in December 1979 underscored the limitations on U.S. capabilities. It also revolutionized the geopolitical picture in the region. The most plausible explanation for the Soviet invasion of Afghanistan is that the Soviets went in to prevent the certain collapse of the Marxist government in Kabul and to replace a recalcitrant leader with one who was more responsive to Moscow's bidding. In so doing, the Soviets may well have been concerned about their own security interests, the effects on their own Muslim population of a failure to move, and the international implications of perceived Soviet weakness. But if, in the short term, the invasion had a defensive quality, in the long term it presented possibilities that were offensive. As such, the invasion was clearly opportunistic: the United States could not prevent it, it put the Soviets in a position to provoke and exploit the region's instabilities and, ultimately, it provided them with strategic ad-

---

20. Sick, "The Evolution of U.S. Strategy."
21. Ibid.; Cyrus Vance, *Hard Choices: Critical Years in America's Foreign Policy* (New York: Simon & Shuster, 1983), pp. 369-370; Zbigniew Brzezinski, *Power and Principle: Memoirs of the National Security Adviser, 1977-1981* (New York: Farrar, Straus, Giroux, 1983), pp. 444-450; and the statement by Matthew Nimetz, Under Secretary of State for Security, Science and Technology, U.S. Department of State, *U.S. Security Framework*, Current Policy No. 221, Bureau of Public Affairs, Washington, D.C., September 16, 1980. For a detailed analysis of the genesis of the Carter Doctrine and its reinterpretation under the Reagan administration, see Maxwell O. Johnson, *The Military as an Instrument of U.S. Policy in Southwest Asia: The Rapid Deployment Joint Task Force, 1979-1982* (Boulder: Westview, 1983), Ch. II.

vantages—even if those advantages had not been part of the original calculation.[22]

"Afghanistan" made more urgent development of the strategic framework that had been under discussion since the fall of the Shah. That framework was now fleshed out and expanded after its rationale was articulated in President Carter's State of the Union message on January 23, 1980:

> Let our position be absolutely clear: an attempt by any outside force to gain control of the Persian Gulf region will be regarded as an assault on the vital interests of the United States of America, and such an assault will be repelled by any means necessary, including military force.

In spite of assertions to the contrary, the so-called Carter Doctrine was carefully considered. Its intent was to put the Soviets on notice that the region was of vital importance to the United States and, in a departure from the Nixon Doctrine, to make clear that the United States assumed ultimate responsibility for regional defense. Less clear was the extent of the area included in "the Persian Gulf region." Pakistan, for example, sought but received no clarification as to whether it was included in the region to which the Carter Doctrine applied. The president's lack of precision, however, was not ill considered. It *was* advisable to be wary of undertaking a commitment that could not be met. Legitimate questions were raised about the matter of vagueness, but if the region was vital there was no escaping the logic of the president's statement, which regional insecurity appeared to require. Until the security framework was broadened, the Carter Doctrine served a useful deterrent function. It did not write off countries whose loss was less than vital, and it kept options open with respect to contingencies in others. If something like the Carter Doctrine was required, however, there was no sense in being too specific about U.S. commitments and by implication spelling out (as Secretary of State Dean Acheson did in 1950 with regard to East Asia) what the United States would not do—particularly since the nature of many contingencies (such as the invasion of South Korea in 1950) made it virtually impossible to know ahead of time how vital a particular

---

22. Nancy and Richard Newell, *The Struggle for Afghanistan* (Ithaca: Cornell University Press, 1981), p. 108; Henry Bradsher, *Afghanistan and the Soviet Union* (Durham, N.C.: Duke University Press, 1983), especially Chapter 8, "The View from the Kremlin," pp. 149-168; Raju Thomas, "The Afghanistan Crisis and South Asian Security," *The Journal of Strategic Studies* 4:4 (1981), pp. 415-434; Rubinstein, *Soviet Policy Toward Turkey, Iran, and Afghanistan*, p. 170; and the comments by Joseph Sisco in *U.S. Security Interests and Policies in Southwest Asia*, Hearings before the Committee on Foreign Relations, U.S. Congress, Senate (Washington, D.C.: G.P.O., 1980), pp. 42-50.

area was and what an appropriate response to a particular contingency might be.[23]

Whatever its merits and shortcomings, the Carter Doctrine defined a U.S. stake in the Persian Gulf region. During the rest of 1980 the Special Coordinating Committee of the National Security Council (NSC) met over 20 times to develop the administration's regional security framework: defense capabilities in the regional states were improved; access to facilities was acquired in Oman, Kenya, Somalia, and Egypt; force capabilities were enhanced; and the U.S.'s NATO allies were pressed to specify shared responsibilities. In spite of more ambitious goals and a change in rhetoric ("strategic consensus" for a time replaced "security framework" until it was recognized that there was no "consensus" on strategy), the Reagan administration in its first years essentially continued and consolidated the security framework initiated by the Carter administration.

If in the early 1980s it was unclear *what* countries in the Persian Gulf region other than Saudi Arabia were vital to the United States or *how* vital they were, and if a *political* strategy for the region was still lacking, it was in part because of the Reagan administration's ideological predisposition to focus on East-West issues and in part because of conceptual inertia. Strategic thinking about the region ignored regional priorities. It also continued to consist of what Gary Sick, an official who served on the National Security Council staffs of both the Carter and Reagan administrations, has characterized as "post-hoc adjustments to unanticipated and largely unwelcome developments." Once such adjustments were made, they tended to become mired in the status quo. Administrations who understood the inadequacy of military power alone to influence political events in the region nonetheless tended to rely on arms sales, military deployments, and occasionally economic assistance as the bedrock for their policies.

On the basis of past performance, prospects for a more enlightened strategy in the 1980s are not particularly auspicious. "Until an administration in Washington is prepared to ask itself soberly what is truly vital to U.S. interests in this region," Sick has observed, "and then to balance that against a realistic appreciation of U.S. political, economic and military capabilities, there is little reason to expect that the future will be more than a perilous reprise of an old refrain."[24] It is to the set of problems that Sick has identified that we must now turn.

23. Jimmy Carter, *Keeping Faith: Memoirs of a President* (New York:Bantam, 1982), p. 483; Brzezinski, *Power and Principle*, pp. 445-450. See also David Newsom, "America Engulfed," *Foreign Policy* No. 43 (Summer 1981), pp. 17-32.
24. Brzezinski, *Power and Principle*, pp. 446-450; and Sick, "The Evolution of U.S. Strategy."

# PART II

# A STRATEGY
# FOR
# THE PERSIAN GULF AND SOUTHWEST ASIA

Since the fall of the Shah of Iran in January 1979, the United States has been restructuring its military posture to deal with contingencies in the Persian Gulf and Indian Ocean. Real progress has been made in that direction. In the urgency of shoring up a crumbling military position, however, neither the Carter Administration nor the Reagan Administration has articulated a viable political strategy which could relate the new military instruments to the broader objectives and purposes of U.S. interests in this complex area.[1] Part II will review the premises and emerging outlines of a U.S. military strategy in Southwest Asia and set forth some ideas about how U.S. military capabilities could be integrated into a broader political framework. Parts III and IV will then examine in greater detail regional problems that must be considered in the development of such a framework.

---

1. In addition to the discussion in Part I, see Paul Bradley, *Recent United States Policy in the Persian Gulf (1971-1982)* (Grantham, N.Y.: Tompson & Rutter, 1982); Chapter 4, n. 16; and Conclusion, n. 2.

**PERSIAN GULF REGION**

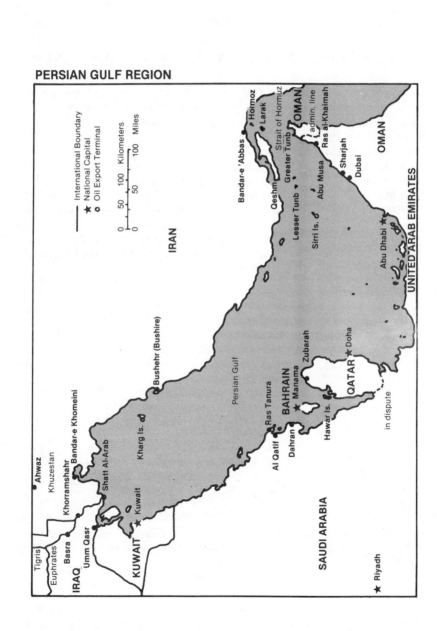

# 3

## U.S. Interests
## and Threat Assessments

### OIL AND OTHER U.S. INTERESTS

The West's main concern in the Persian Gulf Region is oil. The dependence of Europe, Japan, and the United States on oil imported from the Persian Gulf has been well documented. The region holds approximately 55 percent of the world's (and two-thirds of the non-communist world's) reserves and in recent years has provided as much as 28 percent of U.S., 61 percent of European, and 70 percent of Japanese imports. In 1979, Persian Gulf oil as a percentage of total oil *consumed* by industrialized countries was substantial: 13 percent for the U.S.; 32 percent for West Germany; 45 percent for the U.K.; 76 percent for Japan; and 89 percent for France.[2]

Since 1979, a number of factors have contributed to a reduced demand for oil: economic recession, energy conservation, fuel substitution, new oil from the North Sea and the Gulf of Mexico; and the development of alternative sources of energy. U.S. oil imports, meanwhile, declined from 8.344 million barrels of oil per day (MBD) in 1979 to less than 6 MBD in 1981 and slightly over 4 MBD in the first quarter of 1983.[3] While Gulf oil as a percentage of total oil imported initially increased (the U.S. imported 1.9 MBD from the Gulf in the first quarter of 1980), the Iran-Iraq war and the world-wide oil glut led to a reduction of the Persian Gulf's importance as a supplier of oil. By the first quarter of 1983, Mexico, Canada, the United Kingdom and Venezuela ranked as the largest suppliers of petroleum products to the United States.

---

2. *Petroleum Intelligence Weekly*, January 19 and 26, 1981; and April 5, 1982; *Washington Post*, June 15, 1981; *New York Times*, September 8, 1981; and *Monthly Petroleum Statement*, DOE/EIA - 0109 (81/1 - 81/12), United States Department of Energy, Energy Information Administration, Washington, D.C.; John Collins, Clyde Mark, and Elizabeth Severns, "Petroleum Imports from the Persian Gulf: Use of Armed Force to Ensure Supplies," Issue Brief No. IB79046, Congressional Research Service, Library of Congress, Washington, D.C., December 1981.

3. *Ibid.*; Milton Benjamin, *International Herald Tribune*, July 7, 1983; *Christian Science Monitor*, September 29, 1983.

Saudi Arabia ranked fifth, exporting only 200,000 barrels a day (5.1 percent of total U.S. imports). By October 1983 Saudi Arabia had dropped to tenth, and the share of the U.S. oil market held by OPEC's Arab members had dropped to under three percent.[4]

The Strategic Petroleum Reserve (SPR), meanwhile, which by 1989 is expected to hold 750 million barrels of oil and have a drawdown capability (i.e., the amount of oil that can be withdrawn from the reserve) of 3.5 MBD, by October 1983 held 360 million barrels, with a drawdown capability of 1.73 MBD.[5] In spite of premature euphoria over the current oil glut, however, U.S. imports of crude oil still amount to $63 billion (24% of its total import bill in 1982).[6] The continued stockpiling of oil, together with the United States' failure to establish a comprehensive energy program, underscores the vulnerability of the United States to such actions as embargoes and a variety of other political/military measures that could disrupt the flow of oil from the Gulf.

This view is supported by a Congressional Research Service (CRS) study, which used a CRS-constructed model to examine the macroeconomic impacts on the U.S. and six other Western industrialized economies of two hypothetical total disruptions of the West's access to Persian Gulf oil for a period of one year. The disruptions were set in two very different economic contexts: April 1, 1980, a time of economic growth prior to the emergence of significant trends in energy conservation and substitution; and January 1, 1982, a time of economic recession, increased conservation, substitution, and mounting petroleum reserves. The study finds that the 1980 disruption would have produced a dramatic economic decline among the Western industrialized countries, while the 1982 disruption would have resulted in markedly less severe but nonetheless significant economic consequences. Looking to the future, the study asserts that with a resumption of economic growth, the demand for energy is expected to rise. U.S. dependence on imported oil, meanwhile, will grow as domestic oil and gas production declines. The study suggests that if the Western nations relax their efforts to address their energy problems, the United States

4. Peter Grier, *Christian Science Monitor*, October 18, 1983; David Francis, *Christian Science Monitor*, July 15, 1983; Milton Benjamin, *Washington Post*, October 9, 1983.

5. Department of Energy, *Strategic Petroleum Reserve, Annual Report 1981*, U.S. Government Printing Office, Washington, D.C., 1981; *Christian Science Monitor*, December 12, 1980 and April 10, 1981; *Wall Street Journal*, June 9, 1981; *New York Times*, August 22, 1981; *International Herald Tribune*, July 7, 1983.

6. U.S. Department of State, Bureau of Public Affairs, "Oil and Energy," *Gist*, Washington, D.C., November 1983.

(even if it is less dependent than other nations on oil from the Gulf) in the short term would suffer from a Persian Gulf disruption to the same extent as its allies in Western Europe and Japan.[7]

Experts have debated at length the extent of Soviet oil production capacities and needs, which may in turn provide some indication of Soviet interest in gaining access to Gulf oil. The CIA has adjusted its controversial prediction of Soviet oil production in 1985 from 8-10 MBD to 12.1 MBD. The Defense Intelligence Agency estimates Soviet oil production in 1985 at 12.2 to 12.9 MBD, while other sources such as the Economic Commission for Europe go as high as 14 MBD.[8] The trend in predictions suggests that *need* for oil as a potential source of Soviet adventurism in the Persian Gulf is less significant than intially thought; notwithstanding, less urgent needs do not preclude the possibility that the Soviets would be interested in acquiring increased access to oil to supply their allies' energy demands or, under extreme circumstances, damaging the Western economies by *denying* them Persian Gulf oil.

Soviet denial of Gulf oil to the West, however, would confront the Soviet Union with serious economic and military risks. Focusing for the moment on the economic risks (military risks will be addressed later), one must keep in mind that as domestic Soviet demand for oil increases, probable compensating cut-backs in oil exports (Soviet oil exports were between 1.5 and 2 MBD in July 1983) will make Soviet gas an increasingly important hard currency earner. While European dependence on Soviet natural gas will be relatively small (Soviet gas will provide less than 25 percent of total gas consumed and, except for Austria, less than 5 percent of total energy consumed in 1990), Soviet dependence on European consumption for hard currency will be significant.[9]

---

7. *Western Vulnerability to a Disruption of Persian Gulf Oil Supplies: U.S. Interests and Options: An Analysis of the Economic Impact of an Hypothetical Disruption of Persian Gulf Oil Supplies and Policy Implications for the Future*, Congressional Research Service, Report 83-24F, Library of Congress, Washington, D.C., March 24, 1983.

8. *Washington Post*, May 19 and 20, June 15 and 20, 1981; *New York Times*, May 19, and September 3, 1981; *International Herald Tribune*, June 22, 1983. Actual Soviet oil production in 1982 was 12.28 MBD; planned production for 1983 is 12.38 MBD. *Christian Science Monitor*, July 18, 1983.

9. U.S. Department of State, *Soviet-West European Natural Gas Pipeline*, Bureau of Public Affairs, Current Policy No, 331 (Washington, D.C.: U.S. Department of State, October 14, 1981). The pipeline itself was completed in January 1983, but installation of 41 compressors (every 60 miles or so) was delayed and by year's end approximately half were still awaiting installation. Once the compressors are installed, the 53'' pipeline will be capable of deliver-

In 1979, for example, the Soviets relied on energy sales to Western Europe for over 50 percent of their hard currency sales; by 1982 that figure had risen to 60 percent, and natural gas, though less significant, was earning an increasing share. In 1982 the Soviets exported 1.1 trillion cubic feet of gas to Western Europe; according to the Soviet magazine *Foreign Trade*, they have signed contracts for the delivery of an additional 1.1 trillion cubic feet in connection with the 2,759-mile Yamal pipeline (completed in January 1983).[10] Since Soviet gas reserves constitute one-third of total known world reserves, the Soviets will be reluctant to jeopardize the market for this abundantly available and increasingly important resource by carrying out adventurist policies—particularly in the Middle East.

Whatever Soviet intentions may be, the importance of oil to the NATO countries and Japan makes continued access to Persian Gulf oil a primary U.S. interest in the Middle East and one among several interests which, while often in conflict, are nonetheless well-defined and generally agreed upon. These interests include:

— access to oil (on reasonable commercial terms);
— containment of Soviet expansion and influence;
— prevention of arms imbalances, nuclear proliferation and nuclear war;
— regional stability and peaceful change;
— the security of Israel; and
— advancement of the Middle East peace process.[11]

## THREATS TO U.S. INTERESTS

Although analysts generally agree upon the definition of U.S. interests in the Middle East, they disagree in their assessments of the

---

ing up to 20 billion cubic meters of Soviet gas annually. *Christian Science Monitor*, July 18, 1983. According to figures obtained from the International Energy Agency and the European Community, dependence on Soviet natural gas will provide an additional 10% of total gas consumption by the end of this decade in West Germany, Switzerland, France, Italy, and Austria. William Echikson, *Christian Science Monitor*, December 16, 1983; *Durham Morning Herald*, Jan. 2, 1984.

10. Jeanne Robertson, *Christian Science Monitor*, November 1, 1983; David Willis, *Christian Science Monitor*, July 18, 1983. What 1.1 trillion cubic feet of natural gas translates into is approximately 3 billion cubic feet per day, or the equivalent in energy terms of about 500,000 barrels of oil per day.

11. For an extremely thoughtful and full discussion of American interests in the Middle East, see Harold Saunders, *The Middle East Problem in the 1980s* (Washington, D.C.: American Enterprise Institute for Public Policy Research, 1981), pp. 12-73.

threats to U.S. interests in the Persian Gulf. Potential threats to U.S. interests fall into one of three categories: (1) those that come from the Soviet Union itself; (2) those that come from other countries in the region (possibly supported by the Soviet Union); and (3) those that come from within particular countries (also, possibly, supported by the Soviet Union and/or other countries in the region).

*Direct Soviet Attack.* If the Soviets were to conduct limited attacks on areas such as northwest Iran that are close to their borders, they would prevail. The political and military occupation costs, however, would be sufficiently high and the marginal benefits (*potential* air superiority at the head of the Gulf) sufficiently low so as to make such moves unlikely. Soviet attacks on non-contiguous states would be even more risky and difficult, although the build-up of intervention forces and staging areas in the PDRY could make it more costly for the U.S. to combat successfully a Soviet attack.[12]

The two most probable worst-case scenarios for a direct Soviet attack are:

— an overland assault on Iran, possibly coupled with an airborne assault on Khuzestan and a bomber attack on U.S. carriers in the Indian Ocean; or
— an overland assault from Afghanistan into Pakistani and Iranian Baluchistan, coupled with an airborn assault on Chah Bahar or Gwadar and a bomber attack on U.S. carriers in the Indian Ocean.

Such attacks, however, are highly unlikely, not only because of enormous economic and political costs (often ignored by worst-case analysts) but because the logistical difficulties and military costs of such a move would vastly outweigh the potential benefits:

— Only seven of 24 Soviet divisions in the North Caucasus, Transcaucasus, and Turkestan Military Districts could be utilized without seriously degrading Soviet capabilities in other, more important, contingencies (NATO, Poland, Afghanistan, and China).
— These divisions are in a relatively poor state of readiness, would take at least three to four week to mobilize, and would encounter enormous logistical, geographical, and military problems in their movement south—particularly if American forces were deployed according to a strategy designed to delay and cause attrition while allied forces were constructing a defensive perimeter in Khuzestan.

---

12. *Challenges for U.S. National Security, Assessing the Balance: Defense Spending and Conventional Forces, A Preliminary Report, Part II* (Washington, D.C.: Carnegie Endowment for International Peace, 1981), pp. 172-181.

— Aside from the problem of available lift capability to send in air-borne troops (estimates range from a low of one to a high of four airborne divisions—the consensus is two), the Soviets lack the capacity to provide them with fighter escort (Khuzestan is out of range for all Soviet tactical fighters based in Afghanistan or the Soviet Union, and access to Iraqi bases is unlikely).

— Soviet bombers, limited by possible commitments to more important contingencies, and without fighter escorts, would also be vulnerable to U.S. and regional air power once a conflict was joined.[13]

As a result, it is unlikely that a Soviet force could be supported in Khuzestan without penalizing Soviet capacity to handle simultaneous contingencies in more important areas. Such a Soviet force, believes Joshua Epstein, "would be unlikely to enjoy any meaningful superiority over an RDF assembled under the same strategic constraint." In short, he finds that while there are serious challenges to U.S. force deployment, "the current situation warrants neither the kind of pessimism that has been heaped upon it nor an ill-considered 'drive for bases' which may flow from overassessments of the Soviet threat."[14]

Dennis Ross has observed that the Soviet Union's "coalition maintenance" decision-making environment tends to generate lowest common denominator policies that militate against bold departures and high risk actions. A direct attack, he surmises, would be conceivable only in circumstances the Soviets perceived to be defensive or extreme:

— if the costs of inaction were high (e.g., Afghanistan); or

— if the stakes were high (e.g., if the United States were to attempt to recreate the Northern Tier barrier or reestablish Iran as a strategic barrier to the projection of Soviet power).

Short of such high stakes, Ross would agree with Epstein that indirect means of achieving Soviet objectives are much more likely than the direct use of military force.[15]

If, in spite of all calculations to the contrary, the Soviets were to launch a direct attack on Khuzestan, most analysts would probably agree with the staff of the Carnegie Panel on U.S. Security and the

---

13. *Ibid*; and Thomas McNaugher, "Balancing Soviet Power in the Persian Gulf," *Brookings Review* 1:4 (1983), pp. 20-24.

14. The overland assault on Iran scenario, and the obstacles to Soviet power projection, are detailed in Joshua Epstein, "Soviet Vulnerabilities in Iran and the RDF Deterrent," *International Security* 6:2 (1981), pp. 126-158.

15. Dennis Ross, "Considering Soviet Threats to the Persian Gulf," *International Security* 6:2 (1981), pp. 159-180.

Future of Arms Control that, whatever the short-term outcome, in the long run the Soviets would prevail— *if* the battle remained conventional and *if* the Soviets kept pouring in men and materiel at the expense of weakening their forces in other theaters. Both of these "ifs" are important assumptions.[16] The uncertain risks of escalation to nuclear war (vertical escalation) or of widening the war to NATO and other countries (horizontal escalation) would weigh heavily on Soviet thoughts.

The Soviets might in some circumstances be willing to risk a quick military thrust, particularly in northwest Iran, under the assumption that faced with a confrontation the United States and its allies (i.e., Turkey) would be unwilling to assume the onus of initiating an attack on Soviet troops. But such a risk would be high and would, at a minimum, result in the immediate development of U.S. bases throughout the Gulf. Given the stakes involved, an expectation of resistance and, ultimately, confrontation could lead the Soviets to make their first move a surprise attack on U.S. carriers in the Indian Ocean in an effort to undercut U.S. tactical air superiority. Since such a course would risk global war and since, in any case, the Soviets would find it virtually impossible to ensure access to oil in the aftermath of such hostilities,[17] alternative options that focus on denial (e.g. through support of an attack by a surrogate, a massive air strike, or the use of missiles with conventional warheads) would seem to have greater attraction— although their provocative nature makes them extremely risky.

*Regional Threats.* The kinds of threats to U.S. interests caused by differences among countries in the region are limited only by the imagination. While such differences in and of themselves may pose difficult problems, those problems become much more serious to the extent that the Soviets are directly involved in them. Examples of such problems include:

— the historical conflict between Arabs and Israelis, which gave rise most recently to the war between Israel and the Palestinians in Lebanon, and the subsequent confrontation between Israel and Syria, both of which have important implications for the Gulf states;

— historical differences between Arabs and Persians, exemplified

---

16. *Challenges for U.S. National Security,* p. 175.

17. See *Oil Fields as Military Objectives: A Feasibility Study,* prepared for the Special Subcommittee on Investigations of the Committee on International Relations, House of Representatives, U.S. Congress, by the Congressional Research Service, Library of Congress (Washington, D.C.: G.P.O., 1975); and John M. Collins, *U.S.-Soviet Military Balance: Concepts and Capabilities, 1960-1980* (New York: McGraw-Hill, 1980), pp. 391-392.

by the Iran-Iraq war and complicated by differences among Shia and Sunni Muslims;
— Iraqi desires for hegemony in the Gulf, evidenced by threatening maneuvers against Kuwait over the last two decades;
— long-standing tensions between India and Pakistan, which have led to three wars since World War II;
— PDRY attacks on the Yemen Arab Republic (YAR), or PDRY supported attacks on Oman;
— YAR-Saudi border differences; and
— border conflicts between Afghanistan and Pakistan.

All of these problems grow out of historical regional differences. While they may be *influenced* by outside powers, they are much less subject to outside *control.* Any of them could develop into a major war — a war which, in the event of superpower involvement (as threatened in the Yemens in 1979), might escalate out of control. With the exception of a war between two important oil producing states such as Iran and Iraq or a threat to Saudi Arabia (whether from Iran, Iraq, or the PDRY), regional conflicts, while serious, pose much less of a threat to U.S. interests than a Soviet attack, *providing* the Soviets are not or do not become directly involved. If the Soviets are involved, much depends upon the proximity of the area to their borders.[18] If, in the Iran-Iraq war, the Soviets were to use troops in support of either Iran or Iraq, a serious contingency with all the trappings of a direct Soviet attack would arise. Soviet intervention in non-contiguous states, as pointed out earlier, would be risky and difficult.[19]

*Internal Threats to Stability.* Coups, terrorism, insurgencies and revolutions all grow out of complex political, economic, and social problems for which military responses are often inappropriate and counterproductive. Given the rapid pace of modernization in the region, historical, ethnic and religious differences, and discrepancies between rich and poor that exist among countries as well as within them, such challenges to established authority are likely. To the extent that they endanger a regime friendly to U.S. interests, such as that of Sultan Qabus's strategically important Oman, American policymakers

---

18. *Challenges for U.S. National Security,* pp. 172-181. See also Keith Dunn, "Constraints on the USSR in Southwest Asia: A Military Analysis," *Orbis* 25:3 (1981), pp. 607-629.

19. *Ibid.* The Carnegie Study concludes that, in a U.S.-Soviet conflict, Soviet land and air forces would dominate near their border with Iran, U.S. air power would prevail in the southern part of the Persian Gulf area, and there would be a stand-off at the head of the Gulf, with the *immediate* outcome uncertain, although the Soviets would probably prevail (p. 191).

should favor preventive measures (e.g., the prudent creation of structures for political participation) over reactive ones, the political consequences of which could be disastrous. Where such threats endanger the continued production of oil and where production cut-backs in countries such as Saudi Arabia can drastically affect the Western industrial economies, the United States could consider responding to a regime's invitation to protect its oil fields or, in a worst case scenario, contemplate seizing them under hostile conditions.[20] The latter possibility, of course, is precisely what concerns the Gulf states when they seek U.S. assistance, and it dictates their ambivalence toward American offers of protection.[21] Were the United States to attempt the seizure of Saudi Arabia's oil fields under hostile conditions, the oil fields would probably suffer major damage, the risk of inviting a Soviet or Soviet-supported challenge would be high, the military feasibility would be dubious, and the political costs would be so great as to threaten U.S. interests throughout the world.[22] The use of force would also be a long-term proposition since, as the American experience in Lebanon suggests, U.S. troops are unlikely to stabilize a regime otherwise incapable of managing an indigenous challenge to its authority.[23]

If, on the other hand, the Soviets were "invited" to intervene in a civil war in Iran (to support Kurdish or Azerbaijani separatists or a rump Tudeh faction) or in Pakistan (to support Baluch or Pushtun separatists), the problems posed earlier by a direct Soviet attack again would arise. For this reason, military strategists who must plan for such contingencies cannot be too cavalier in dismissing the probability, however small, of a Soviet attack.

---

20. See Robert Tucker, "Oil: The Issue of American Intervention," *Commentary* 59:1 (1975), pp. 21-31; Miles Ignotus (Edward Luttwak), "Seizing Arab Oil," *Harper's* 250 (March, 1975), pp. 45-62; subsequent articles by Tucker, "Further Reflections on Oil & Force," *Commentary* 59:3 (1975), pp. 45-56, "Oil and American Power-Three Years Later," *Commentary* 63:1 (1977), pp. 29-36, and "Oil and American Power-Six Years Later," *Commentary* 68:3 (1979), pp. 35-42; and J.B. Kelly's discussion of the issue in *Arabia, The Gulf and the West: A Critical View of the Arabs and their Oil Policy* (New York: Basic Books, 1980), pp. 494-504.

21. See, for example, Abdul Kasim Mansur (Anthony Cordesman), "The American Threat to Saudi Arabia," *Armed Forces Journal International* 118:1 (1980), pp. 47-60; and "The Military Balance in the Persian Gulf: Who will Guard the Gulf States from the Guardians?" *Armed Forces Journal International* 118:3 (1980), pp. 44-86.

22. Collins, *U.S.-Soviet Military Balance*, pp. 391-392.

23. Jeffrey Record, *The Rapid Deployment Force and U.S. Military Intervention in the Persian Gulf* (Cambridge, Mass.: Institute for Foreign Policy Analysis, 1980), p. 17.

Devising appropriate responses to these threat assessments is a difficult task. The most serious threat (a direct Soviet attack) is the least likely, while the more likely threats (those from within the region) are least responsive to military influence. Finally, the threats are not mutually exclusive—one can easily lead to or be part of another. If American policymakers prepare to counter the most serious threats, they may encourage and even precipitate other problems. The United States could look to Jordan, Pakistan, or Turkey as surrogates for American power, or attempt to establish a ground presence in the Gulf in order to give real as well as symbolic support to "moderate" regimes and thereby strike a credible deterrent posture.[24] Such policies, however, could foster the development of a radical, anti-American opposition in those countries or in the region as a whole, undermining rather than supporting regional stability. Depending on their circumstances, such actions could also result in Soviet pressures on Iraq, Iran, or even Kuwait to establish a countervailing presence in the region, thus bringing great power rivalry to the head in the Gulf.

On the other hand, when the United States discounts the utility of military force in addressing these problems and when it downplays the Soviet threat, keeping a low profile out of sensitivity to the political vulnerability of the Gulf's fragile regimes, it may be leaving the Gulf states open to coercion and attack. Such attitudes could contribute to a perception that U.S. influence is waning and to a belief among the local states that they should reckon with the Soviet Union. In so doing, the United States could encourage regional initiatives that increase a destabilizing Soviet influence to the detriment of American interests.

Finally, in the event of a great power confrontation in the Gulf, it would be infinitely more difficult for the United States or the Soviet Union to *ensure* access and control over the oil fields than it would be for either to *deny* the other such access and control. The relative ease that either would have in denying access and control to the other constitutes an important limitation on any military strategy in the Gulf and underscores the current asymmetry between U.S. and Soviet interests: the United States must ensure access and control; the Soviet Union, which in the short run does not need the oil, has only to deny it to the industrialized nations of the West to have a major impact on their economies.

---

24. For a belief within the armed services that forces stationed within the Gulf are necessary for its defense, see *The Economist*, December 11, 1983; for discussion of a U.S.-Turkish Agreement to build a new air base and modernize two others in Eastern Turkey (making it possible for NATO fighter-bombers to be within striking distance of Soviet forces in the Transcaucasus and within 700 miles of the Persian Gulf), see the *Washington Post*, November 7, 1982. See Chapter 5, fn. 13-16, Chapter 9 and Chapter 10 for Jordan's, Turkey's, and Pakistan's respective roles in the Gulf.

# 4

## Developing a Military Strategy

### U.S. MILITARY CAPABILITIES AND PLANS

United States capacity to respond to Soviet threats and to project its forces into the Persian Gulf Region currently is built around naval superiority in the Indian Ocean, substantial tactical air power, and ground forces that are readily deployable though lightly armed. Essential elements include:

— One and occasionally two carrier battle-groups (with up to 110 fighter and attack aircraft) deployed in or near the Indian Ocean; since 1983, supporting naval forces include a total of three carrier battle groups.

— Facilities in the region (in Kenya, Somalia, Oman, Diego Garcia, Egypt, Morocco and Israel, along with potential facilities in other areas depending upon the contingency).[1]

— AWACS and associated command, control, and communications equipment currently in Saudi Arabia and occasionally Egypt.[2]

— B-52 bombers staged in Spain or Guam and capable of operating out of Diego Garcia;

— Prepositioning of a 30-day supply of ammunition, fuel and spare parts for a Marine Amphibious Brigade aboard seven Near Time Prepositioning Ships (NTPS) capable of putting the brigade ashore in 48 hours at well-equipped ports (this does not include

---

1. For elaboration of the role and function of these facilities, see James Wooten, *Regional Support Facilities for the Rapid Deployment Force*, Report No. 82-53F, Congressional Research Service, Library of Congress, Washington, D.C., March 25, 1982; Lewis Sowell, Jr., *Base Development and the Rapid Deployment Force: A Window to the Future*, National Security Affairs Monograph Series 82-5 (Washington, D.C.: National Defense University Press, 1982); and John D. Mayer, Jr., "The U.S.-Moroccan Agreement and its Implications for the Rapid Deployment Forces," Congressional Budget Office, Washington, D.C., March 1983. For the difficulties posed by the lack of port facilities, see Dan Beakey, *Logistics Over the Shore*, National Security Affairs Monograph Series 82-6 (Washington, D.C.: National Defense University Press, 1982).

2. For the role and function of the AWACS, see the sources cited in Chapter 8, n. 21.

steaming time); these ships form part of a larger Near Time Prepositioning Force that includes additional stocks, ammunition, fuel, water, two 400-bed Army field hospitals and one 200-bed combat support hospital aboard 11 additional ships.

— Various elements of the Rapid Deployment Force (as of January 1, 1983, the United States Central Command, or CENTCOM), including one Marine Amphibious Force (MAF), three army divisions and seven tactical fighter wings (totalling over 200,000 troops and 400 fighter and attack aircraft). By the end of 1983, CENTCOM was to include five army and two Marine divisions, and was to have the equivalent of ten tactical air wings.[3]

By 1987, the United States will also have completed a number of strategic mobility initiatives currently underway:

— Prepositioning of a 30-day supply of ammunition, fuel, and spare parts for a Marine Corps division aboard 13 Maritime Prepositioning Ships (MPS) in the Indian Ocean;

— Prepositioning of support equipment at Diego Garcia, Masirah (Oman), and Ras Banas (Egypt), as well as over-building and over-stocking of maintenance sets at selected sites such as Dhahran and King Khalid Military City in Saudi Arabia;

— Acquisition of eight SL-7 fast deployment logistics container ships capable of moving a mechanized division to the Persian Gulf via the Cape of Good Hope from ports in the United States in 15-19 days (this does not include loading and off-loading, which will take an additional ten days);[4]

— Enhanced strategic airlift, including extension of the service life of the C-5A, an increase in the cargo capacity of the C-141, procurement of 56 additional KC-10 tanker aircraft and 50 C-5B's,

---

3. CENTCOM generally refers to the planning headquarters, the RDF to the forces that are available to CENTCOM. For discussion and elaboration of the mission, organization, training, logistical support facilities, and tactical doctrine of the RDF, see Maxwell Johnson, *The Military as an Instrument of U.S. Policy in Southwest Asia: The Rapid Deployment Joint Task Force, 1979-1982* (Boulder: Westview, 1983); Thomas McNaugher, "Balancing Soviet Power in the Persian Gulf," *Brookings Review* 1:4 (1983), pp. 20-24. For further details, the policy implications of alternative RDF levels, and the budgetary implications of such levels, see *Rapid Deployment Forces: Policy and Budgetary Implications* (Washington, D.C.: Congressional Budget Office, February 1983).

4. More than 400 ships are available for an RDF contingency: 37 from the Military Sealift Command Controlled Fleet; 29 from the Ready Reserve Fleet; 216 commercial U.S.-flag ships from the U.S. Merchant Marine available under the Sealift Readiness Program; and 141 in the National Defense Reserve Fleet. *Rapid Deployment Forces*, pp. 35-36.

modification of commercial aircraft for a military transport role, and, possibly, development and production of the costly and controversial strategic transport C-17.[5]

Although estimates vary, it is reasonable to conclude that these initiatives will give the commander of CENTCOM the capability of deploying the equivalent of four to five divisions, or 80-100,000 combat troops, to the Persian Gulf in thirty days.[6]

Beyond these initiatives, some have proposed prepositioning stocks in Saudi Arabia, together with the development in Saudi Arabia of a capacity for a region-wide, integrated defense network, to support the projection of U.S. tactical air and ground forces in the event of serious contingencies.[7] Development of a similar infrastructure in eastern Turkey will give the United States even greater flexibility in the region and, by its very existence, serve to deter Soviet adventurism in Iran. In principle, these developments are clearly desirable; but the Reagan Administration must be sensitive to regional limitations on its policies, being careful not to let design considerations, based in part on a worst-case analysis of the potential threat and in part on interservice rivalries

---

5. The United States currently has 70 "outsized" cargo C-5A and 234 smaller C-141 transport aircraft, which can be supplemented by as many as 367 commercial transports (Boeing 707 or 747 equivalents) under the Civilian Reserve Air Fleet Program. By 1988, assuming 127 of these commercial transports are provided (a number used by the Department of Defense in the Congressionally Mandated Mobility Study), the U.S. will be capable of generating 161 cargo airlift sorties daily for Southwest Asia (as opposed to 123 in 1983). *Rapid Deployment Forces*, pp. 31-33. The extraordinary logistical requirements involved in transporting supplies by air from the United States to the Middle East are evidenced by the fact that during the emergency resupply of Israel in 1973 six tons of aviation fuel were required to deliver every ton of supplies. James Wooten, *Regional Support Facilities for the Rapid Deployment Force*, p. 8.

6. The Reagan administration apparently intends to double the size of the 220,000-man RDF to 440,000 by the end of the decade. *Rapid Deployment Forces*, pp. 11-15. For earlier assessments, see: *Challenges for U.S. National Security*, pp. 165-69; Record, *The Rapid Deployment Force*, pp.47-52; and various issues of the *Armed Forces Journal International*, 1980-82; for later assessments, see: *The Economist*, December 11, 1982, pp. 62-64; and Johnson, *The Military as an Instrument of U.S. Policy in Southwest Asia*, pp. 102-110, and 113, who notes that the most severe constraints on the RDF's capability to engage in combat operations are deficiencies in water production, fuel supplies, medical evacuation and treatment facilities.

7. Interviews with officials in the Department of Defense. Development of a similar infrastructure in eastern Turkey would give the U.S. even greater flexibility in the region and—by its very existence—serve to deter Soviet adventurism in northern Iran.

within the Pentagon, confuse the strategy that the United States pursues. At present, in spite of improvement in the United States' *capacity* to deal with military contingencies in the Persian Gulf, debate continues over the military *strategy* that undergirds American military readiness.

## PREEMPTION, TRIPWIRES, AND DIRECT DEFENSE

At a minimum, most analysts agree that the United States must be capable of "beating" the Soviets to the Persian Gulf if the Soviets are to be deterred from adventurism there. They disagree, however, on whether possessing that preemptive capacity is sufficient to safeguard U.S. interests.

Some who minimize the Soviet threat believe that if the United States develops the capability for quick preemptive intervention, it can prevent Soviet adventurism.[8] Because a Soviet attack would result in direct conflict with the United States and the costs of such a venture would clearly outweigh the gains, they argue that the Soviets would back away from any situation where the United States has established a trip-wire. A corollary to this argument is that a relatively limited, "over-the-horizon" sea-based force (with land-based air support) is sufficient to establish a trip-wire if necessity so dictates, and that a more elaborate force is not only unnecessary and costly but also counterproductive. According to this interpretation, the asymmetry of the two countries' interests in the region is sufficient to underscore U.S. determination and dictate Soviet caution.

Critics have pointed out that preemptive intervention is a theory of deterrence, not a strategy, since it fails to address the question of what to do if deterrence fails.[9] If deterrence should fail (and it could, they argue, because most Western nations don't act as if their vital interests are at stake), fairly elaborate conventional forces would be essential to back up the trip-wire force. Without such a back-up, the United States would have recourse only to a nuclear threat, which lacks credibility unless the U.S. has previously committed sizable numbers of troops whose lives are jeopardized. The Soviets, recognizing Western impotence, might be prompted to disregard problems posed by a small

---

8. Christopher Van Hollen, "Don't Engulf the Gulf," *Foreign Affairs* 59:5 (1981), pp. 1064-1078; Stanley Hoffman, "Security in an Age of Turbulence: Means of Response," *Third-World Conflict and International Security (Part II)*, *Adelphi Papers*, No. 167, September 1980.
9. F.J. West, "NATO II: Common Boundaries for Common Interests," *Naval War College Review* 34:1 (1981), pp. 59-67.

conflict with the United States, particularly if they could outmaneuver American forces and establish themselves in some trouble-spot before the United States could get there. The Soviets could also provoke the United States to move preemptively in response to a Soviet feint, and then use U.S. intervention as justification for actions elsewhere.

As a result, most analysts see the need for an American strategy that goes beyond a capacity for preemptive intervention. Some have advocated a direct theater (or regional) defense by the United States with a view to entangling Europe either through Turkey or through the requirements of U.S. operations in Southwest Asia, which would be contingent upon allied assistance.[10]

A strategy of direct regional defense relies on quick reaction to Soviet initiatives. In the event of a Soviet move into Azerbaijan, for example, it requires early intervention (e.g. the insertion of airborne troops in the Zagros Mountains) as a means to buy time. Simultaneously, it seeks to create a buffer between Soviet forces and the Gulf through more elaborate military operations, with a view to building a coalition of allies that would make it very difficult for the Soviets to succeed in any aggressive action in Southwest Iran. The operating assumption of this strategy is that the Soviets' most significant advantage is not strategic but tactical, and that theater linkage (i.e., a linkage between the Middle East and Western Europe), with its escalatory risks, is necessary to counter that advantage. A corollary to coalition politics is that a more elaborate regional framework (i.e., facilities and prepositioned materiel) is necessary if a deterrent strategy is to be credible. How elaborate the regional framework should be depends on one's interpretation of the magnitude and likelihood of the Soviet threat. Those who seek the military capacity to counter a sizable Soviet attack generally argue for more elaborate and expanded facilities and discount the political costs in regional stability associated with an increased U.S. presence.

## MARITIME VS. COALITIONAL STRATEGIES

Within the defense establishment, interservice rivalries and competition for a larger share of the defense budget continue to fuel debate

---

10. Interviews with officials in the Department of Defense; see also John Hackett, "Protecting Oil Supplies: The Military Requirements," in *Third-World Conflict and International Security (Part I)*, *Adelphi Papers*, No. 166, September 1980, pp. 41-51; Albert Wohlstetter, "Meeting the Threat in the Persian Gulf," *Survey* 24:2 (1980), pp. 128-88; W. Scott Thompson, "The Persian Gulf and the Correlation of Forces," *International Security* 7:1 (1982), pp. 157-80.

over the role the United States should play vis-a-vis its allies, the division of labor among the services in responding militarily to developments in the Middle East, and the kind of conventional defense appropriate to the problem. A maritime strategy, articulated by F.J. West before he became Assistant Secretary of Defense for International Security Affairs and endorsed at least in part by the Reagan Administration's defense program (which plans for three new nuclear carrier battle groups), supports a policy of horizontal escalation which links NATO to any U.S.-Soviet conflict in the Persian Gulf.

West argues that a theater defense is not feasible. Nonetheless, he believes that sustaining a toehold in the Persian Gulf is necessary since Soviet control of the Gulf means Soviet control of Western Europe. He also believes that naval operations, unlike ground operations, cannot be limited by geography. As a result, he argues, NATO agreement to reinforce U.S troops is an agreement to naval combat because the naval threads of NATO forces are too intertwined. In the event of Soviet aggression, he asserts, the Soviets would be confronted by a conjunction of unacceptable threats. These include: (1) the threat of catastrophic naval losses; (2) a full NATO build-up; (3) mobilization of U.S. and European military might; and (4) a hair-trigger nuclear balance. The uncertain threat of vertical escalation, presumably, is expected to be more credible given the actions already taken. At the root of West's argument is the assumption that command of the sea confers a distinct advantage upon the United States, and that superior naval power is a category of military power separate from the capacity to fight a land war in the NATO countries. Articulation and implementation of a policy based on this assumption will, in West's estimation, provide the most credible defense possible for the United States.[11]

Critics of West's argument, led by former Under Secretary of Defense Robert Komer, argue that maritime supremacy is essential, but that primary reliance on it to project offensive forces will build the wrong kind of costly navy (Komer estimates that the three carrier battle groups will cost over $50 billion) at the expense of our larger strategic interests. Such a strategy, Komer argues, will not prevent Soviet domination of Europe and the Middle East. As a result, its implications ("at best a form of unilateral U.S. global interventionism and at worst a form of neoisolationism") will pressure America's allies to consider accommodation with the Soviet Union. Komer believes that America's efforts to rejuvenate the security relationship with its NATO allies, subject to more rational and efficient burden sharing, and benefiting from a

---

11. F.J. West, "NATO II: Common Boundaries for Common Interests," pp. 59-67. See also Secretary of the Navy John Lehman's letter to the editor, *Foreign Affairs* 61:2 (1982/1983), pp. 455-56.

more balanced force structure, offer a better prospect for achieving a conventional deterrence/defense in Western Europe, the Persian Gulf, and Northeast Asia.[12]

Those who agree with Komer's criticism of a maritime strategy built around a few super carriers for projecting power do not always share his enthusiasm for a coalition approach. Former Director of Central Intelligence Stansfield Turner, for example, emphasizes the importance of smaller carriers exercising traditional maritime capabilities (i.e., control of the sea lanes and air lanes above them). Turner believes that more small ships, in conjunction with a revised doctrine that includes smaller amphibious assault operations and more mobile follow-on ground and air forces, would give the United States the flexibility it must have to move forces where unexpected contingencies dictate. This could be done, he argues, *without* threatening the programs that presently support the defense of Europe and Northeast Asia. The strategy that Turner advocates would not be as dependent on the NATO alliance as that espoused by Komer and would provide insurance against European failure to cooperate with the United States.[13]

Finally, two members of the Strategic Studies Institute of the U.S. Army War College have criticized the deterrent posture of both schools. In their judgment, the continental/coalition school's reliance on theater nuclear weapons (vertical escalation) and the maritime school's reliance on war-widening options (horizontal escalation) both threaten a fundamental concern: the avoidance of super-power conflict. Their preference is to keep political-military objectives limited; otherwise, their recommendations do not appear that different from Komer's. They advocate a balance of conventional capabilities, seeking to combine a coalitional approach with a policy of force procurement that emphasizes strategic mobility assets. A policy built on these recommendations, they believe, would be flexible enough to allow for non-nuclear deterrence in the Persian Gulf, which they regard as significant but secondary in importance to Europe.[14]

---

12. Robert Komer, "Maritime Strategy vs. Coalition Defense," *Foreign Affairs* 60:5 (1982), pp. 1124-1144; and "Security Challenges of the 80's," *Armed Forces Journal International* 119:3 (1981), pp. 64-77. See also Komer's letters to the editor, *Foreign Affairs* 61:2 (1982/1983), pp. 453-454 and 456.

13. Stansfield Turner and George Thibault, "Preparing for the Unexpected: The Need for a New Military Strategy," *Foreign Affairs* 61:1 (1982), pp. 122-135. See also Turner's letters to the editor, *Foreign Affairs* 61:2 (1982/1983), pp. 454-457.

14. Keith Dunn and William O. Staudenmaier, "Strategy for Survival," *Foreign Policy*, No. 52 (1983), pp. 22-41; see also the exchange of letters between the authors and Robert Komer, *Foreign Policy*, No. 53 (1983-84), pp. 176-178.

Since these two analysts regard the Persian Gulf as more unstable than Europe, they also see it as more likely to require U.S. assistance. They circumvent the question of cost by recommending that the United States shift its defense budget priorities and pursue military operations sequentially rather than simultaneously. While they acknowledge that shifting budget priorities would be difficult politically, they never confront the crucial importance of the Gulf region to the security of Western Europe and Japan, a factor that created the problem of simultaneous fronts in the first place. As a result, they also ignore the tough question of how successful a publicly declared non-nuclear policy in the Gulf would be in deterring the Soviets. Finally, they do not provide any insight into what the United States should do if non-nuclear deterrence fails and conventional forces, once committed, are on the verge of defeat.[15]

As debates within the defense establishment continue, the Reagan Administration, while leaning toward the strategy advocated by F.J. West, has yet to make clear its preference between maritime and coalition strategies. If the FY 1983 Defense Posture Statement is any guide, the administration appears to have endorsed both.[16] Perhaps, as Komer points out, it is unlikely that a choice would or should be made between them. Political realities, underscored by Pentagon estimates that implementing the administration's declaratory strategy would take $750 billion more than the $1.6 trillion in defense authorization requested for 1982-1986, suggest nonetheless that choices between various weapons and capabilities must be made and that such choices, cumulatively, may result in the predominance of one strategy over another. Relative in-

---

15. For a thoughtful examination of the implications of the RDF for nuclear escalation, see Christopher Paine, "On the Beach: The Rapid Deployment Force and the Nuclear Arms Race," *MERIP Reports* 13:1 (1983), pp. 3-11, and 30.

16. *Report of Secretary of Defense Caspar Weinberger to the Congress on the FY 1983 Budget, FY1984 Authorization Request and FY1983-1987 Defense Programs* (Washington, D.C.: G.P.O., February 8, 1982). More recently, Air Force General David Jones, retired chairman of the Joint Chiefs of Staff, has complained about the United States "trying to do everything," and Senator Sam Nunn has observed that "spending more money without a clear sense of ultimate purpose or priority will not result in a sound strategy or an adequate security." When administration officials such as Secretary of Defense Weinberger attempt to defend defense programs on the basis of jobs that will be lost, they are making the wrong argument. Robert DeGrasse of the Council on Economic Priorities has found that for every billion dollars spent on military procurement, 28,000 direct and indirect jobs are created. The same money spent on personal consumption would yield 57,000 jobs; on education, 71,000 jobs. Brad Knickerbocker, *Christian Science Monitor*, June 15, July 28, 1983.

creases in the Navy's share of the FY 1983 budget, for example, including funding for two large carriers (at $3.4 billion a carrier), mean that by and large the other services have had, and (with one OMB analysis estimating the cost of a carrier battle group at $15.4 billion)[17] will have, their force structure increases deferred. When it comes to claims of the Navy's ascendence over the other services, however, skepticism is warranted. An analyst who is critical of the administration's failure to settle on a strategy has observed that the Navy has received fewer than 50 percent of the ships contained in the past 15 completed Five Year Defense Plans.[18] More recently, in August 1983, a Defense Department spokesman observed publicly that the Army's share of military funding had not been "as equitable as it should have been," lending credence to a published report that the Navy might lose as much as $10 billion to the Army in the next five years.[19] The debate, clearly, is far from resolved.

## WHERE DO WE GO FROM HERE?

Given the political context within which the United States must operate in the Persian Gulf, the most sensible military strategy for it to pursue there would seem to be that which is consistent with current American military capabilities and plans to enhance sea-lift and air-lift. This strategy should allow for a conventional force sufficient to:

— assist American allies (e.g., Saudi Arabia);
— help defend them against threats from other regional forces (e.g., Iran, Iraq, or the PDRY); and
— deter a Soviet attack by means of (a) a capacity to deploy a preemptive force in readiness; (b) a capability to transport (by air and sea) conventional reinforcements that would serve as a significant obstacle to Soviet aggression in the unlikely event that it were to occur; and, ultimately, (c) the uncertain threat of vertical and horizontal escalation.

The level of forces required to throw back, rather than impede, a determined Soviet attack on the Gulf would be far in excess of what is

---

17. Interview with an official in the Office of Management and Budget.

18. William Van Cleave, "Strategy and the Navy's 1983-87 Program: Skepticism is Warranted!" *Armed Forces Journal International* 119:8 (1982), pp. 49-51. For Secretary of the Navy Lehman's belief that he already has his 600 ship navy (the United States already has 514 ships, and by "front loading" it has 106 more ships under contract), see Michael Getler in the *New York Times,* Dec. 2, 1982.

19. George Wilson, *International Herald Tribune,* August 11, 1983.

required to accomplish these three goals. A sizable ground presence would also be politically counterproductive, and it is not at all clear that sizable forces could prevent the Soviets from destroying the oil fields and terminals or denying the United States access to Gulf oil anyway. As a result, the strategy recommended here eschews a ground presence. Rather, it relies, initially, on airborne divisions and sizable sea-based capabilities that could react quickly; secondly, on air-lifted and sea-lifted forces; and ultimately, on the uncertain threat of nuclear weapons and war-widening capabilities (both at sea and on the ground) to deter a Soviet attack. In short, it places its confidence in a force that is quick, no larger than necessary to perform its regional functions, but large enough to require Soviet military intervention to defeat it. A trip-wire force, Kenneth Waltz has observed, must be thick enough so that only a national military force—not a loose band of irregulars—can snap it. "This then gives the United States the target for retaliation and establishes the conditions under which deterrence prevails."[20] Should deterrence fail, a full range of options would still be available to decision-makers, providing that the options of vertical and horizontal escalation have not been renounced.[21] The United States may never intend to resort to either option, but public declaration of such a policy would weaken its deterrent posture.

There are a number of ways in which such a strategy could be implemented, one of which is articulated by an analyst who advocates "a small, agile, tactically capable intervention force that is based on and supplied from the sea, governed by a single, unified command, and supported by expanded sea power, especially forcible-entry capabilities."[22]

---

20. Kenneth Waltz, "A Strategy for the Rapid Deployment Force," *International Security* 5:4 (1981), pp. 49-73. The emphasis on *rapid* is crucial because rapid deployment of even a small force makes counter-intervention by the Soviet Union extremely risky. Given the difficulties discussed earlier of seizing oil fields under hostile conditions, a reasonable interpretation of what should constitute "an asset-seizing, deterrent force" is that which would allow the United States to respond—rapidly and effectively—to a regime's *invitation* to protect its oil fields. To move without an invitation, or to conduct a preemptive operation without regional support, would probably not work and be extremely risky.

21. For discussion of this issue, see "A Conversation with Zbigniew Brzezinski," *Bill Moyer's Journal,* Show # 702, PBS Air Date November 14, 1980, p. 9.

22. Record, *The Rapid Deployment Force,* p. 69. See Robert Hanks, "Rapid Deployment in Perspective," *Strategic Review* 9:2 (1981), pp.17-23, and Albert Wohlstetter, "Meeting the Threat in the Persian Gulf," pp. 128-88. Providing that the U.S. force is sea-based, its capacity to meet a threat at its own level makes the threat of escalation more credible, and remains politically tolerable to the regional states.

Such a force would stress quality over size, prompt responsiveness over the nonetheless important capacity for delayed augmentation from the United States, sea-based power projection capabilities over land-based tactical air power, and air transported forces and logistical self-sufficiency over a dependency on facilities ashore. Air transported forces and facilities ashore, it should be stressed, would be extremely important in the event that the Soviets were involved.

Such a force, operating under the strategy outlined above, would have several virtues:

— While the proposed strategy recognizes that the United States must improve its capacity to move tactical air and ground forces rapidly, the strategy directs attention to regional and lesser threats, both of which are much more likely than a worst-case Soviet attack.

— A sea-based force, supplemented by a rapidly deployable airborne force and an increasingly developed infrastructure (i.e., overbuilding, enlarged airstrips, and prepositioned material in selected locations), would afford the United States the option to intervene, but would also allow American decision-makers the choice of avoiding situations that would engulf a land-based American force in hostilities.

— The Soviets, who currently do not have a capacity equal to that of the United States to project force without bases, would have greater difficultly (politically and militarily) matching the U.S. presence.

— As a result, the proposed strategy, while giving the United States a qualified capacity to respond credibly to a Soviet attack, would also be more responsive to the internal problems of countries in the region and to the fact that American forces stationed there would be a serious liability to their interests and those of the United States alike.

— A corollary is that it would allow for greater receptivity to the needs and concerns of the regional states, and greater flexibility in American dealings with those states.

# 5

## Formulating a Political Strategy

A military strategy toward the Persian Gulf Region is meaningless unless it is conceived in the context of a political strategy. As Rouhollah Ramazani has observed, the United States must share with the region a policy based on a common vision of its priorities and stability; in short, the soldier must remain the servant of the diplomat.[1]

## PREREQUISITES AND OPERATING ASSUMPTIONS

The imperatives that condition the development of a political strategy deserve some elaboration. Washington officials must acknowledge that relations with the states of the Gulf region are symbiotic and that regional imperatives must have equal footing with mutual concerns about the Soviet threat. They must also recognize that, while there are no reliable substitutes for America's military power, political constraints nonetheless limit its use and efficacy. Finally, they must accept the uncertainties that attend the development and maintenance of a flexible political strategy toward a rapidly changing region. If American policymakers accept these premises, they will be in a position to consider a broader range of viable political options toward the Persian Gulf and Southwest Asia.

Because operating assumptions implicit in a discussion of such options are crucial, it will be useful before proceeding to identify them. To begin with, a Soviet (or other national) threat to certain countries in the region must anticipate the possibility of a credible conventional response by the United States on behalf of those countries. Since conventional U.S. forces are constrained both in size and in manner of deployment by regional sensitivities, the United States, in confronting a Soviet threat, can rely on conventional forces only to a certain point. Beyond that point, the United States must rely on the *uncertain* threats posed by horizontal and vertical escalation. This is not to say that the United States would ever resort to either course, but it is to acknowledge that the U.S. possesses a capability for doing so that the Soviet Union cannot ignore.

---

1. Rouhollah Ramazani, "Weapons Can't Replace Words," Newsweek (International) (September, 1980), p. 23.

The balance so struck between Soviet land forces (in the Transcaucasus and Central Asia) and the U.S. Rapid Deployment Force (operating out of the Indian Ocean) could, if appropriately nurtured, allow for the gradual creation of what should be the central component of any strategy toward the region: a *de facto buffer zone between East and West*—a zone for which there is historical precedent.[2] If the United States could come to some agreement with the Soviet Union about their policies in such a zone (i.e., a code of conduct), it is reasonable to assume that Iran and Afghanistan would be amenable to it. Iran has already chosen to follow a non-aligned role, evident in the slogan "neither East nor West," that follows traditional policies and currently characterizes its foreign policy.[3] Afghanistan's traditional policy of *bitarafi* (without sides), which seeks to balance external influences,[4] is one of the few policies that most Afghans, should they ever reconstitute themselves as a nation, could agree upon. In the context of such an understanding, regional states could be relatively free of great power influence and pursue non-aligned policies to the benefit of all parties.[5]

Meanwhile U.S. military capabilities, if properly deployed, could impede regional adventurism against vital Western interests; they could also stimulate regional cooperation. Secure from pressures to accommodate Soviet demands, though still vulnerable to situations that excite great power rivalry, regional states would have a strong incentive to head off those situations through regional cooperation.

The military balance would also make it possible for Gulf states, short of policies that directly threaten vital U.S. or Soviet interests, to control their own destinies. As a result, while relying ultimately on the balance of power between the United States and the Soviet Union, regional states to varying degrees could and would have to play a primary role in the management of regional conflicts.

---

2. For discussion of this issue, see Bruce Kuniholm, *The Origins of the Cold War in the Near East: Great Power Conflict and Diplomacy in Iran, Turkey, and Greece* (Princeton: Princeton University Press, 1980).

3. See Chapter 7.

4. Alvin Rubinstein, *Soviet Policy Toward Turkey, Iran, and Afghanistan: The Dynamics of Influence* (New York: Praeger, 1982), pp. 131, 141, 147.

5. Greece and Turkey also recognize the limitations of U.S. commitments and, because of internal pressures, have periodically gravitated at least partially back to a traditional posture in which they carefully balance their relations with the great powers. If the October 1981 elections underscore these developments in Greece (where substantive changes have yet to match rhetorical promises), less dramatic indices have periodically suggested them in Turkey. Reference is not to Turkish constraints on U.S. use of its military facilities, but to the fact

Such a development would make it easier for the United States and the Soviet Union to accommodate political change and avoid involvement within the region, as long as neither country seeks to change the status quo by drastic measures. While the United States could support particular states within the broader region, especially Turkey and Saudi Arabia, and to a lesser extent Pakistan, it would have to be sensitive to the various regional contexts within which those states operate. Turkey, for example is a NATO ally; but it is also a rival of another ally, Greece. Its Islamic identity, moreover, may become increasingly significant and its historical role as a buffer between the great powers is still applicable.

The regional contexts within which states operate change with time. Iran's and Pakistan's pro-U.S. orientation and membership in CENTO, for instance, have been replaced by an Islamic orientation. Accordingly, the United States would have to anticipate changes and constantly evaluate the significance of changing circumstances so that its policies could be adjusted. To facilitate the process, policymakers would have to acquire the habit of thinking in terms of, cooperating with, and encouraging sub-regional groupings of states (e.g., a non-aligned "Northern Tier," the GCC or a bloc of states on the subcontinent) which constitute discrete if not always cohesive sources of political, economic, or military strength, and which could address collective problems and advance common interests.

The role of America's NATO allies and Japan would have to be carefully thought through and closely coordinated.[6] Operational problems and political concerns associated with joint military responsibilities might lead the United States to rely essentially on its own reaction forces in the Indian Ocean, although it would continue to coordinate

---

that as recently as the late 70s, prior to the improvement of U.S.-Turkish relations in the early 80s, the Soviet Union was Turkey's largest single source of credit and economic aid as well as its strongest trading partner. In addition, the Cyprus conflict and related Aegean problems make it difficult for the United States to support either of its NATO allies completely, and hence impedes good relations with both. See Bruce Kuniholm, "Turkey and NATO: Past, Present, and Future," *Orbis* 27:2 (1983), pp. 421-446.

6. For a discussion of peacetime contributions of European forces, guaranteed provision of facilities for Persian Gulf contingencies, and financial support of military construction efforts in the region, see Dov Zakheim, "Of Allies and Access," *The Washington Quarterly* 4:1 (1981), pp. 87-96. See also David Newsom, "America Engulfed," *Foreign Policy* No. 43, (1981), pp. 17-32 (esp. pp. 24-25); and "Will Europe Help America Help Europe?" *Economist*, December 11, 1982, which notes the potential value of France's Alpine division, Italy's five Alpine brigades, and a number of European paratroop forces. For a discussion of the role Japan could play, see Takashi Oka in the *Christian Science Monitor*, March 30, 1981.

with France, Britain, and Australia on naval deployments. The United States could explore a division of labor with its NATO allies and Japan whereby they increase their defense responsibilities in Europe and in the Pacific, respectively, to balance increased American efforts in the Persian Gulf and Indian Ocean. The United States could also encourage its NATO allies to exercise their influence in particular countries of the region (e.g., Germany in Turkey, France in Iraq, Japan in Iran, Britain in Oman).[7]

As European commercial ties with the Soviet Union improve (a development which the gas pipeline will encourage), the Soviet Union might be more amenable to allowing European influence to serve as a "third alternative" to that of the two superpowers. The Germans and the Japanese saw themselves providing Turkey, Iran, and Afghanistan with an alternative to Soviet and British influence earlier in this century, and the French, certainly, aspire to such a role in the Gulf in the 1980s.[8] Though the rest of the European countries and Japan have been more reserved about playing such a role, they too may seek to develop special relationships with individual countries in the region.

Were the United States to encourage such efforts, the Soviet reaction would be difficult to predict. Because implementation of the strategy could result in the creation of a buffer zone between East and West in the region, and would encourage the region's developing and non-aligned countries to use their collective influence to restrain either Soviet or U.S. inclinations to take risks, it would lessen the chances of confrontation between the United States and the Soviet Union. It would encourage regional stability, would reassure the Soviet Union of American interest in amicable relations *if the Soviets desire them*, and might even make possible a resolution of the Afghan problem.

These arguments, clearly, would be far more persuasive if presented along with other initiatives in the context of a thaw or a least a "tough-minded" detente in U.S.-Soviet relations. If the Soviets reacted

---

7. See the discussion in Chapter 7. For evidence that the Iranians would welcome Japanese and other contracts, see William Drozdiak, *International Herald Tribune*, May 31, 1983; Peter Maas, *Washington Post*, July 23, 1983; and Claude Van England, *Christian Science Monitor*, August 8, 1983. While the Japanese would like to resume work on the $3.5 billion petrochemical complex at Bandar Khomeini, they have been warned not to by Iraq, which considers the project a war target. *International Herald Tribune*, May 13, 1983.

8. France, the third largest manufacturer and exporter of arms in the world, until recently received 25% of its oil from Iraq and has been processing Iraqi jets since 1977. *Christian Science Monitor*, January 27, and February 2, 1981. Foreign Minister Francois-Poncet, in a press conference in the UAE in December 1978, referred to France as the "third alternative." See also Chapter 7.

cooperatively, Moscow and Washington might agree to take advantage of this opportunity to reach a *modus vivendi* and go back to some of the rules of the "Great Game" that the great powers have played in the region since the eighteenth century.[9] If the Soviets believed U.S. initiatives were a guise for recreating a pro-U.S. Northern Tier barrier, Moscow would probably attempt to subvert the strategy. The strategy's success would then depend on the extent to which countries of the region believed U.S. policy to be in their best interests, and the degree to which they could be convinced of both the strategy's efficacy and U.S. good will.

A strategy that builds on such assumptions and follows along the lines suggested below would provide convincing evidence of American support for the sovereignty and territorial integrity of existing states and would best safeguard U.S. interests in the region. It would address realistically the regional constraints on American policies. It would be consistent with American ideals, would be more acceptable to states of the region, and would provide for a potentially significant and politically effective voice against aggression from any front (especially the Soviet Union). At the same time, it would avoid repetition of the American experience with other formerly conservative regimes (Libya, Iraq, Ethiopia, and Iran) — all of which established close military cooperation with the United States, all of which were overthrown, and all of whose successors are among the most rabidly anti-U.S. regimes in the world. Oman may one day experience a similar fate, while Russia's experience in Egypt should also be instructive.

The strategy proposed here could be characterized as one of "strength through respect," for it acknowledges that pluralism has come of age and that support for regionalism is in the security interests of all countries.[10] It could signal the beginning of a constructive and fruitful U.S. policy toward the Third World.

---

9. The "Balkan problem," the "Eastern Question," the "Persian Problem," and the "Great Game," all refer to different geographical foci of the rivalry between East and West (initially between Russia and Great Britain and later between the Soviet Union and the United States) that began in the area stretching from the Balkans to India as long ago as the eighteenth century. The term "Great Game" was used by Rudyard Kipling to describe what he saw as Britain's attempts to contain Russia's expansion southward into Southwest Asia. J.B. Kelly, "Great Game or Grand Illusion," *Survey* 24:2 (1980), p.118, argues that "over the past decade, through inattention rather than design, the West has failed to abide by the rules of the Great Game as it is played in Persia, thereby inadvertently paving the way for the Soviet Union, in their turn, to break them in Afghanistan."

10. An essential component of this strategy, which should be underscored, is a comprehensive energy program. Such a program is necessary if we are to

## A GENERAL POLITICAL STRATEGY

Examples of how such a strategy could operate in the context of the Middle East and Southwest Asia will illustrate, but by no means exhaust, the possibilities. The United States could develop a general three-pronged strategy whose components would consist of:

— A regional coalition of Arab Gulf states such as the Gulf Cooperation Council (GCC), under Saudi leadership, whose defense systems the United States could help to integrate.

— A *de facto* regional coalition of old CENTO countries (an aligned Turkey, a non-aligned Iran, and a quasi-aligned Pakistan) which would constitute a buffer zone between the Soviet Union and the Gulf states.

— Quiet support for the Islamic Conference (IC). The IC is the best forum for subsuming the interests of the two groupings of states. It makes the Soviets uncomfortable because of its religious focus and its possible effect on the Soviet Muslim population. It would also keep Afghanistan in the public eye and undercut the influence of secular radical coalitions.[11]

As a complement to the above three-pronged strategy, the United States might also wish to support a concept designed to support Egyp-

---

reduce our vulnerability to OPEC and convince the countries of the Middle East that the strategy is more than a ruse to trick them out of their oil. For the desirability of such a program, see the conclusion of the CRS study cited in Chapter 3, n. 7.

11. For a discussion of the Soviet Muslim population, see Helene Carrere d'Encausse, *Decline of an Empire: The Soviet Socialist Republics in Revolt* (New York: Newsweek Books, 1981); and Edward Mortimer, *Faith and Power: The Politics of Islam* (New York, Vintage, 1982), pp. 377-95, whose book is a useful corrective to many of the broad and misleading generalizations that are made about Islam. Hermann Eilts, "Security in the Persian Gulf," *International Security* 5:2 (1980), p. 112, urges that we avoid misguided efforts to *harness* the Islamic world, as represented by the Islamic Conference, to the American Policy bandwagon. He underscores our poor understanding of it and emphasizes that tying it to superpower policies taints the limited, moral effectiveness it may have. The argument here is not to tie the IC to our policies, but to make it possible for the IC to support them. Since Islam is the single most important cultural and political fact in the region, one of those universal movements which can mobilize human energy in a devoted and concentrated way, it is advantageous to have its attention — to the extent that it is negative — focused on our adversaries. For the difficulties of this endeavor, see Chapter 6. For a discussion of the spiritual and psychic needs that have stimulated the recent quest for a return to the Islamic ethos, see R. Hrair Dekmejian, "The Anatomy of Islamic Revival: Legitimacy Crisis, Ethnic Conflict and the Search for Islamic Alternatives," *Middle East Journal* 34: 1 (1980), pp. 1-12.

tian,[12] Jordanian,[13] Pakistani,[14] or possibly Turkish[15] troops with U.S. airlift capabilities, and build closer ties between those Muslim countries and the Gulf states. To the extent that it relies on Islamic states to protect mutual interests, this concept would be more acceptable than the introduction of American forces into the region. It would also facilitate a mutually beneficial arrangement between countries rich in manpower, but poor in oil, and those that have small populations, but are oil rich.[16] Such a scheme could, however, commit the United States to greater involvement in the Gulf or cause it to incur more far-reaching responsibilities in the region (especially to Pakistan) than presently envisioned — all desirable options only to the extent that some regional power, perhaps Iran, poses a serious threat to regional security or gravitates toward the Soviet Union. Such a shift would change the political and

---

12. For a report of 12,000 Egyptian "volunteers" already serving with Iraqi troops, see *Christian Science Monitor*, July 5, 1983. In October 1983, President Mubarak warned that if Iran blocked oil shipments through the Gulf, Egypt would take military action against Iran. "Egypt's army is Arab and will intervene to help its brothers," he said. *International Herald Tribune*, October 20, 1983.

13. For discussion of U.S. involvement in the training of a two-brigade, 8,000-man Jordan strike force (conceived after the takeover of the Great Mosque in Mecca in 1979) for use in military emergencies in the Gulf, see the *Washington Post*, October 22; and the *New York Times*, October 24, 1983.

14. For discussion of the Pakistani connection with the Gulf states (President Zia ul-Haq also took part in the Jordanian civil war in 1970-71), see Chapter 10.

15. While more problematic than relations with other countries mentioned above, the rapprochement between Turkey and the Gulf states, discussed in Chapter 9, nonetheless makes an arrangement between them a possibility. The Turks, for example, have recently intervened in northern Iraq to deal with a common Kurdish problem. See the *International Herald Tribune*, May 28-29, 1983.

16. Turkey has almost $15 billion in investments in the Middle East (primarily Saudi Arabia, Iraq, and Libya), where 250,000 Turks have found new jobs. *New York Times*, September 9, 1981; see also Chapter 9, n. 5. Reliable reports of Pakistani Air and Army units in Saudi Arabia have estimated their number as anywhere from 6-25,000 (President Zia-ul-Haq has acknowledged 1,500-2,000). *Christian Science Monitor*, December 6, 1980, February 6, 20, March 5, 1981, and December 6, 1982. See also Chapter 10, n. 13. Since March 1981, Egypt has been sending the Gulf state quarterly shipments of arms, spare parts, and ammunition; in April 1982 it agreed to supply Iraq with $1.5 billion worth of military equipment and ammunition, all financed by the Saudis; at about the same time, the Egyptians discussed with the Omanis the possibilities of Egyptian cooperation with the Gulf Cooperation Council. *Christian Science Monitor*, April 14, 1982.

strategic contexts within which U.S. forces operate and create the opportunity to change policies in response to regional "shocks."[17] In the absence of such an opening, these options must be developed cautiously because of the consequences that a heavy-handed American influence could have on the often tenuous power bases of leaders in the region. The extent of Gulf cooperation would hinge on a number of variables, including perceptions of the Soviet threat, Soviet relations with Iran, progress on the Palestinian question, the role of Israel in America's strategic posture, the relationship at the time between Iran and Iraq, and the climate of opinion within the Gulf.

In the event of serious differences between the United States and Saudi Arabia, the United States might have little recourse but to fall back on Israel and Egypt as its only important allies in the region, with Oman being America's primary Gulf partner. Under this scenario, American options would be extremely grim, suggesting the importance of preventing U.S.-Saudi relations from deteriorating and the desirability of operating within the framework of the strategy outlined above. Before examining the components of a political strategy toward the region, however, the crucial connection between the Palestinian problem and the Persian Gulf deserves brief attention.

---

17. This is what economists call "the displacement effect." Examples of past "shocks" would be the fall of the Shah or the Soviet invasion of Afghanistan. An example of a future "shock" would be an Iraqi decision to bomb Kharg Island and an Iranian decision to mine the Strait of Hormuz, or, less likely, a Soviet decision to send troops (invited or otherwise) into northwest Iran. Such a decision clearly would affect the magnitude of our relationship with Turkey as well as Gulf attitudes toward U.S. bases in the Gulf and would open up an entirely different set of options for the U.S. in the region. Planning for such options, of course, must anticipate their likelihood.

# 6

## The Palestinian/Arab-Israeli Problem
## and the Gulf

A number of writers have asserted that the Arab-Israeli problem is not the key issue in the Gulf, that it is tenuously related, and that even if one were to resolve it the main sources of conflict and instability in the region would not be removed.[1] Others have insisted that, while not the sole issue, nor the solution to all American problems in the region, the Palestinian problem is regarded by Arab leaders of the Gulf as the prime political issue—one which, as long as it exists, will continue to impede American efforts to elicit closer security cooperation from the Gulf states.[2]

### THE GULF CONNECTION

Whether or not the Palestinian question is resolved, serious problems will continue to develop in the Gulf—the Iran-Iraq War has made that clear. What seems equally clear, particularly in the aftermath of the Israeli invasion of Lebanon, is that if there *were* progress toward a resolution of the Palestinian question, Gulf problems would not develop in the context of a situation that threatens so completely to counter U.S. interests in the region. *Until* there is such progress, American efforts at security cooperation with the Gulf states will be at best impeded and at worst fundamentally challenged.[3]

---

1. See Robert Tucker, "American Power and the Persian Gulf," *Commentary* 70:5 (1980), pp. 25-41; "The Middle East: Carterism Without Carter?" *Commentary* 70:3 (1981), pp. 27-36; and J.B. Kelly, "A Response to Hermann Eilts' 'Security Considerations in the Persian Gulf,' " *International Security* 5:4 (1981), pp. 186-95.

2. See Hermann Eilts, "Security Considerations in the Persian Gulf," *International Security* 5:2 (1980), pp. 79-113; "A Rejoinder to J.B. Kelly," *International Security* 5:4 (1981), pp. 195-203; David Newsom, "Miracle or Mirage: Reflections on U.S. Diplomacy and the Arabs," *Middle East Journal* 35:3 (1981), pp. 299-313.

3. If, for example, the United States fails to address the Palestinian question, Israel continues its annexation of the West Bank, and symbolic incidents (e.g., the April 1982 slaying of Arabs in Al Aqsa mosque by an American-born

This judgment derives from the assumption that Israeli retention of the West Bank and Gaza will become increasingly unacceptable to the Palestinians who live there, inevitably forcing Israel to intensify security measures and progressively weakening its political and moral position in international forums.[4] In time, increased tensions and longstanding hostilities in the region, fueled by the resources of the Arab world and on occasion by the Soviet Union, will force Israel, as in 1973, to increase its requests for U.S. security assistance. At some point, U.S. officials will be confronted with disconcerting choices as they look at the U.S. Israeli relationship and its implications for U.S. policy in the Gulf.

If the United States fails to meet Israeli security requests, Israelis will feel increasingly vulnerable. They will also be more likely to strike preemptively at their foes (e.g., the bombing of Iraq's nuclear research center, which was not related to the Palestinian problem, and the invasion of Lebanon, which was). They might even involve themselves in wars that could escalate out of control. As the 1973 War made clear and as Israeli-Syrian confrontations over Lebanon suggest, Israeli policies have the potential for involving the United States in serious—and possibly nuclear—confrontations with the Soviet Union as well.

Yet if the United States meets Israeli security requests, the U.S.-Israeli relationship will reinforce Arab and Muslim perceptions that American assistance is the prime reason why Israel is able to deny Palestinians their "legitimate rights." These perceptions, in turn, which aggravate the radical Arab regimes and have long separated them from the United States, will generate growing internal and external pressures on conservative regimes to distance themselves from the United States as well.

A regime's response to such pressures is conditioned by complex trade-offs. Arab rulers in the Gulf, for example, recognize that the U.S. presence in the Indian Ocean exercises a deterrent function with respect to Soviet pressures. In conjunction with a symbolic show of force in the Persian Gulf (MIDEASTFOR), it also provides them with some protection from intimidation by regional powers such as Iran. Nonetheless,

---

Israeli and the so-called "strategic cooperation agreement" between Israel and the United States in 1983) continue to enflame the Arab world, it becomes much more difficult for the Saudis to cooperate with the United States.    Constructive mediation that addresses the Israeli search for security and the Palestinian quest for self-determination, on the other hand, could allow for a *modus vivendi* which satisfies the aspirations of both Palestinians and Israelis, and is compatible—both politically and militarily—with the policies advocated in this book.

4. For a detailed elaboration of this argument, see Bruce Kuniholm, *The Palestinian Problem and U.S. Policy* (Claremont, Cal.: Regina Books, forthcoming).

since the Palestinian cause is an Arab cause, Arab regimes cannot ignore the fact that U.S. and Israeli policies toward the Palestinians constitute an affront to their dignity as Arabs. Hundreds of thousands of Palestinians live throughout the Gulf, often occupying important administrative, civil, commercial, educational, journalistic and political positions. One quarter of Kuwait's population, for example, is Palestinian. However cynical some regimes (i.e., that of Hafez al-Asad in Syria) may have been, and continue to be, about the Palestinian question and however badly they have treated the Palestinians themselves, the common Arab and Muslim bonds they share with others throughout the Arab world are periodically solidified by common outrage over certain Israeli policies (i.e., in Lebanon and on the West Bank) and apparent support for those policies by the United States.

The visceral responses of many Arabs to what they perceive as a lack of respect (on the part of non-Arabs and non-Muslims) for the concerns of the Arab world and the legitimate rights of the Palestinian people should not be discounted. Regardless of what Arabs do to each other, their perceptions of what non-Arabs do to them contribute to a reservoir of collective hostility that erodes what otherwise might be a far more favorable attitude toward the policies of the United States.[5] A recent example is the Arab attitude toward U.S. alarm at the Soviet invasion of Afghanistan. Many Arabs, while profoundly disturbed by events in Afghanistan, saw Israeli occupation of the West Bank and Gaza as a greater threat to the Arab world than the Soviet occupation of Afghanistan. They gave Israel's policies on the West Bank more than equal time in international forums such as the Islamic Conference or the Non-Aligned Movement, complicating U.S. attempts to marshall world opinion against Soviet actions in Afghanistan.

Continued stalemate of the Palestinian question and the imperatives that flow from it directly affect a host of issues, from a solution to the problem of political reform in Lebanon to a *modus vivendi* between Arabs and Israelis. In the Gulf, these issues could create serious complications for U.S. relations with friendly regimes and inhibit their receptivity to American concerns about larger security issues. The Saudis, to cite but one of many complicated examples, under certain circumstances could find it increasingly difficult to associate themselves with U.S. policies and interests. To the extent that the Palestinian question is not addressed, criticism of the royal family's "irresponsible" use of the national patrimony (oil) to subsidize (through the United States)

---

5. This judgment is based on conversations with editors, educators and public officials in the Persian Gulf states, March and April 1983.

Zionist aspirations in the West Bank and Jerusalem is likely to challenge the House of Saud's Islamic and Arab credentials and thus directly affect its legitimacy.[6] Israeli actions such as the bombing of Iraq's newly constructed nuclear reactor in June 1981,[7] or the invasion of Lebanon in June 1982, reinforce perceptions of the threat posed by Israel and the risks associated with too close a relationship with its primary ally the United States. Recognizing these threats to its legitimacy, the House of Saud might well consider reducing its ties with the United States, expanding its ties with Western Europe and Japan, and one day normalizing its relations with the Soviet Union.[8] American influence in the region would diminish, while U.S. interests and capabilities to counter Soviet intimidation of regional states would suffer.

Other Gulf states, meanwhile, could turn increasingly to Western European markets for their armaments needs and to European markets and Japan to meet their technological, infrastructural, and business requirements. In isolation, these developments would pose few problems. But most of the Gulf states, as previously mentioned, have sizable Palestinian populations. They are also responsive to Palestinian concerns and fear Arab radicalism, which the Palestinian problem has consistently provoked and which polarization of the Palestinian national movement by Syria may exacerbate. As a result, they could insist on a more pro-Palestinian line from the European Common Market countries (the EC-10) as a *quid pro quo* for their business or their oil. If and when the current oil glut diminishes, and as the Gulf states gain control of oil deliveries "downstream," the oil weapon—directed against U.S.

---

6. For elaboration of this issue, see Chapter 8.

7. For discussion of this issue, see U.S. Congress, Senate, *The Israeli Air Strike*, Hearings before the Committee on Foreign Relations, 97th Congress, 1st Session (Washington, D.C.: G.P.O., 1981); Shai Feldman, "The Bombing of Osiraq — Revisited," *International Security* 7:2 (1982), pp. 114-42; Jed C. Snyder, "The Road to Osiraq: Baghdad's Quest for the Bomb," *The Middle East Journal* 37:4 (1983), pp. 565-93.

8. For a former State Department intelligence analyst's perception of Saudi attempts to distance themselves from the United States, see Malcolm Peck, *Christian Science Monitor*, August 12, 1983, who notes that the Saudis "view the Arab-Israeli conflict as the main cause of Arab radicalism and divisiveness and, therefore, as the principal threat to their security." As a consequence of the belief that the United States is unwilling or unable to compel Israeli acceptance of American ideas, many want a less close alignment with the United States. For a report of the "thaw" between the Soviet Union and Saudi Arabia, see Dusko Doder, *International Herald Tribune*, June 7, 1983. Foreign Ministry officials in Saudi Arabia, however, play down the Soviet option. Conversations with Foreign Ministry officials, Riyadh, Saudi Arabia, April 1983.

policies toward Israel—could exacerbate U.S.-European differences and directly undermine NATO.[9]

What is remarkable about some of these speculations is not that there is a reasonable basis for them, but that the United States, not the Soviet Union, could set them in motion and the Soviet Union, not the United States, would benefit from them. Israel, in some abstract sense, may constitute a strategic asset in the region because of its military capability and its apparent reliability, but it also constitutes a strategic liability. The close association between Israel and the United States, to the extent that it leads the United States to ignore the Palestinian problem, to disregard other U.S. interests, and to alienate most states within the region, has the clear potential for undermining regimes that cooperate with the United States, thereby creating massive inroads for Soviet influence. This argument has been voiced since 1948 and has only partially been borne out. Developments of the last decade and a half, however, beginning with the advent of the Palestinian national movement in the wake of the 1967 War, coupled with Britain's departure from the Gulf in 1968-1971, and followed by the increased leverage over oil prices exercised by the Arab states after the 1973 War, make it more likely than before. The financial power of the Gulf states to address regional concerns is a mixed blessing in that it also makes them increasingly vulnerable to the charge that they have done nothing to resolve them—and in fact have helped to *prevent* their resolution. All that is necessary to set in motion the process described above is continued inactivity on the Palestinian question in conjunction with the development of serious internal difficulties within one of the Gulf states closely associated with the United States. As a result, although this is not the place for detailed discussion of the Palestinian problem, nor for elaboration of proposals to address it, it seems clear that a determined effort must be made to resurrect and nurture the dialogue initiated by President Reagan's statement of September 1, 1982, and sustain the momentum behind the presidential initiative.[10]

## WHAT IS TO BE DONE?

If one can accept the logic of these arguments, it follows that the Reagan Administration, in the aftermath of the Israeli invasion of Lebanon, has basically three options: (1) letting things drift, as it did

---

9. See discussion of this possibility in *The Wall Street Journal*, April 8, 1981.

10. For President Reagan's initiative, see "President Reagan's Middle East Peace Initiative," a statement by Secretary of State Shultz before the Senate Foreign Relations Committee, September 10, 1983.

when Alexander Haig was Secretary of State; (2) revitalizing the peace process briefly resuscitated after George Shultz became Secretary of State by the Reagan initiative of September 1, 1982; or (3) pursuing an alternative strategy for addressing the Palestinian question in all its aspects. If the United States chooses to let things drift, it will leave the initiative to others. In such circumstances, it will have little option but to respond to events created by Israeli policies, such as the invasion of Lebanon or de facto annexation of the West Bank, with all the consequences that such actions entail. This may well be the policy that is pursued during the 1984 election campaign.

If the United States chooses to confront the Arab-Israeli conflict and to address the Palestinian question in all its aspects, whether through pursuit of the Reagan Plan or some alternative, it must, in part, be able to count on Arab receptivity to the idea. Such receptivity was evidenced by President Anwar Sadat's willingness to go to Jerusalem in November 1977. Whether the opportunity will present itself again under King Hussein depends on Israeli policies in Lebanon and the West Bank and on King Hussein's assessment of U.S. political will and seriousness of purpose.

Israel's annexationist policies toward the occupied territories more than any other problem, Carter administration officials believed, kept the United States from facilitating a process of mutual accommodation between the Israeli desire for security and the Palestinian desire for self-determination.[11] If this is still so, and if one can accept the argument that the practical problems of peace are not insurmountable,[12] the

---

11. See Cyrus Vance, *Hard Choices: Critical Years in American Foreign Policy* (New York: Simon & Shuster, 1983), pp. 237, 254.

12. Concerned individuals such as those who collaborated in the Brookings Report in 1975, and thoughtful public officials such as former Assistant Secretary of State Harold H. Saunders, have isolated problems that need to be addressed; they have attempted to define principles that would govern a settlement and to explore the contents of what a settlement might look like. In the course of their endeavors they have examined the importance of safeguards, demilitarized zones, great-power guarantees, and various forms of assistance in reinforcing commitments. In an effort to avoid pressures for one-sided implementation of any agreement, they have considered carefully the role of stages in the process of implementation, pondering the linkages between stages of withdrawal from occupied territory and manifestations of peaceful intent. To preclude military actions, they have looked hard at the interposition of force, limitations on military equipment, the creation of physical barriers, and zones of separation and denial. Their writings lead one to believe that practical implementation of a solution is not impossible, and that it is not even the main problem. The most

crucial question is the extent to which the United States can exercise the political will necessary to set the peace process in motion. Massive U.S. assistance to Israel to a great extent determines the constraints on Israeli policies, and Israeli policies have the potential not only to work against U.S. interests in the Middle East but to draw the United States into a global confrontation with the Soviet Union as well. Thus, it is only reasonable that the U.S. government, in addressing the Arab-Israeli conflict, consider carefully how and to what degree it can constructively influence Israel to cooperate in the peace process. If history is any guide, the problem will not be addressed until after the 1984 election.[13]

---

difficult problem, recent history suggests, is mustering the political will necessary to get the peace process in motion and encourage it on its way. For the Brookings Report, see "Toward Peace in the Middle East," Report of a Study Group (Washington, D.C.: The Brookings Institution, 1975). Its members included Zbigniew Brzezinski, Nadav Safran, and William Quandt, whose book *Decade of Decisions: American Policy Toward the Arab-Israeli Conflict, 1967-1976* (Berkeley: University of California Press, 1977), is particularly thoughtful. See also Harold Saunders, "An Israeli-Palestinian Peace," *Foreign Affairs* 61:1 (1982), pp. 100-121.

13.   For a detailed discussion of the problems that the Palestinian question poses for U.S. policy, see Bruce Kuniholm, *The Palestinian Problem and U.S. Policy* (Claremont, Cal.: Regina Books, forthcoming).

## THE PERSIAN GULF
## AND SOUTHWEST ASIA

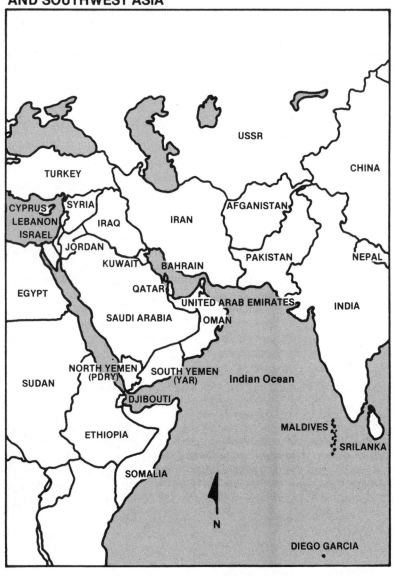

# PART III

# THE PERSIAN GULF

The major problem of any political strategy toward the Persian Gulf as a region is the question of how to think about its littoral states. The difficulty of safeguarding U.S. interests in the Gulf is complicated by three separate sets of problems:

- the historical animosity between Iran and some of the Arab states;[1]
- the possible disintegration of either Iran or Iraq, which could make the regional role of one or the other particularly significant;[2] and
- the ideological differences between Iraq and Saudi Arabia.[3]

These threats to regional stability suggest the practicability of a policy whose essential thrust is to prevent domination of the Gulf by any single power (i.e., Iraq or Iran) and to foster a sense of cohesion among Saudi Arabia and the states of the northern Arabian Peninsula littoral.

Chapter 7 will take a look at the motives behind the Iran-Iraq war and address the problems that the war poses for the Gulf states and U.S. interests. One difficulty with formulating a policy toward Iran and Iraq is

---

1. While relationships between the Arab states and Iran are extremely complex, the historical character of Arab-Persian differences, particularly when compounded by ideological and religious factors, cannot be ignored. For the manner in which they have been played out in Iran and Iraq in recent years, see the works of Rouhollah Ramazani and Majid Khadduri cited in the bibliography.

2. Iraq's disintegration could occur in the aftermath of a major Iranian victory, Iran's in the aftermath of Khomeini's demise. For the prospect of Iraq's being divided up into a Shiite South and a Sunni-Arab/Kurdish/Turkoman North, see Nameer Ali Jawdat, "Reflections on the Gulf War," *American-Arab Affairs* No. 5 (Summer 1983), p. 95; see also Hanna Batatu, "Iraq's Underground Shia Movements: Characteristics, Causes And Prospects," *Middle East Journal* 35:4 (1981), p. 594.

3. In spite of their current good relations brought about by the common threat from Iran, Iraq and Saudi Arabia have profoundly different outlooks on the world that have affected their past and will continue to affect their future relations. In some departments of the Saudi Foreign Ministry, the threat from Iraq, Syria and the PDRY is seen as even greater than the threat from Iran. Discussion with Saudi Foreign Ministry officials, Riyadh, May 1983.

that, as a result of the 1967 Arab-Israeli war and the 1979-81 hostage crisis, the United States has formal diplomatic relations with neither country. U.S. long-term interests, however, preclude total support of, or opposition to, either country, and dictate the desirability of better relations with both. Chapter 7 will examine what the United States might do to improve its relations with Iran and Iraq, and suggest what it could do to help prevent the Gulf's domination by either country. Chapter 8 will look closely at Saudi Arabia's role in the international arena and explore how the United States could improve its understanding of regional priorities and foster a greater sense of cohesion among the members of the Gulf Cooperation Council (GCC).

# 7

## Iran and Iraq

### IRAQI WAR AIMS

The long and bitter war between Iran and Iraq raises serious concerns among all the states of the region. The war began over three years ago, on September 22, 1980, when Saddam Husayn, invoking the Arab victory over Sassanid Persia at Qaddissya in the 7th century A.D., sent his armies into Iran. Judging, perhaps, that the United States was preoccupied with the hostage crisis in Iran and the Soviet Union with occupying Afghanistan, Saddam sought a number of related objectives:

— to bring down Khomeini and remove the threat of a revolutionary ideology that encouraged the majority Shiite population of Iraq (55%) to overthrow Saddam's Bathist regime;
— to reduce Iraq's vulnerability to attack by regaining control over strips of territory occupied by Iran (which under the terms of the 1975 Algiers Accord should have been returned to Iraq by the Shah);
— to gain control over the Shatt al-Arab waterway (Iraq's only outlet to the Gulf and the means by which it exported most of its oil);
— to secure a border that had seen 240 military incidents (largely initiated by Iran) in the year prior to the attack;
— to further Saddam's aspirations to regional leadership, which Iran's apparent weakness seemed to invite and which return of Abu Musa and the Tunbs to the UAE would legitimate (the return of the three islands occupied by Iran in 1971 was cited by Saddam in 1980 as one of his initial war aims); and, finally,
— to "liberate" Khuzistan ("Arabistan" to the Arabs), so depriving Iran of the oil fields needed to rival Iraq as a regional power.[4]

---

4. U.S. Foreign Broadcast Information Service. Special Memorandum. *Teheran Radio Arabic-Language Broadcasts* (Springfield, Va.: FBIS, January 7, 1980); Adeed Dawisha, "Iraq: The West's Opportunity," *Foreign Policy* No. 41 (Winter 1980-81), pp. 134-53; Stephen Grummon, *The Iran-Iraq War: Islam Embattled* (Washington, D.C.: Praeger, 1982); and Anthony Cordesman, "Lessons of the Iran-Iraq War: The First Round," *Armed Forces Journal International* 119:8 (1982), pp. 32-47; "Lessons of the Iran-Iraq War: Part Two, Tactics, Technology, and Training," *Armed Forces Journal International* 119:10 (1982), pp. 68-85.

The Iraqi offensive, while initially successful, was not well conceived and bogged down in mid-November 1980 before Iraq had advanced far enough to cut off Iran's key pipelines east of Ahwaz and Bandar Khomeini. The ensuing stalemate, brought on in part by the rainy season (which starts in November and continues through April), was perpetuated by the difficulties of maintaining lines of communication and projecting force. It was made more likely by Saddam's desire to avoid casualties and the failure of the Arab minority in Khuzistan to support Iraq as Saddam had hoped. The Khomeini regime, meanwhile, its extremism apparently justified by what the Iraqis referred to as the "Second Qaddissya," was able to mobilize the population and in early May 1981 to counterattack.

## IRANIAN WAR AIMS

The Iranian counterattack was aided in considerable part by the *Basij-i Mostazafin* (Mobilization of the Oppressed). Exhibiting a religious-based willingness to embrace martyrdom[5] and an ability to absorb extensive casualties, these young Iranian volunteers (who averaged 15 years of age) attacked the Iraqis in human waves, often with little ground or air support, wearing shrouds, chanting prayers and waving penants marked "Next Stop, An Najaf." Najaf is the burial site of the Imam Ali, Muhammad's cousin and son-in-law and, for all Shiites, the legitimate caliph after Muhammad's death. Many Iranian Shiites make an annual pilgrimmage to Najaf as well as to Karbala, where Ali's martyred son Hussein is buried. In addition to being one of the four most revered shrines in Shia Islam, Najaf also is the place where Khomeini spent 14 years in exile. Before being deported by Saddam Hussein in 1978, the Ayatollah was given a choice of desisting in his attempts to overthrow the shah or leaving. While the event was crucial to Khomeini's later prominence, the Ayatollah apparently remembers it with bitterness. Whatever the Iranians' immediate objectives, their war aims increased as they drove the Iraqis back across the Shatt al-Arab. After the battle of Khorramshahr in the Spring of 1982, Iranian demands included:

— a complete and unconditional withdrawal from Iran of all Iraqi troops;
— extensive war damages and reparations (sums mentioned ranged from $50 to $150 billion);
— Iraqi acknowledgment of war guilt, or an international arbitration committee to determine the aggressor;

---

5. See Christine Helms, "The Iraqi Dilemma: Political Objectives Versus Military Strategy," *American-Arab Affairs* No. 5 (Summer 1983), p. 82.

— repatriation to Iraq of approximately 100,000 Shiite Muslims (who are Arabs of Iranian extraction) exiled from Iraq by Saddam Husayn; and

— the overthrow of Saddam Husayn and the Bathist regime.

Most of these demands posed serious problems. Iraqis felt that the Iranians had provoked the attack, that the sum for reparations was exhorbitant, and that repatriation of Iranian Arabs was a gambit to establish a fifth column in Iraq. The Ba'athist regime, moreover, did not want to give up power. The most fundamental problem, however, was a sense that giving in on any or all of these demands would only pave the way for new ones.[6]

## IRAQI DIFFICULTIES

By 1983, mounting casualties and economic difficulties began to create serious problems for Saddam. Estimates of the number of dead on both sides ranged between 120,000 and 300,000, with another 250,000 wounded. While more Iranians were killed than Iraqis, Iran had a rising oil income, almost three times the population of Iraq, and a greater ability to withstand enormous losses. Iraq had an advantage in its defensive position, its superior armor, and its airpower, but it was beginning to suffer from the rising cost of the war.

The source of Iraq's problem can be found in the fact that Iraqi oil production, at 2.6 MBD before the war (with a peak production of 3.5 MBD), has been drastically reduced. Iranian control of Gulf waters at the head of the Gulf has cut off Iraqi exports by sea, and Syrian closure in April 1982 of the Iraqi pipeline through Syria (which carried 1.2 MBD) shut off another important channel. Since April 1982, the only means left for exporting oil has been a pipeline through Turkey, which delivers approximately 650,000 barrels a day and which Iran, out of deference to its relations with Turkey, has been reluctant to destroy. According to one authority, the capacity of this pipeline, improved by chemicals and added compression, may reach 1.4 MBD by April 1984. Plans for linking a pipeline from Iraq to Saudi Arabia's Petroline pipeline are also under consideration (it has a capacity of 1.85 MBD and is currently functioning at 0-50% of capacity). Realization of such plans

---

6. In addition to the sources cited above, see H.A.R. Gibb and J.H. Kramers, eds., *Shorter Encyclopaedia of Islam* (Ithaca: Cornell University Press, 1953); Edmund Ghareeb, " 'The Forgotten War,' " *American-Arab Affairs* No. 5 (Summer 1983), pp. 59-75; Jawdat, "Reflections on the Gulf War," p. 90; *Christian Science Monitor*, June 17, July 1, July 15, August 3, September 28, and October 7, 1982; *Time*, August 16, 1982; *New York Times*, July 31, 1982; *Washington Post*, May 27, 1983; *International Herald Tribune*, August 2, 1983.

is at least two years away and while the Saudis have agreed to let the Iraqis build a 1.5 MBD pipeline across Saudi Arabia, that enterprise, if it goes forward, will not be completed until the end of the decade. In the interim, Iraq's oil revenues have dwindled to less than $1 billion a month—a total that is insufficient to cover the costs of the war estimated by U.S. government analysts to be around $1.5 billion a month. Nor will it cover Saddam Husayn's once ambitious development and social programs, Iraq's food imports, and rising veterans' benefits. Iraq's financial reserves which amounted to around $35 billion at the beginning of the war have been virtually exhausted. Real economic activity, which declined 33% in 1981, and another 4.8% in 1982, is expected to fall a further 5.7% in 1983; in monetary terms, according to the Wharton Middle East Economic Service, this means a cutback in spending from $20 billion to $4 billion. Gulf assistance, meanwhile, which previously amounted to around $1 billion a month, was cut in 1983 to less than $600 million a month as a result of the pinch brought on by the oil glut.[7] In early 1984 Gulf assistance may have risen again in response to Iraq's increased difficulties with Iran.

## TACTICAL MANEUVERING

Economic hardship, evident in widespread shortages in Iraq and in consequent Iraqi pressure on European countries to reschedule debts, has led Saddam to consider desperate measures in order to seek relief from the inexorable war of attrition being waged by Iran.[8] Operating on the assumption that without oil Iran cannot continue the war, Iraq has attempted to deter Iran by warning that if attacks on Iraq do not cease, its ports and petro-chemical complexes will be bombed, its harbors mined, and ships carrying cargo to or from Iran struck. Some of these threats have been carried out. Countries such as France (which is owed at least $5 billion by Husayn's regime and by some estimates has over

---

7. Anthony Cordesman, "The Iraq-Iran War: Attrition Now, Chaos Later," *Armed Forces Journal International* 120:9 (May 1983), pp. 36 ff.; Christine Helms, "The Iraqi Dilemma," p. 82; *Christian Science Monitor*, August 3, 1982; October 11 and 17, 1983; *New York Times*, August 5 and 16, 1982; *International Herald Tribune*, May 5-6, and September 30, 1983; *Washington Post*, October 9, 1983. Another source has the pipeline capable of moving 1.6 MBD and operating at only 60% of capacity. *International Herald Tribune*, October 18, 1983.

8. In April 1983 in the aftermath of limited progress in a series of Iranian offensives, the speaker of Iran's parliament Hashemi Rafsanjani said that Iran, while making limited advances where possible, would concentrate on waging a war of attrition. Paul Eedle, *International Herald Tribune*, July 26, 1983.

$15 billion in capital investments, export orders, and long term contracts with Iraq) have become concerned about Iraq's vulnerabilty and sought to aid it in deterring further Iranian attacks.

In a deal worked out in May, revealed in June, and consummated in October 1983, France sold Iran five of its 61 Super Etendard fighter bombers. These planes are capable of flying at 750 miles per hour, detecting ships 81 miles away, and firing surface-skimming Exocet missiles that have a range of 43 miles (out of the range of Iran's Hawk missiles on Kharg Island). There is disagreement over the damage that these missiles could do: a number of experts have discounted their utility against Iran's main oil terminal at Kharg, arguing that they are meant to be used against ships. Japanese authorities in the Gulf who are familiar with the island also note that few storage tanks there are now in use and that the Iranians are pumping oil directly from land to the jetties directly off of the island. As a result, it appears that the most damaging Iraqi move would not be to attack the storage tanks, but rather to attack tankers in the process of loading, hoping thereby to impede as well as deter others from loading, and by raising insurance rates to bring about the cessation of Iranian exports.[9]

Concerned about the possibility of new weapons being used in such attacks, Iranian Foreign Minister Ali Akbar Vellayati has warned Iraq that if such weapons were used, Iran would retaliate either by blocking the Strait of Hormuz or bombing the oil facilities of the Gulf states. In September 1983, President Khameini and Ayatollah Khomeini reiterated Iran's retaliatory threats as Iran took up positions on strategic islands in the Strait of Hormuz (e.g., Larak), strengthened defenses at Kharg, Bushire, and Bandar Abbas, and, according to one report, began to militarize Chah Bahar in the Gulf of Oman.[10]

The United States has maintained neutrality since the beginning of the war, and President Ronald Reagan has reaffirmed President Carter's

---

9. *Christian Science Monitor,* August 3, September 20, 1983; *International Herald Tribune,* June 7 and 29, July 19, October 24 and 26, 1983; *Washington Post,* August 25, October 12, November 3, 8, and 11, 1983; *Sunday Times,* October 16, 1983. An alternative course of action contemplated by Iraq is to repair its oil loading jetties at the head of the Gulf (which some oil sources say could load as much as 2 million barrels a day), warning Iran that if it strikes those jetties, Iraq will retaliate against Kharg. *Washington Post,* October 9, November 11, 1983. Based on data cited by James Bill, *Politics in the Middle East,* 2nd ed. (Boston: Little, Brown, 1984), p. 372, a good guess is that approximately 50 ships (mostly tankers) transit the Strait of Hormuz every day. While U.S. officials estimate that approximately 70 ships have been sunk since the beginning of the Iran-Iraq war, none of these have been tankers. *Washington Post,* November 24, 1983.

10. *Washington Post,* September 20, 28, 1983; *Christian Science Monitor,* June 26, September 20, November 10, 1983.

pledge to preserve freedom of navigation in the Gulf. The Iranian foreign minister, however, has retorted that such a pledge is an insult to the Gulf countries and constitutes an assault on their territorial integrity and sovereignty. (The shipping channels, it should be noted, are in Omani territorial waters, and any Iranian attempt to impede traffic through them would constitute a breach of maritime law.) In October 1983 the Pentagon asserted that the U.S. Navy could thwart attempts to cut off traffic in the Gulf, and in November the Commander of MIDEASTFOR (a U.S. command that includes an LPD and four destroyers or frigates, and operates out of Bahrain) observed that the United States was prepared to respond quickly and effectively in the context of joint international action to ensure freedom of navigation there.[11]

Blocking the Strait of Hormuz is not the problem that some commentators suggest. The waterway is navigable to supertankers over a width of 20 miles at its narrowest point. The main shipping channel through the strait has no unique characteristic other than the fact that it provides the shortest route in and out of the Gulf. This route, moreover, is five to eight miles wide and 300 to 350 feet deep—wide and deep enough to enable shipments to continue even if a tanker were sunk there. If this route were temporarily blocked, ships could simply move outside the main channel.

The most effective Iranian tactic—both in terms of its probable success and its psychological effect—would be to sabotage Kuwait's or

---

11. *International Herald Tribune*, October 16, November 7, 1983; *Christian Science Monitor*, November 7, 1983; *Durham Morning Herald*, November 26, 1983. The U.S. naval command shared base facilities at Jufair with a British command from 1949 until 1971 when, with Britain's withdrawal, a new agreement was reached. The agreement was cancelled in 1973, following the 1973 Arab-Israeli war, but renewed in 1974 and extended in 1977. According to the former commander of MIDEASTFOR, the government of Bahrain understands that the U.S. naval contingent deters Iranian adventurism in Bahrain and that Iranian seapower could present serious problems for Bahrain without the presence of MIDEASTFOR—particularly in view of Iranian attempts to subvert Bahrain. As a result, the government has been more than accommodating, allowing three ships to tie up along side each other to count as only one of the limited "ship days" the U.S. is allotted in port. The point that U.S. officials should understand, Rear Admiral Guerney observed, was that many of the Gulf states were prepared to give the United States as much space as necessary to set up whatever infrastructure and preposition whatever materials it required—*providing* the United States did not make it public. They preferred that we keep a low profile and not make a big production of detailed agreements over access. Conversation with Rear Admiral Guerney, Bahrain, March 1983.

Saudi Arabia's piers and loading facilities. A suicide mission would be difficult to stop. Another possibility would be to mine the strait by dropping mines into the transit lanes from a dhow. Since ground mines are ineffective in deep water, the Iranians, if they were to pursue this course, would probably use unsophisticated floating mines that cannot be controlled or selectively targeted. Because tankers enroute to Iran's own Kharg terminals would also be vulnerable, the Iranians, presumably, would undertake such a course only if their exports had been cut off. American CH-53 helicopters deployed in the Indian Ocean, meanwhile, have the capability to clear such mines, but a successful mining operation nonetheless would have considerable impact. Insurance rates would rise rapidly. Over the short term, oil prices could even double. Except for Japan, however, most U.S. allies would suffer less than one might expect. At the time of writing, only 80% of Gulf production must transit the strait—the rest is (or could be) exported via pipeline through Turkey and the Red Sea. Of the 80% that must transit the strait, moreover, 90% is destined for Asian states and only 10% for Europe and the West. OPEC countries outside the Gulf, meanwhile, have at least 3 MBD spare capacity, which could offset almost half of Gulf production.[12]

Saddam Husayn, for his part, is willing to accept (and in fact eagerly seeks) a truce. Mediation efforts by members of the United Nations Security Council, the Organization of the Islamic Conference, the Nonaligned Movement, and the Gulf Cooperation Council, however, have all failed. Efforts to arrange a cease fire in order to contain a massive oil

---

12. Milton Benjamin, *Washington Post,* October 9, 1983; and Earl Foell, *Christian Science Monitor,* October 17, 1983. In June 1983, U.S. Government statistics indicated the following production and export figures in millions of barrels per day for the Gulf states:

|              | Production | Export |
|--------------|-----------|--------|
| Saudi Arabia | 4.738     | 3.571  |
| Iran         | 2.400     | 1.815  |
| UAE          | 1.150     | .975   |
| Kuwait       | 1.038     | .760   |
| Iraq         | .900      | .655   |
| Oman         | .375      | .363   |
| Qatar        | .298      | .242   |
| Bahrain      | .042      | .020   |
| TOTAL        | 10.941    | 8.401  |

Source: *Washington Post,* November 11, 1983. For a concise analysis of trends in oil capacity (installed, maximum sustainable, and available), see Anthony Cordesman, "The 'Oil Glut' and the Strategic Importance of the Gulf States," *Armed Forces Journal International* 121:3 (1983), p. 41.

spill from Iran's Nowruz offshore oil field were no more successful, although the oil leak finally appears to have been contained.[13] The reason for the impasse between Iran and Iraq is that Ayatollah Khomeini wants Saddam's ouster and appears willing to continue sacrificing lives for that goal. Even if Saddam were removed, it is not clear that Khomeini, who has called on the Iraqis to overthrow their secular government and replace it with an Islamic one, would stop at anything less than total victory.[14] His desire to export the revolution, moreover, not just to Iraq but to the Arabian peninsula as well, has alarmed a number of Gulf states.[15] As a result, when officials in the Arab Gulf states look for a way out, as they have on many occasions, they see no alternative to continued support for Iraq. They subsidize Saddam's efforts because they genuinely fear the triumph of Khomeini. They also fear a desperate move by Saddam that will bring Iranian retaliation—not only

13. See *Arabia: The Islamic World Review*, June 1983, p. 17; David Lamb, *International Herald Tribune*, July 25, 1983; and *International Herald Tribune*, September 26, 1983.
14. Fred Halliday, "Year IV of the Islamic Republic," *MERIP Reports* 13:3 (1983), pp. 3-8, has observed that Iranian government leaders are divided amongst themselves about war aims. Khomeini, however, has stated that if Iran defeated Iraq, Iraq would be annexed to Iran, and as Rafsanjani told Elaine Sciolino, "the Imam is not the kind of man who ever changes his mind." Elaine Sciolino, "Iran's Durable Revolution," *Foreign Affairs* 61: 4 (1983), pp. 906-908.
15. The Islamic revolutionaries in Iran do not see the revolution as confined to the Gulf, nor do the Arab states of the Gulf. Shiite grievances against the Wahhabis of Saudi Arabia are also longstanding. The Saudis, for example, destroyed the tomb of the Imam Hussein at Karbala in 1892, and more recently, Iranians believe, had full knowledge of and gave support to Saddam Husayn's plan to attack Iran. Even before the war, in part because the Saudis increased production of oil to make up for reductions caused by the Iranian revolution, Saudi Arabia was second only to Iraq as the target of hostile propaganda. These factors, along with different political styles and Islamic ideologies, coupled with Saudi Arabia's close ties with the United States, help to explain Iranian attempts to undermine the Saudi regime and some of the smaller states in the Gulf. Edward Mortimer, *Faith and Power: The Politics of Islam* (New York: Vintage, 1982), pp. 356-59; W.G. Millward, "The Principles of Foreign Policy and the Vision of World Order Expounded by Imam Khomeini and the Islamic Republic of Iran," in *The Iranian Revolution and the Islamic Republic: Proceedings of a Conference* (Washington, D.C.: The Middle East Institute, 1982), pp. 189-204 and the discussion on p. 209; James Bill/ Carl Leiden, *Politics in the Middle East*, pp. 395-405; Elaine Sciolino, "Iran's Durable Revolution," pp. 909-910; and the FBIS Special Memorandum cited in n. 4.

against Iraq, but also against them.[16] Such an attack could take the form of the mining of a tanker or an airstrike against oil terminals in the Gulf. In spite of serious aircraft maintenance problems and the existence of the AWACS in Saudi Arabia, U.S. military experts in the Gulf acknowledge that such an attack is possible.[17] The thrust of this line of thinking is that Saddam's threats against Iran are also threats against the Gulf states, whose "generous" support (which will probably never be repaid) is precisely what those threats are designed to elicit.[18]

Ultimately, Gulf officials conclude, the most probable catalyst for a solution will be the death of Ayatollah Khomeini, the overthrow or death of Saddam Hussein, or some other event that allows a face-saving truce to replace the current stalemate. Face-saving mediation is possible, but first there must be a desire for it. At present, there is none in Iran.[19] In the meantime, according to knowledgeable observers, the key to Saddam's survival is the strength, discipline, and loyalty of party workers in the Ba'athist Party, the loyalty of the army (whose lower ranks are dominated by Shiites), and financial aid from the Gulf.[20]

## FUTURE OPTIONS FOR THE UNITED STATES

Looking beyond the present, U.S. relations with Iran and Iraq will be determined to a great extent by the interplay between internal and external factors: between Iranian politics in the wake of Khomeini's demise, the ability of the Ba'athist regime in Iraq to survive the war, and traditional geopolitical realities that will continue to operate in the region long after the Iran-Iraq war winds down.

---

16. Discussions and interviews with government officials in Kuwait, Bahrain, Qatar, the UAE and Saudi Arabia, conducted in March and April 1983. According to one report, Iraq has approximately 400 servicable Soviet and French combat aircraft. Iran had 430 and has lost 80. Only a third of the remaining aircraft are known to be airworthy, however, and they have to be used primarily for defense purposes. Dilip Hiro, *International Herald Tribune*, November 7, 1983.
17. Discussions with U.S. military advisors in the Gulf, March and April 1983.
18. This point was underscored by a number of influential Gulf officials in March and April 1983.
19. A story making the rounds of the Arab Gulf states in early 1983 was that one of Khomeini's siblings had recently died. (After a pause) He was 104 years old. (After a pause) His parents were very upset. The point of course is that if one is waiting for Khomeini's death to resolve the Iran-Iraq war, one may have to wait a long time (Khomeini apparently does have a brother who is 15 years older than he is).
20. Phebe Mar, *New York Times*, July 27, 1982; Stephen Grummon, *The Iran-Iraq War*, p. 38.

*Iran.* American relations with Iran are limited by the fact that the United States has no influence over internal factors and would create greater problems for itself were it to try to exercise what little it had. As a result, U.S. policy must be essentially passive in regard to Iran's internal affairs. What room there is for influencing creatively Iran's international posture depends on many variables, from the outcome of the Iran-Iraq war, to the effect of new Soviet initiatives in the region. What is crucial is the extent to which the United States can respond constructively to internal developments and exercise flexibility in fostering an external environment conducive to mutual U.S.-Iranian interests.

There is relatively little that the United States can do in its relations with Iran until the Iran-Iraq war ends or the two countries reach a *modus vivendi.* Should the war end, and if Iranian animosity toward the U.S. begins to abate,[21] the United States could seek to establish relations with Iran at a joint commission office established in Europe. It has little choice but to maintain a low profile and gradually work to restore Iranian confidence in American intentions. Such confidence will be restored only when Iranian leaders who enjoy wide popular support feel sufficiently secure in their leadership and convinced of the desirability of better relations with the U.S. to marshall public opinion along these lines.

In the interim, the United States should encourage European and Japanese economic relations with Iran in order to strengthen those elements and groups wishing to rebuild Iran's relations with the West.[22] Americans could seek to resolve their commercial/financial tangle with Iran as amicably as possible and, when it is prudent, resume limited commercial ties. Even under current conditions trade has begun to improve. Once Iran is willing to reach a *modus vivendi* with Iraq, the United States could encourage Iran's private sector through certain European subsidiaries of American companies, indirectly supporting Iranian economic development and increased oil production. Over a period of several years, a basis might be laid for broader U.S.-Iranian relations.

---

21. The U.S. should not underestimate Iranian hostility toward the United States. For a useful chronology of U.S.-Iranian relations and events that fed Iranian animosity during the fall of the Shah and throughout the hostage crisis, see *The Iran Hostage Crisis: A Chronology of Daily Developments*, a report prepared by the Congressional Research Service, Library of Congress (Washington, D.C.: G.P.O., 1981).

22. Japan currently exports over $1 billion a year to Iran (some experts believe this figure could rise to $2.5 billion in 1983). It also imports 10% of its oil from Iran. Geoffrey Murray, *Christian Science Monitor*, August 1, 1983.

On the political level, American leaders could gradually encourage (through Turkey and Pakistan) Iran's informal cooperation with its former CENTO allies. Their aim should be to support independence from Soviet pressure and influence, without suggesting that the Iranians should participate in a defensive military association aimed at Moscow. Recent trends suggest that Iran is receptive to playing the role of not only an anti-American bulwark, but an anti-communist bulwark as well, and that it has attempted to improve ties and trade relations with Pakistan and Turkey, much to Moscow's annoyance.[23] These trends, one should note, are not so much pro-Western as they are traditionally Iranian. Historically the Iranians have rejected the influence of the great powers, using one as a counterweight against the others when necessary, and seeking aid from third parties when possible to extricate Iran from its geopolitical predicament. A traditional response to geopolitical pressure is also evident in the slogan, "neither East nor West," that currently governs Iranian policy toward the two superpowers.[24]

This strategy avoids an overactive U.S. posture in a period when the political situation will be turbulent. It reduces the likelihood that Americans will be made the scapegoats for internal Iranian problems. At the same time, it encourages pro-Western influence as a counter to Soviet influence in Iran in a manner (e.g. Turkish and Pakistani initiatives) that is acceptable to the Iranians. It facilitates Iran's gradual cooperation with other regional states in security areas that are of concern to Iran, and it minimizes conflict as much as can be expected in the short run with other U.S. security interests in the Gulf.

Were the Iran-Iraq war to end, the Iranian government to change, and an opportunity to arise, the United States might be tempted to move quickly to build its relations with the government in power. It might be tempted to reestablish diplomatic relations at the embassy level (although with a small presence), to respond to spare parts and limited arms requests, and to support Iran's economic development

---

23. See Chapter 9 for a discussion of developing relations between Turkey and Iran. For President Zia ul-Haq's attitude toward Pakistani-Iranian relations, see Elaine Sciolino, "Iran's Durable Revolution," p. 910; for the Soviet attitude toward Turkish and Pakistani relations with Iran, see Muriel Atkin, "The Islamic Republic and the Soviet Union," in Nikki Keddie and Eric Hooglund, eds., *The Iranian Revolution and the Islamic Republic*, pp. 143 and 149, n.15. According to Gary Sick, a former member of the National Security Council, if we get to the point where we can have a relationship with Iran, it will be because of the relationships we share with intermediate countries.

24. For traditional Iranian policies, see Rouhollah Ramazani, *The Foreign Policy of Iran: A Developing Nation in World Affairs* (Charlottesville: University of Virginia Press, 1966), pp. 53, 68, 70-71, 91.

requirements, with an eye to reviving the Iranian economy and reconstituting Iran, along with Turkey and Pakistan, as an anti-Soviet buffer between East and West. This course, although it could under certain conditions be a logical extension of the strategy outlined above, is unlikely to be viable in the short run. If pursued without inhibition, it could precipitate a destabilizing Soviet response. Since the main interest of the United States is not to acquire influence but to prevent undue Soviet influence in a country that is commonly recognized as the region's strategic prize, policymakers would be wise to move with caution and avoid a policy that legitimates precisely what they should be trying to prevent.

A course sometimes advocated is for the United States actively to support certain groups in Iran that oppose the present government, with a view to creating a new government more favorably disposed to U.S. interests.[25] Exile groups which are divided into monarchist and "republican leftist" movements and which are hopelessly dispersed will prove relatively useless for such purposes. There are others in Iran that may appear to be more attractive: factions within the military, bazaaris, selected political and religious moderates, and various tribes.

The impracticability of such suggestions, however, should be clear. It is virtually impossible to stay attuned to the shifting attitudes and splits within the government. Rivalry between the technocrats and the free-market advocates, or between the ultraconservative fundamentalists and the social reformers is illustrative of the problem and suggests the difficulty of manipulating the amorphous groups that could one day vie for power in Iran. Analysts believe that if Khomeini were to die tomorrow, no group in the army or the Revolutionary Guard would be able to topple the regime. No opposition group, moreover, has the necessary popular support. The concept of *Valayat-e Faqih* ("the governance of the jurisprudent"), considered by many to be the hallmark of the new order, has yet to lose legitimacy. Until it does, debate will continue and most discussion will center around whether Khomeini will be succeeded as supreme jurisprudent by a single indvidual such as Ayatollah Montazeri or a small group of three to five clerics elected by the 83-man Council of Experts.[26] In short, while a government favorably disposed

25. For rumors of a strategy along these lines, see Leslie Gelb, *New York Times*, March 7, 1982, whose report was subsequently discounted by Marvine Howe, *New York Times*, April 5, 1982.

26. See "Khomeini & the Opposition," *MERIP Reports* No. 104 (1982), entire issue; and "Iran Since the Revolution," *MERIP Reports* 13:3 (1983); Amir Taheri, *International Herald Tribune*, May 12, 1983; Elaine Sciolino, "Iran's Durable Revolution," pp. 913-915; Shahram Chubin, "The Soviet Union and Iran, *Foreign Affairs* 61:4 (1983), pp. 942-943; Shahrough Akhavi, "Clerical

to the United States would be desirable in the abstract, the process of effecting it would be fraught with difficulties. An activist U.S. policy, meanwhile, could result in undesirable consequences such as the partition of Iran, which would be extensively destabilizing for the region, or Soviet intervention, which would be catastrophic. The Iranians themselves have renounced the Soviet-Iranian treaty of 1921, but the Soviets have not and have declared that any foreign intervention in Iran would be considered a threat to Soviet security (i.e., cause for invoking the treaty).[27]

An activist U.S. policy toward Iran, in addition to working against U.S. interests in the region, would also be contrary to the notions of territorial integrity and sovereignty which are essential to U.S. policies toward other states in the region. The United States, therefore, should reject an activist posture unless Soviet policies, such as massive support for the Tudeh Party in the struggle for power that follows Khomeini's demise, result in a situation where the U.S. has no other option. The Tudeh was the object of three major purges in 1982 and it was again the

---

Politics in Iran Since 1979," and W.G. Millward, "The Principles of Foreign Policy and the Vision of the World Expounded by Imam Khomeini and the Islamic Republic of Iran," *The Iranian Revolution and the Islamic Republic,* pp. 17-28, and 189-204 (see also the remarks by Ervand Abrahamian, p. 210); Liz Thurgood, *Washington Post,* August 6, 1983; and Claude Van England, *International Herald Tribune,* August 16, 1983. For the two best studies of religion in Iran, see Shahrough Akhavi, *Religion and Politics in Contemporary Iran: Clergy State Relations in the Pahlavi Period* (Albany: State University of New York Press, 1980), and Michael Fischer, *Iran: From Religious Dispute to Revolution* (Cambridge: Harvard University Press, 1980).

27.  Article VI of the treaty states in part:

"If a third party should attempt to carry out a policy of usurpation by means of armed intervention in Persia, or if such power should desire to use Persian territory as a base of operations against Russia, or if a foreign power should threaten the frontiers of federal Russia or those of its allies, and if the Persian Government should not be able to put a stop to such a menace after having once been called upon to do so by Russia, Russia shall have the right to advance her troops into the Persian interior for the purpose of carrying out the military operations necessary for its defense. . . ."

For discussion of the treaty and previous references to it, see Bruce Kuniholm, *The Origins of the Cold War in the Near East: Great Power Conflict and Diplomacy in Iran, Turkey and Greece* (Princeton: Princeton University Press, 1980), pp. 133, 134n, 277n, 281, 285-86, 305, 313-14, 325. Premier Brezhnev's implicit reference to the treaty on November 19, 1979, when he declared that any foreign intervention in Iran would be considered a threat to Soviet security (see Muriel Atkin, "The Islamic Republic and the Soviet Union," p. 141), was underscored by Soviet use of their 1978 treaty with Afghanistan as a source of legitimacy for intervention later in the following month.

object of a major purge in 1983[28] when posters that served as backdrop to the purge trials ranked them as second in their deviltry only to the United States. Since the Iranians have always regarded the Tudeh as a Soviet puppet organization, U.S. policymakers should be cautious lest they exaggerate the Tudeh Party's influence and overreact to inflated reports about its activities.[29]

*Iraq.* To the extent that the Iraqis are severely threatened by an Iranian offensive and/or the Soviets move closer to Iran, the United States could, and perhaps should, move closer to Iraq. President Francois Mitterand of France, asserting that France has friends but no enemies in the Gulf, did precisely that in late 1983 by warning that France would not allow Iraq to collapse because such a development would destabilize the entire region.[30] In conjunction with its NATO allies, the United States could play a more supportive role in helping the Iraqis to resist continued Iranian attacks. It could also play a quiet but important role in consolidating local resistance to possible Iranian aggression in the Gulf. In the unlikely event of Soviet aggression in Iran, such a role would also allow consideration of U.S. support for anti-Soviet forces in southwest Iran—a "Khuzestan option"—based on a pre-1957 defense line at the Zagros Mountains that protects the oil fields.

Better U.S. relations with Iraq, if handled with care, are not necessarily harmful to or incompatible with an improvement in U.S.-Iranian relations, particularly if U.S. support for Iraq is solely defensive.[31] If Saddam Husayn survives, and can reach a *modus-vivendi* with a post-Khomeini Iran, better relations with *both* Iran and Iraq would be consistent with American support for nonalignment—a policy position to which both states subscribe. Overzealous pursuit of U.S.-Iraqi relations,

---

28. See Claude Van England, *Christian Science Monitor*, July 22, 1983.

29. The issue of Tudeh strength is constantly debated in the government and among academics. See, for example, the discussion in Keddi et al., *The Iranian Revolution and the Islamic Republic*, pp. 157-158; Shahram Chubin, "The Soviet Union and Iran," pp. 930-931, 943.

30. *International Herald Tribune*, October 29-30, 1983. For indications that the U.S. has made moves to prevent an Iraqi loss, see the *Washington Post*, January 1, 1984,

31. Nameer Ali Jawdat observes that "it is an article of faith in Teheran that Saddam Hussein would never have dared attack without specific instructions from America. . . ." He implies that, since the U.S. is already credited with the worst motives, it would not have much to lose by tilting a little bit toward Iraq. Nameer Ali Jawdat, "Reflections on the Gulf War," p. 97. It should be noted that one impediment to U.S.-Iraqi relations has been the presence of Abu Nidal (a radical Palestinian terrorist group) in Baghdad. The office was closed and Abu Nidal's men expelled from Iraq in November 1983. Don Oberdorfer, *Washington Post*, November 24, 1983.

of course, would jeopardize American interests in Iran. Support for an Iraqi *resistance* effort such as both the Soviets *and* our NATO allies are currently undertaking, however, is less dangerous. The normalization of U.S.-Iraqi relations would not be especially harmful to U.S. interests and would be welcomed by the Gulf states, who remain concerned about Saddam's aspirations to play an important regional role but are more concerned at present about his survival.[32]

Developments in progress in Saudi Arabia and the Arab Gulf, meanwhile, should enhance Gulf security and allow those states, with some assistance, to serve as a countervailing force to Iranian and Iraqi desires for hegemony within the region. The most significant of these developments is that Saddam Husayn's difficulties with Iran have encouraged an alliance among Iraq, Jordan, and Saudi Arabia. Formed in response to regional developments such as the Iranian revolution, Soviet activities in the PDRY, Ethiopia, and Afghanistan, and Iraqi difficulties in the Iran-Iraq war, this alliance has fostered a gradual rapprochement between Egypt and Saudi Arabia. The alliance may bring Egypt back into the Arab system, as suggested by the Islamic Conference Organization's decision in early 1984 to invite Egypt to join its ranks. The alliance may even provide a balance to the threat that Iran now poses to the Arab Gulf states. It is to the Arab Gulf dimension of this problem that we now turn.

---

32. Eilts, "Security Considerations in the Persian Gulf," p.105, correctly observes that any U.S.-Iraqi axis aimed at Iran would only miscarry. See also Steven Kashkett, "Iraq and the Pursuit of Nonalignment," *Orbis* 26:2 (1982), pp. 477-495; see also n. 3.

# 8

## Saudi Arabia and the Arab Gulf States

An examination of U.S. policy options toward Saudi Arabia and the Arab Gulf states requires not only a keen sense of the Gulf's regional dynamics but careful attention to the priorities that shape the foreign policies of the states themselves. This is particularly true of Saudi Arabia, which has emerged as the cornerstone of U.S. policy in the Gulf. With the "loss" of Iran, the demise of America's "two pillar" policy, and the problems posed by the Iran-Iraq war, a closer relationship with Saudi Arabia and the smaller Gulf states is the only real option left open to the United States. The Carter Doctrine, to which President Reagan has added his corollary (i.e., the United States will not permit Saudi Arabia "to be an Iran"), provides a general framework for the continuing "special relationship" between the United States and Saudi Arabia. The essence of this relationship, at its most fundamental level, revolves around the exchange of security for oil. This exchange was evident most recently in two episodes: (1) Saudi willingness to make up for the world's short-fall in oil production after the Iranian revolution and the onset of the Iran-Iraq war; and (2) President Reagan's personal intervention with Congress to ensure the sale of Airborne Warning and Control System (AWACS) planes to Saudi Arabia in the Fall of 1981.[1]

U.S.-Saudi relations, however, are much more complex than the simple exchange of security for oil. As a result of the relationship's complexity and, perhaps, because of cultural barriers, the two countries

---

1. *Congressional Quarterly Weekly Report*, Oct. 31, 1981, pp. 2095-2100. The President's comparison, of course, is misleading. In Saudi Arabia, as in Sunni theory, religious activities come within the domain of the state; as a result, the ability of the Iranian ulama to act independently of the Shah is not possible in Saudi Arabia, where the House of Saud is strongly identified with the Wahhabi movement, and the descendents of Ibn Abdul Wahhab and other leading ulama of Saudi Arabia continue to uphold the political authority of the House of Saud. Edward Mortimer, *Faith & Power: The Politics of Islam* (New York: Random House, 1982), pp. 159-184, 300. Other important differences include the fact that the Pahlavi dynasty was extremely small (as opposed to the large Saudi family that has married into many of the tribes of the kingdom), had nearly ten times the population of Saudi Arabia and only a third of its income. For a thoughtful discussion of other differences, see John Duke Anthony, *Baltimore Sun*, December 31, 1978.

have occasionally experienced serious misunderstandings. At the heart of these misunderstandings are the U.S. government's imperfect notions about the royal family's room for maneuver and the American tendency to overestimate its own importance in Saudi calculations. During the Carter presidency, for example, Washington expected that the Saudi regime could and would support, or at least would not actively oppose, the 1978 Camp David agreement. This expectation precipitated, in March 1979, the visit to Saudi Arabia of a high-powered U.S. team under Zbigniew Brzezinski to pressure the Saudis to support the agreement. The administration's failure to understand what the Saudis told that delegation, and a previous delegation under Secretary of Defense Harold Brown in February 1979, was mirrored in an unintentionally ironic editorial in the *Washington Post* that hailed Saudi support for Camp David.[2]

The Reagan administration, when it took office, expected that the Saudi regime could and would provide bases for the Rapid Deployment Force. According to one Saudi prince, Riyadh was concerned that the United States would come to them with great hopes: "Ronald Reagan will offer us weapons in return for ports and bases in Saudi Arabia. We will say no, and he will be disappointed because he expects too much."[3] The Saudis were right. Other disappointments followed over Saudi failure to support the Hussein-Arafat rapprochement in the Spring of 1983, and over Saudi failure to exert pressure on Syria to withdraw its forces from Lebanon in the Summer of 1983.[4] Saudi behavior, in short, has created puzzlement in U.S. official circles about what the Saudis want. Since informed assessments of Saudi priorities are essential to judgments of what U.S. policies toward Saudi Arabia should be, it is necessary to give careful attention to what it is that the Saudis really want—not to what U.S. officials *think* they want.

## SAUDI PRIORITIES

U.S. uncertainty about Saudi Arabia results, in part, from the shifting saliency of one or another threat to the House of Saud, from the complexity of Saudi Arabia's consensual decision-making process, and from the Saudis' inclination to play the role of mediator between their

---

2. "Baghdad II," April 1, 1979. (See also the editorial for April 2, 1979.)
3. *Wall Street Journal,* November 4, 1980. On President Reagan's belief that the United States needed a ground presence in the Persian Gulf, see the *Christian Science Monitor,* February 4, 1981.
4. See Robin Wright, *Christian Science Monitor,* May 16, 1983; Trudy Rubin, *Christian Science Monitor,* May 18, 1983; and Joseph Fitchett, *International Herald Tribune,* June 5, 1983.

quarreling friends. This latter role particularly lends itself to misinterpretation when the Saudis try to be all things to all people. The primary cause of puzzlement in U.S. official circles about what the Saudis want, however, is a misunderstanding of Saudi priorities, which lie on several distinct but intersecting planes, and which deserve careful attention if U.S.-Saudi relations are to be built on a firm foundation.

*The Royal Family.* Of primary concern to the Saudi leadership is the preservation of the family and its dominant role in the kingdom. While intrafamily bickering between King Fahd and Crown Prince Abdallah over their respective roles and responsibilities in the wake of King Khalid's death in June 1982 may receive considerable attention outside Saudi Arabia,[5] nearly all members of the royal family assign top priority to family unity and continuity. Differences are reconciled through the agonizing process of achieving a consensus.

*The Kingdom.* Next to the family, the kingdom is of primary importance. Indeed, the interests of the kingdom tend to be indistinguishable from those of the royal family, whose numbers are in the thousands (there are approximately 3,000 princes) and whose leading members occupy key positions throughout the country. At the same time, the Saudis feel obligated to improve living conditions, to respond to human needs, and to articulate the concerns of Saudis at large.

*The Arab Nation.* Beyond the borders of the kingdom, the Saudis feel a strong identity with other Arabs. They have a sense of obligation as the protectors of Arabism. A primary goal of the Saudis on any major international issue is to obtain a consensus that will enable the Arabs to function as one nation. Even those Arabs who are philosophically opposed to the Saudis are not rejected; instead, they are considered errant members of the larger Arab family who must be brought back into the fold. In this light, the breaking of diplomatic relations with Libya in October 1980 was unusual. It was warranted only by Colonel Qaddafi's vitriolic accusations that the AWACS planes sent to Saudi Arabia by the United States after the onset of the Iran-Iraq war had desecrated Muslim holy places, and by the Libyan leader's call for *jihad* (holy war) to liberate Mecca. More typical of Saudi practice is the royal family's care in keeping open its ties with the Baathists in Damascus and in continuing financial aid to Syria, despite Syria's friendship treaty with the Soviet Union and Syria's differences with Jordan, Iraq, and Lebanon.

*The Islamic World.* After the Arabs, other Muslims are of greatest concern to the Saudis. The Saudis view themselves as, and most Muslims consider them to be, guardians of the Islamic holy places and protectors of the faith. As such, they feel a great obligation to ensure

---

5. David Ottoway, *Washington Post,* May 31, 1983.

that Muslim interests in the international arena are protected. The pattern of Saudi financial assistance reflects this priority; whereas Muslim nations have received generous financial assistance, non-Muslim Asian and African states have obtained relatively little.[6]

*The Anticommunist Bloc.* Another important Saudi interest lies in shoring up the anticommunist bloc. Relations with the United States, the closest powerful ally the Saudis have in this common interest, are quite different from relations with Arab and Muslim states. From Riyadh's perspective, though, anticommunism is directly related to the Saudis' interest in protecting the family, the kingdom, the Arab nation, and the Islamic world from the threat posed by radicalism. As a result, these very different concerns are at times indistinguishable.[7]

## SAUDI DILEMMAS

The basic problem the Saudis face is that of most countries in a complex world; their fundamental concerns are often in conflict with one another. Faced with a decision, therefore, they must weigh its impact

---

6. While statistics vary, most analysts believe that well over 90 percent of Saudi Arabia's foreign aid (which in recent years has run close to $3 billion per year) goes to the Arab and Muslim world. See, for example, Ralph Braibanti, *The Recovery of Islamic Identity in Global Perspective* (Durham, N.C.: Duke University, Islamic and Arabian Development Studies, Reprint Series, No. 1, 1979); Ralph Braibanti and Fouad Al-Farsy, *Saudi Arabia: A Developmental Perspective* (Durham, N.C.: Duke University, Islamic and Arabian Developmental Studies, Reprint Series, No. 2, 1979); and Adeed Dawisha, "Saudi Arabia in the Eighties: The Mecca Seige and After," a paper presented at the Wilson Center, Smithsonian Institution, Washington, D.C., November 6, 1980.

7. The themes of family, the kingdom, the Arab nation, the Islamic world, and anticommunism are examined in detail in H. St. John Philby, *The Heart of Arabia*, 2 vols. (London: Constable, 1922) and *Arabia of the Wahhabis* (London: F. Cass, 1977); Gerald De Gaury, *Faisal: King of Saudi Arabia* (New York: Praeger, 1966); Derek Hopwood, ed., *The Arabian Peninsula: Society and Politics* (Totowa, N.J.: Rowman & Littlefield, 1972); Joseph Malone, *The Arab Lands of Western Asia* (Englewood Cliffs, N.J.: Prentice-Hall, 1973); David Long, *Saudi Arabia* (Beverley Hills, Ca.: Sage, 1976); Richard Nyrop et al., *Area Handbook for Saudi Arabia*, 3rd ed. (Washington, D.C.: G.P.O., 1977); Fouad Al-Farsy, *Saudi Arabia: A Case Study in Development* (London: Stacey International, 1978); Willard Beling, ed., *King Faisal & the Modernization of Saudi Arabia* (Boulder, Col.: Westview Press, 1979); Christine Helms, *The Cohesion of Saudi Arabia: Evolution of Political Identity* (Baltimore: Johns Hopkins University Press, 1980); Alvin J. Cottrell et al., *The Persian Gulf States: A General Survey* (Baltimore: Johns Hopkins University Press, 1980); Robert Lacey, *The Kingdom: Arabia and the House of Saud* (New York: Harcourt Brace Jovanovich, 1981); David Holden and Richard Johns, *The House of Saud: The Rise and Rule of the Most Powerful Dynasty in the Arab World* (New York: Holt, Rinehart & Winston, 1981).

on all their concerns and not just on one. The resulting decision often reflects the immediacy of a particular threat—the Saudi perception of a threat is never static—as well as a temporary compromise between contradictory interests. The decision, therefore, is likely to be one with which the Saudis themselves are uncomfortable, and, given the Saudi decision-making process, Riyadh will appear to outsiders to vacillate even on key issues. As the complexion of a particular threat changes, so will the evaluation of the compromise that must be made. The Saudis confront such choices in virtually all of their current policy problems, the three most important of which are outlined below.

*The Peace Process.* The Saudis regard the Arab-Israeli issue in general, and Zionism and "Israeli expansionism" in particular, as a direct threat to their security. The Israeli occupation from 1967 to 1982 of two Saudi islands at the entrance of the Gulf of Aqaba and occasional Israeli overflights of Saudi territory (the Israelis have dropped empty fuel pods on Saudi air-strips) remind Saudi leaders of Saudi Arabia's vulnerability. In addition, the Saudis regard the Arab struggle with Israel as undercutting fundamental Saudi interests because the close relationship between a major Saudi ally, the United States, and Israel provides the Soviets with an immense opportunity to create divisive factions—whether within the family, the kingdom, the Arab nation or the Islamic world. As a result, the Saudis want a just and lasting peace. This, they believe, can be established only by (1) Israel's withdrawal to its pre-June 5, 1967 boundaries, including the return of East Jerusalem to the Arab-Muslim fold, and (2) granting the Palestinians their full legitimate rights, including the right to self-determination and to an independent state in their homeland.[8]

To respond to U.S. initiatives such as the Reagan Plan and acquiesce publicly in anything less than the conditions listed above would, in the Saudi view, polarize the Arab world even more than it already is over the Iran-Iraq war and threaten virtually every one of Saudi Arabia's

---

8. This assessment of Saudi perceptions of the Arab-Israeli issue was corroborated in conversations with Saudi officials in the foreign and defense ministries and professors in King Abd al-Aziz and King Saud Universities in Riyadh and Jidda, Saudi Arabia, April 1983. For one of many statements on the question of the requirements for peace, see Foreign Minister Saud's statement of August 1, 1979, in Taif. (Foreign Broadcast Information Service, *Daily Report*, MEA-79-150). See also George Rentz, "The Fahd Peace Plan," *Middle East Insight* 2: 2 (1982), pp. 21-24; and Adeed Dawisha, "Saudi Arabia and the Arab-Israeli Conflict: The Ups and Downs of Pragmatic Moderation," *International Journal* 38: 4 (1983), pp. 674-689. On the question of Saudi vulnerability, see William Quandt, *Saudi Arabia in the 1980s* (Washington, D.C.: Brookings Institution, 1981), p. 61.

major interests. The Saudis are convinced that the survival of the monarchy depends on the solidarity of the Arab nation. Should the Arab world become polarized over the Arab-Israeli question, Saudi Arabia would face increased internal and external threats. The royal family's claim that it is responsible for the Muslim holy places and the preservation of the Islamic way of life, a claim that is a crucial component of its legitimacy, would be undermined.[9] If the Saudis need a reminder of their vulnerability on this issue, they need only look at the rhetoric of those who attempted to take over the Grand Mosque of Mecca in November 1979, or at Colonel Qaddafi's attacks on them in October 1980.[10]

The primary threat to their leadership, the Saudis recognize, will come from those who can challenge the House of Saud's legitimacy— either within Saudi Arabia or in the Muslim world. Legitimacy derives from the House of Saud's unification of the peninsula and imposition of stability on the warring tribes of the peninsula. It depends on the people's consent and is grounded in the concepts of *shurra* (consultation) and *ijma* (consensus). These foundations of Saudi authority, however, were called into question by the seizure of the Grand Mosque in November 1979 and Shiite disorders in the Qatif Oasis in November 1979 and February 1980—disorders that had been stimulated by the Iranian revolution and the rhetoric of Ayatollah Khomeini.[11]

The House of Saud's sensitivity to the threat posed by Khomeini's continuous challenge to its legitimacy was exemplified most recently in the Fall of 1983 after the Ayatollah's encouragement of Islamic oil-producers to cut off supplies to the United States in retaliation for U.S. "oppression of Lebanon," and his urging of Muslims to use their annual pilgrimage to Mecca to denounce the United States. Responding to Iranian charges that the 95,000 Iranians who intended to go on the *hajj*, or pilgrimage to Mecca, would be prevented from doing so, Saudi minister of the interior Prince Naif denied the Iranian allegations and,

---

9. See David Holden and Richard Johns, *The House of Saud*, pp. 511-27.

10. Juhayman bin Muhammad bin Seif al-Oteibi and his followers asserted that the royal family had betrayed Islamic ideals and had therefore forfeited its role as a leader of Islam. *New York Times*, February 25, 1980. Colonel Qaddafi asserted that the AWACS planes constituted a desecration of the Muslim holy places in Mecca and called on the 2 million pilgrims to the Muslim shrines to engage in a holy war to liberate Mecca. *Washington Post*, October 23 and 29, 1980. The attacks on the royal family as well as the royal family's response evidence a need to seek legitimacy within the context of Islam.

11. David Holden and Richard Johns, *The House of Saud*, pp. 529-531. For the reaction of Saudi officials to the shiite riots, see David Long, "U.S.-Saudi Relations: A Foundation of Mutual Needs," *American-Arab Affairs*, No. 4 (1983), pp. 12-22.

at the same time, made it clear that the House of Saud would not abandon its duties to safeguard the peace and tranquillity of the pilgrimage. Among political and demagogic activities that Prince Naif condemned were calls for revolution against any Islamic government (i.e., Saudi Arabia) that did not conform to the principles of the Iranian revolution. The Saudis were particularly concerned by mass meetings held by the Iranians within the courtyards of the mosques at Mecca and Medina, the Iranian claim that any form of monarchy was incompatible with Islam, and the Iranian call for the Saudi people to rise up against their rulers.[12]

If legitimacy depends on the people's consent, it also depends to a great degree on perception and is influenced considerably by the image that the royal family projects at home and abroad. An awareness of this problem explains the strong Saudi reaction to the BBC film "Death of a Princess" in the Spring of 1980. In Saudi society a woman's conduct reflects the honor of her male blood relatives; the film's portrayal of a Saudi princess was thus seen as bringing shame upon the royal family. "A man who does not correct a shame," a Saudi proverb advises, "has no future." The imperatives of Saudi culture required that the royal family seek sanctions against the British to avoid a loss of face within their own society—even at the expense of increased publicity—and that the British show evidence of contrition before the injury could be excused. If moral behavior is a source of legitimacy, it is important to recognize that to the Saudis, it is not so much what you do (to which the notion of guilt speaks), but how actions are perceived (to which the notion of "face" speaks) that counts.[13] Sensitivity to the need for main taining "face" within their own society, and hence safeguarding the legitimacy of the Saudi royal family, explains the need for taking a strong stand against the showing of the film. The need for legitimacy also explains why, in August 1980, Crown Prince (now King) Fahd raised the possibility of *jihad* against Israel over a Knesset law affirming united Jerusalem's status as the "eternal" capital of Israel, and why, in January 1981, the Saudis endorsed the Islamic summit's Mecca Declaration, which asserted that the primary mission of the present generation would be to prepare for *jihad* in order to liberate East Jerusalem and all Israeli-occupied Arab lands.[14]

---

12. See Michael Collins, *Christian Science Monitor*, August 9 and September 27, 1983; *International Herald Tribune*, August 2 and September 14, 1983; *Durham Morning Herald*, August 18 and December 8, 1983.

13. For a brief but valuable discussion of "face," see Peter Iseman, "The Arabian Ethos," *Harper's*, February 1978, pp. 43-44.

14. *Durham Morning Herald*, August 15, 1980; *Washington Post*, January 29, 1981.

The Saudis, with the rest of the Arab and much of the Islamic world, share a similar concern for the plight of the stateless Palestinians who, lacking any means of obtaining a political identity, will continue to remind the Arab world that they cannot be ignored. The Kuwaiti National Assembly was dissolved in 1976 partly because of tensions emanating from popular support within the assembly for the Palestinian cause.[15] To the extent that the Saudis, like the Kuwaitis, experiment with more representative structures for political participation,[16] tensions over the Palestinian question are likely to increase rather than abate, and call into question the Islamic and Arab credentials of the royal family. Private criticism of the royal family's "irresponsible" use of the national patrimony (oil) to subsidize indirectly, through the United States, Zionist aspirations in the West Bank and Jerusalem is likely to become public and more acute. Concern about such criticism helps to explain Saudi concern about recent Iranian charges, which tend to portray Khomeini as more Islamic than the House of Saud. It also explains the Saudis' vociferous reaction to the so-called strategic cooperation agreement between Israel and the United States in the Fall of 1983, which the Saudis feel has generated Arab support for Syria and puts Saudi Arabia in the difficult position of either accepting a radicalized PLO supported by Syria or appearing to reject the principle of Palestinian rights.[17] Neither choice provides much comfort to the Saudis, who perceive themselves as extraordinarily vulnerable to radical pressures— both because of their small native population (only about 4.3 million, as opposed to inflated public figures of over double that number) and their

---

15. Elections were held once again in February 1981 and the assembly is now back in session. It is worth mentioning that once expatriates, women, and children are eliminated and "grandfather clauses" applied, the number of eligible voters is quite small. Nonetheless, the Kuwaiti assembly is the most representative one in the Gulf.

16. While there has been much talk of the establishment of a shura, or consultative council (for which there is a precedent in the Hijaz), and of the publication of basic statutes of government, King Fahd has apparently let a draft of these reforms sit on his desk for almost two years. He has been considering, however, a proposal to increase the governors' administrative and budgeting authority, a move which would give the Saudi system more flexibility. *New York Times,* February 17 and 22, 1980; *Wall Street Journal,* August 20, 1980; *International Herald Tribune,* July 5, 1983; *Washington Post,* October 31, 1983; and Majid Khadduri, *Arab Personalities in Politics* (Washington, D.C.: Middle East Institute, 1981), p. 49. Khadduri also notes, p. 56, the necessity of integrating the emerging political system with the larger social structure and allowing the participation of an increasing number of people. If there are lessons to be learned from the fall of the Shah, this, surely, is one of them.

17. See Justin Coe, *Christian Science Monitor,* December 8, 1983.

large expatriate population (approximately 2 million as opposed to deflated public figures of about half that number).

The Saudis would prefer not to have to reconcile the inherent conflict between their U.S. connection and their Arab and Islamic roles, a conflict which, in their eyes, will continue so long as the United States fails to confront the Palestinian problem. The Saudis want to maintain close relations with the United States. Nevertheless if the Reagan administration, like the Carter administration in 1979, were to pressure them to give public support to the Reagan Plan, their policy would be fairly predictable. In the absence of what the Palestinian leadership (now in disarray) considers to be acceptable, Riyadh will again conclude, as it did at the time of its rejection of the Camp David agreement in 1979, that Saudi Arabia must devote primary attention to the agreement's shortcomings rather than U.S. support for Saudi security concerns in the Gulf. An agreement that is unacceptable to the Palestinians, or the Syrians who now control a sizable radical faction of Palestinians, would be seen as a more direct threat to the survival of the family, the maintenance of Arab unity, the protection of Muslim rights, and the containment of radicalism in the Arab world.

To argue that the Saudis can ignore such factors is to make the same mistake as those who argue that Israel can ignore what it views as real threats to its survival.[18] The threat to Saudi Arabia may be less dramatic, but it is as real. Just as the United States must accommodate within its political system the complex of moral, political, and military factors that influence its policies toward the peace process, so must Saudi Arabia. Such factors must be weighed against the political realities peculiar to each country as well as against their mutual long-term interests.

*Regional Security.* In the wake of events on the Horn of Africa, the revolution in Iran, the Yemen war, the Soviet invasion of Afghanistan and, most recently, the war between Iran and Iraq, the Saudis recognize the need for an effective U.S. shield to protect them from the externally sponsored forces of communism and radicalism. This explains their request for four AWACS early warning planes in the Fall of 1980. At

---

18. See, for example, Phillip J. Baram's "Op-ed" piece, "Don't Forget How the U.S.-Saudi Romance Began," in the *Christian Science Monitor*, August 1, 1980: "The case can be made that today the monarchy is increasingly and seriously hurting, not helping, the U.S.—and the U.S. government is doing very little about it." The obvious implication, repeated by many in Washington, is that the U.S. should be a lot tougher with the Saudis. This line of reasoning assumes that the Saudis can ignore the factors discussed above and that we can pressure the Saudis into doing what we want them to do.

the same time, the Saudis recognize that dependence on a close relationship with the United States is dangerous because (1) it makes the Saudis beholden to Washington and vulnerable to American pressure on issues such as the Camp David accords and the Israeli-Lebanese agreement; (2) it subjects them to the charge that they have foresaken their Arab and Muslim brothers for association with an imperialist power; and (3) it threatens what is left of Arab solidarity. All of these factors militate against the stability of the House of Saud and lead the Saudis to fear that they embrace the United States at their own peril.

The Yemen war in 1979 was a microcosm of the Saudi dilemma. Saudi vulnerability was clear, and Riyadh wanted strong U.S. support. When American aid was forthcoming, however, the Saudi response was mixed, not only because the Saudis feared Yemeni strength, but because the United States played up the conflict as a great-power confrontation. The Saudis thus found themselves accused by their fellow Arabs of aiding and abetting the internationalization of an *essentially Arab problem* by encouraging a superpower confrontation on the Arabian Peninsula. While an Arab League solution relieved the Saudis of Arab wrath, it also illustrated their dilemma.

The uproar later in the year over the Strait of Hormuz, resulting from Oman's call for a multilateral approach to the security of the strait, elicited a reaction from the Persian Gulf states that again illustrated the Saudis' dilemma. While they and their Arab Gulf friends might benefit from a U.S. role in Gulf security arrangements, they also feared what might flow from American involvement. As a result, they wanted a *limited* U.S. presence in the region, a *low profile* in the provision of desired assistance, and *no U.S. rhetoric.* Even publicity necessary to garner domestic support for U.S. policies is seen in Saudi Arabia as a potentially dangerous lack of discretion. The Iran-Iraq war that began in September 1980 and is now in its fourth year continues to illustrate the same themes. As in the case of Yemen, Saudi requests generated a quick U.S. response: AWACS planes and a guided-missile cruiser were dispatched to Saudi Arabia. In the face of an immediate threat, the Saudis were more than willing to explore the possibility of some form of regional security and were, at least temporarily, willing to accept a greater U.S. presence in Saudi Arabia. But there are limits, as the Saudis have reminded us.[19]

_____

19. Consider, for example, the comment of Foreign Minister Prince Saud, repeated in the *Wall Street Journal* for September 30, 1980: "If one speculates and prepares for every eventuality, one tends to increase the threat. . . . The dynamics of such logic is what is dangerous." Or Crown Prince Fahd's opening remarks at the January 1981 Islamic summit in Taif which included the assertion that "the security of the Islamic nation won't be assured . . . by taking refuge under the umbrella of a superpower." *Ibid.*, January 26, 1981.

The Saudi dilemma in this instance is that a serious American guarantee of Persian Gulf security, as implied in President Reagan's assertion on October 1, 1981, that the United States would not permit Saudi Arabia "to be an Iran," would require U.S. actions that would make shambles of other Saudi goals. To increase dramatically the U.S. presence in the region, beyond the prepositioning of project stocks, and to raise the profile of U.S. forces in the Gulf would have serious repercussions. The Soviets, for example, could seek a comparable presence, thereby making more likely a superpower conflict in the region. Depending on how the conflict between Iran and Iraq is resolved, there could be others. Iraq, it may be recalled, initially distrusted U.S. intentions and feared great-power involvement in Gulf affairs. If Iraq had eliminated Iran as a threat, the Iraqis undoubtedly would have seen an American presence in Saudi Arabia as directed against them. In such circumstances, external pressures might seriously have threatened the kingdom's security and could have stimulated internal forces which would have exacerbated that threat. Once the fortunes of war were reversed, however, Iran became the threatening power. The Iranians condemn the United States for blocking their intentions to undermine the Saudi regime which, they are convinced, plotted with Iraq in the initial attack on Iran. The rhetoric they are now directing toward Saudi Arabia is more than a mere threat to the House of Saud. Along with the bombing of Kuwaiti oil installations three times in the last two years and attempted coups in Bahrain and Qatar, Iranian rhetoric is seen as part of a widespread attempt to export the Iranian revolution and bring down the conservative regimes of the Gulf.[20]

As a result of the interplay between these factors, the Saudis welcome the gradual rapprochement with Egypt. When it comes to the United States, however, they can be expected to vacillate on the key issue of regional security, while desiring symbolic reassurances of support in the form of an unrealistically extensive military supply relationship—a desire whose fulfillment congressional legislation makes extremely difficult. In the Summer of 1980, a Saudi request for bomb racks, conformal fuel pods, and KC-135 refueling tankers (for F-15s

---

20. Ned Temko, *Christian Science Monitor*, December 14, 1983. An Iranian victory in its war with Iraq, aside from its impact on the shia populations of Kuwait, Bahrain, and Saudi Arabia, would mean that three Iranian mechanized divisions could march right down the Gulf to the Ghawar oil fields in Saudi Arabia with virtually nothing to stop them. The Saudis have one brigade east of Riyadh that they could deploy, a divisional cantonement (lacking troops) near their northern border, and would undoubtedly get expected support from Pakistan, Jordan, and, possibly, Egypt (see Chapter 3, n. 24), but they have little in the way of manpower resources of their own.

that were scheduled for delivery starting in 1981) was turned away and a decision on the request postponed until 1981. In October 1980, a campaign statement by President Carter ruling out the sale of bomb racks was reported to have led Crown Prince (now King) Fahd to consider requesting a withdrawal of the AWACS planes. Additional equipment for the F-15s, which the Saudis correctly felt was essential to their long-range intercept and all-weather missile-launch capabilities as well as to their protection against low-altitude attack, became a test of Saudi-U.S. relations until President Reagan's intervention narrowly convinced Congress to resolve the issue in favor of selling the equipment to the Saudis.[21]

If Washington had not been forthcoming on the F-15 issue, particularly on the fuel pods, which a Defense Department study concluded did not constitute a threat to the Israelis, the Saudis undoubtedly would have pursued with greater urgency the Mirage-4000 option offered by France. Recent agreements with France and Germany suggest an increasing Saudi inclination to diversify the sources of military assistance available to them anyway, a trend which U.S. officials see as giving the United States less influence over the Saudis. From the Saudi point of view, however, this course of action has the additional attraction of allowing them to consider using the weapons systems they acquire to assist other countries—an option not open to them with U.S. systems.

*Oil Policy.* Saudi oil also presents the kingdom's rulers with a serious dilemma. The Saudis are under constant pressure from other Arab states and Iran to reduce oil production and raise prices. The goals of these states are to increase their own incomes and, secondarily, to influence U.S. and indirectly Israeli policies toward the Middle East

---

21. The telling argument on the AWACS sale (although not the key political argument) was that the total time for an F-15 intercept of Iranian F-4s based in Bushire was 25 minutes with ground radar and no AIM-9L missiles (10 minutes too late), as opposed to 10-11 minutes with AWACS and the AIM-9L missiles (time enough to complete a short-range pass at the approaching F-4s and ready the defensive batteries). For full discussion of these issues, see U.S. Congress, Senate, Arms Sales Package to Saudi Arabia, Parts 1 & 2, Hearings before the Committee on Foreign Relations, Washington, D.C., G.P.O., October 1981; *Military and Technical Implications of the Proposed Sale of Air Defense Enhancements to Saudi Arabia,* Report of the Hearings before the Committee on Armed Services, Washington, D.C., G.P.O., 1981; and Anthony Cordesman, "Saudi Arabia, AWACS, and America's Search for Strategic Stability in the Near East," Working Paper No. 26A, The Woodrow Wilson Center for International Scholars, Smithsonian Institution, Washington, D.C., September 1981, portions of which appeared in the September and December 1981 issues of the *Armed Forces Journal International.*

peace process. In the period before the current oil "glut," if the Saudis had heeded the call to cut back production, they would have increased world oil prices substantially, thereby creating serious economic and political problems not only for the West but ultimately for themselves as well.[22]

On the other hand, as the Saudis saw it, acceding to U.S. desires to keep prices down and increase production angered the other Arab states and discouraged conservation by consumers. In a time of scarcity such as that which followed the Iranian revolution and the beginning of the Iran-Iraq war, moreover, the Saudi capacity to influence oil prices beyond a certain point diminished greatly because Saudi Arabia no longer had sufficient excess capacity to be an oligopoly price leader. Finally, Saudi "conservationists" such as Minister of Planning Hisham Nazer attributed much of the oil problem to the inability of the West to adopt an effective energy policy.[23]

Faced by these unpalatable alternatives, the Saudis made some difficult choices. The decision in July 1979 to increase oil production from 8.5 to 9.5 million barrels per day (MBD) reflected essentially a compromise between two sets of fundamental concerns: (1) the economic health of the United States and the West, as well as Saudi investments in the West; and (2) solidarity with OPEC and the Arab world. These concerns related to the very security of the kingdom and appeared to be mutually exclusive. They made the compromise that the Saudis reached an extremely tenuous one. Riyadh reluctantly acquiesced in the OPEC demand for a significant price increase and set the price of Saudi Arabian light crude—the OPEC benchmark—at $18 per barrel. While increased oil production clearly served their own economic interests, it also enabled them to meet international responsibilities.

---

22. In a statement on August 14, 1979, Minister of Petroleum Sheik Ahmad Zaki Yamani explained the problem: "Saudi Arabia is undertaking a unique role, because when it adopts an oil resolution, it does so in light of seemingly contradictory factors. For example, if we raise prices to a higher level than we should, we will cause a world recession which could lead to a standstill in our industrialization programs. That is why we must be aware of the balance between the price that should be applied and the price that is harmful. The same process would apply to an increase in production since this would affect the oil life span while the lack of increase would affect the world economy." Foreign Broadcast Information Service, *Daily Report*, MEA-79-159.

23. Imputations by "liberals" such as Sheikh Yamani are generally, but not always, more ellipitical: "Saudi Arabia cannot be expected to go on forever using its production to save the world from the consequences of unrestrained greed....A global energy program is necessary to move the world away from the edge of an abyss." *Saudi Report*, March 31, 1980. Cf., however, the *Wall Street Journal*, November 18, 1980.

The July 1979 decision to increase oil output was attributed by the Saudi state radio to the additional needs of the kingdom's 1976-1981 development plan—an obvious attempt to rationalize the decision for public consumption. A more convincing explanation would refer to a combination of factors: (1) an attempt to control the spot market and to stabilize prices, thereby softening the impact of OPEC price increases on Western economies and Saudi investments, and demonstrating to OPEC that the Saudis were still a force to be reckoned with; (2) a response to President Carter's letter to the heads of OPEC countries, possibly seen by the Saudis as a strong indication that the United States was prepared to reduce energy consumption but needed relief on the production side to proceed in an orderly fashion; and (3) an opportunity to earn political credit with consumers, to repay the United States for its support of North Yemen in February-March and, implicitly, to induce Washington to use its leverage on Israeli in the peace process.

Many of the factors outlined above were influential in a subsequent Saudi decision, in September 1979, to maintain oil production at 9.5 MBD. The same was true a year later at Vienna, where the Saudis agreed to raise the price of a barrel of oil to $30 but maintained production at 9.5 MBD. It was demonstrated again at Bali in December 1980 when the Saudis, acting to restrain price increases demanded by the OPEC countries, reluctantly raised the price of oil to $32 a barrel but kept to an even higher production increase of 10.3 MBD that followed the Iran-Iraq war.

The shortfall in world oil supplies in 1980 and Washington's failure at the time to enact a comprehensive energy program made clear to Saudi Arabia the heavy dependence of the United States and its Western allies on imported oil. The Iran-Iraq war underscored the West's dependence and resulted in the Saudi decision to increase production by approximately 1 MBD (to 10.3 MBD) in order to bring OPEC prices down to the Saudi level and make up for the Iraqi shortfall. This shortfall, because of extensive damage to refineries, pipelines, pumping stations, oil-loading terminals, and other facilities, continued through most of 1981, by which time the world economic recession and conservation measures together began to have their effect. These developments, meanwhile, led the Saudis—who were well aware of their own vulnerability and who depended on the United States to be more forthcoming on military assistance—to expect more consideration in return for their oil.[24] The U.S. decision in late 1981 to go ahead with the

---

24. For further discussion of this issue, see Bruce Kuniholm, "What the Saudis Really Want: A Primer for the Reagan Administration," *Orbis* 25:1 (1981), pp. 118-119.

sale of additional equipment for the F-15s can be seen as partial confirmation of the fact that those expectations were justified.

What an analysis of Saudi oil policies reveals is that the conflicting pressures to which Saudi Arabia is subject allow the Saudis to go only so far in responding to any one that seems particularly threatening. As the Saudis see it, their only choice is to compromise between competing pressures with the hope of gradually improving the difficult situation in which they find themselves. In this context, cartoon stereotypes of unkempt, gouging, and backstabbing Arabs which can be seen throughout the press, project a totally misleading image of Saudi Arabia that makes even more difficult any understanding of Saudi Arabia's options and what it is the Saudis want from us.[25]

Psychological and sociological factors help to explain what the popular press inappropriately refers to as "blackmail," and what should be understood as a more subtle linkage between the Saudis' oil production policies and their perceived military-supply needs. The Saudis have a deeply ingrained aversion to the use of threats. This attitude makes any blunt use of the oil weapon, such as occurred in 1973, an exception. To the Saudis, threats and blackmail directly challenge fundamental Bedouin norms and are regarded as tactically counterproductive. If a Saudi wants to influence a friend, he does so in the context of reciprocity. In the Saudi system, friends have mutual obligations that oblige one to help another in time of need. In the process, influence is exercised and expectations are met without confrontation. For these reasons, perhaps, the Saudis have avoided an explicit linkage between oil and the peace process. Saudi leaders both privately and publicly, have denied repeatedly that these two matters are interconnected.[26] Commentators, in turn, have asserted that Islamic fatalism, combined with a fixation on divine will, has enabled the Saudis to compartmentalize issues and to view specific events as separate exercises of fate or of God's will, having no association with related events.[27] Such denials and explanations, however, should not blind Washington to the expectations that the Saudis do have.

The Saudis have repeatedly hinted at the linkage between their production of oil and U.S. assistance for Saudi security, whether in the

---

25. See, for example, Herblock's cartoon in the *Washington Post,* July 12, 1979.
26. For example, see Foreign Minister Prince Saud's explicit rejection of the use of Saudi oil as a weapon against Israel's Western supporters. *Washington Post,* February 1, 1981.
27. See David Long's analysis in *The Government and Politics of the Middle East and North Africa* (Boulder: Westview, 1980), pp. 23-24, which expresses a point of view widely shared by many government analysts.

form of military equipment or progress in the peace process. Saudi perceptions that Washington has failed to recognize this linkage could result in the reduction of oil production levels, supposedly for technical reasons, as well as in a serious setback for U.S. policies in the Gulf. Such reductions, clearly, would not be likely at a time when supply was outstripping demand. But the oil market, as oil economist Morris Adelman has pointed out, is "utterly unstable."[28]

In spite of the unpredictability of the oil market, the 1983 oil "glut" has led some individuals such as Secretary of Energy Donald Hodel to question the strategic importance of the Gulf.[29] Such individuals ignore the fact that the world did not suffer a worse oil crisis in 1979-1981 because Saudi Arabia raised its oil production, and that it was an economic recession, not demise of the energy crisis, that made the glut possible. There is no doubt that significant developments *did* occur in the international oil market in the first half of 1983. Saudi Arabia's average monthly production level dropped to roughly one-third its 1980 level of 9.6 MBD (and OPEC's from 26.9 MBD in 1980 to monthly levels as low as 14.3 MBD in early 1983). But these developments should not obscure another fact: projections in 1983 by the Energy Information Agency, the International Energy Agency, and the big oil companies all suggest that OPEC production levels will rise to around 25 MBD in 1985 (the lowest major independent projection of demand is 21 MBD). These projections, moreover, are based on limited levels of world economic growth.[30]

What the foregoing analyses suggest is that the United States should not be too complacent about the energy situation and that it cannot write off its good relations with the Gulf states. The Gulf states still have 55% of the world's proven oil reserves. Saudi Arabia alone has 25% of the world's proven reserves and 30% of OPEC's sustained production capacity. As Britain's output declines later in the decade, and if alternative energy projects continue to be cancelled, the prediction of a number of analysts, including former Secretary of Energy James Schlesinger, will come true: the West will be increasingly dependent on OPEC in the second half of this decade. If OPEC's 1978-81 production levels are more typical of production levels in the 1980s and 1990s, we can also expect that the market will continue to be unstable and that it will be punctuated by oil shocks.[31]

28. Cited in David Francis, *Christian Science Monitor*, December 1, 1983.
29. Cited in Anthony Cordesman, "The 'Oil Glut' and the Strategic Importance of the Gulf States," *Armed Forces Journal International* 121: 3 (1983), pp. 30-47.
30. Ibid.; *International Herald Tribune*, July 6, 1983.
31. Ibid.; Bob Hagerty, *International Herald Tribune*, July 13, 1983; see also the warning by Daniel Yergin, *International Herald Tribune*, July 20, 1983.

In the interim, while supply outstrips demand, Iran and Libya continue to put enormous pressures on Saudi Arabia to cut production. The Saudis, however, have slashed prices and made credible the threat of doing so again, shocking others into curbing their outputs. After a series of akward compromises, OPEC in March 1983 agreed to cut the price of oil from $34 to $29 per barrel and to create a 17.5 MBD ceiling, with Saudi Arabia acting as the "swing producer" (i.e., it could increase or decrease whatever was necessary to keep the market tight).[32] By the end of the year, the kingdom had increased production to around 5 MBD, and OPEC sales had edged over the 17.5 MBD ceiling with a short-lived bulge in demand that normally accompanies the onset of winter. If Saudi Arabia's income from oil in 1983 amounted to less than half what it was in 1981 (when it was $112 billion) and if it would have to spend $26 billion more in 1983 than it earned, its reserves (variously estimated between $123-150 billion) were more than adequate for the short haul.[33] Many Saudis, in fact, welcomed the neccessity of taking stock and reassessing their domestic priorities.[34] Of greater immediate concern to them was how they could prevent cheating on production quotas and prices sufficient to keep the market relatively stable, and whether they could withstand the pressures of the OPEC states to increase production until demand picked up.[35]

## VELVET GLOVE OR MAILED FIST?

Analyzing the full range of their interests, many Saudis feel that despite the interdependence between our two countries, Saudi Arabia is of greater importance to the United States than the United States is to Saudi Arabia. When the Saudis feel particularly threatened, they will

---

32. Joseph Fitchett, *International Herald Tribune,* July 6, 1983; Thomas Stauffer (October 11), John Yemma (November 22), and David Francis (December 1, 1983), *Christian Science Monitor.*

33. Ibid.; *International Herald Tribune,* August 16, 1983; *Time,* November 23, 1983. As far back as February 1981, Sheikh Yamani asserted that the Saudis could cut oil production to 6MBD and still finance their needs. He predicted at that time that Saudi production, then at 10.3 MBD, might drop to as low as 5 MBD by 1982. *Wall Street Journal,* Feb. 2, 1981; *Christian Science Monitor,* February 5, 1981.

34. This opinion was expressed to me by Saudis in various ministries in Riyadh, April 1983. As one official put it, "Like going to a dentist, its good for you." Another compared it to the useful affects of an oil price hike on the West's "irresponsible" energy consumption.

35. *International Herald Tribune,* June 9, 1983; *Christian Science Monitor,* July 19, 1983.

seek U.S. assistance if it seems appropriate. But such threat perceptions—as materialized during the early stages of the Yemen civil war, the period immediately following the ouster of the Shah of Iran, and at certain times during the Iran-Iraq war—have short lives. The Saudis also understand the politics of survival and have other means of accommodating them. Their perceptions eventually tend to gravitate back to the generalization that oil for the West weighs more heavily on the scale of U.S.-Saudi relations than American promises to safeguard the security of Saudi Arabia. This is particularly so when the most *immediate* threats to Saudi security come not from Soviet-supported forces operating in the Horn of Africa, in the People's Democratic Republic of Yemen, or in Afghanistan but, rather, from within the Persian Gulf region, if not from within Saudi Arabia itself. As a result, the Saudis look to Washington to balance the scale by (1) using its influence with Israel to help resolve the Jerusalem and Palestinian issues, and (2) providing Saudi Arabia with the military equipment it needs and with a regional security umbrella that will not upset its Arab neighbors.    The Saudis consider close ties with Washington an essential element of their foreign policy. Nevertheless, they cannot afford to sacrifice their even more essential ties with other Arabs and Muslims, or to risk domestic instability, for their relationship with the United States. In short, what the Saudis really want—a clear choice that protects their interests—they cannot have. Instead, they must pursue policies that balance extremely difficult choices and sometimes violently conflicting interests, thus unavoidably creating misunderstandings among those who share some of those interests with them.

By the same token, what the United States wants—an ally that can be counted on to support its general policies in the region—it cannot have either. After recovering from its disappointment over Saudi endorsement of the Baghdad Resolution of March 31, 1979, the Carter administration acquired a better understanding of Saudi ambivalence. Saudi support for U.S. policies toward the peace process as it then stood, undue Saudi acquiescence in the projection of military force in the Persian Gulf, and increased production of Saudi oil all were potentially as harmful as they were helpful to Saudi interests and risked undermining the very institutions that U.S. policies were said to be protecting.[36]

The Reagan administration has learned to be sensitive to the same considerations, although the current glut of oil has made the increased production of Saudi oil less of an issue in the last two years. The message of the disappointments chronicled earlier in this chapter has

---

36. These judgments are derived from my experience in the Department of State during the Carter Administration as well as from conversations with officials at State, Defense, and the NSC.

become increasingly clear. Any attempt to push the Saudis beyond what their instinct for survival tells them is acceptable, and we must remember that their interpretation of what is threatening to their survival is markedly different from ours, can only result in failure and damage to our common interests. At the same time, the constraints under which Saudi Arabia must operate do not preclude constructive U.S. policies. Delivery of some of the equipment that the Saudis feel they must have (providing it does not pose a threat to Israel) or, more importantly, progress toward resolution of the Palestinian question, will not *necessarily* change Saudi oil-pricing and production policies, or *necessarily* render the Saudis capable of withstanding regional pressures against an enhanced U.S. presence in the Gulf. Such policies *would* diminish the threats to which the Saudis are most vulnerable, however, and would alter the nature of the political pressures operating on Saudi leaders.

Progress toward a resolution of the Palestinian question would reduce a number of threats to the legitimacy of the House of Saud. It would also make it easier for the Saudis to focus the attention of the Islamic states on the Soviet occupation of Afghanistan, which many Middle Eastern Muslims regard as little different from the Israeli occupation of the West Bank. The Saudis, who for obvious reasons will continue to be responsive to the West's energy needs as economic growth returns, would also be in a position, both internally and regionally, to be more receptive to U.S. concerns about Persian Gulf security. In short, there is room for maneuver, but such maneuvers should be conducted with a velvet glove, not a mailed fist. Heavyhandedness in dealing with the Saudis is self-defeating and will only impede the continuation of what has been, up to now, a mutually beneficial special relationship.

## THE SMALLER GULF STATES

An appreciation of the domestic concerns and priorities of the smaller Gulf states, coupled with an understanding of their interaction with each other and the larger Gulf states, is essential to the formulation of a broader U.S. policy in the region.[37] Unfortunately, space prohibits our conducting such an analysis here and requires that we

---

37. There are a host of books on these subjects, many of which are listed in the bibliography. Those that deserve especial mention include: John Duke Anthony, *Arab States of the Lower Gulf: People, Politics, Petroleum* (Washington, D.C.: The Middle East Institute, 1975); Rouhollah Ramazani, *The Persian Gulf and the Strait of Hormuz* (Alphen aan den Rijn, the Netherlands: Sijthoff & Noordhoff, 1979); Robert Litwak, *Security in the Persian Gulf 2: Sources of Interstate Conflict* (Montclair, N.J.: Allanheld, Osmun, 1981); and portions (but not all) of the books in the series edited by Shahram Chubin.

confine ourselves, briefly, to a discussion of those relationships that most directly affect the formulation of U.S. policy in the region as a whole.[38]

The Lower Gulf states of Bahrain, Qatar, and the United Arab Emirates act independently in their domestic policies but consult with Saudi Arabia before taking any actions in the realm of foreign policy, where their priorities follow those of the Saudis. Bahrain's ruling Al Khalifa family needs and gets economic and political support from the Saudis. Qatar's Al Thani dynasty and the various sheikhs of the UAE—particularly Sheikh Zayid, the ruler of Abu Dhabi (which is by far the richest emirate), and Sheikh Rashid, the ruler of Dubai, whose emirate has good economic relations with Iran—are not dependent on the Saudis economically. They nevertheless almost always wait to see what Saudi policies will be before moving politically themselves.

The Lower Gulf states, in addition to their solicitude to Saudi concern over security issues, are attuned to the Middle East peace process and the Iranian revolution, both of which directly concern their large Palestinian, Iranian and/or Shiite populations. There are over 1,500 Palestinians in Bahrain, where over half the country's population of 360,000 are Shiites; approximately 40,000 Palestinians and 50,000 Iranian Shiites in the UAE, whose population is around 1,000,000; and approximately 20,000 Palestinians and 40,000 Arabs of Iranian extraction in Qatar, whose population is about 230,000.

As a result of these figures, the sheikdoms are necessarily sensitive to Palestinian radicalism. They are concerned about Islamic pressures and apprehensive about nationalist claims such as Ayatollah Rouhani's reassertion of Iran's claim to Bahrain in 1979. Islamic pressures, some fear, could radicalize not only Shiites or Palestinians but also the Gulf's large, mostly male expatriate populations and thereby seriously threaten the position of the ruling families. Their fears acquire credibility when one considers that in the UAE expatriates outnumber the indigenous population by a ratio of approximately five to one.

Kuwait, with a larger Palestinian population (almost 25% of 1.4 million) than any Gulf state, a sizable Shiite population (30% of the total), and an extremely vulnerable position at the head of the Gulf,[39] is forced to manage a complex array of conflicting forces in order to ensure its survival. As a result, the Kuwaitis do not necessarily follow Saudi

---

38. The discussion that follows is largely based on extensive conversations with Gulf, American, British and French officials in the Gulf states, March and April, 1983.

39. Various metaphors used to describe Kuwait's geopolitical position include that of "a nut in a nutcracker" and "between Iraq and a hard place." Kuwait borders Iraq and is only 12.5 miles from Iran at its nearest point.

guidelines. Regarding themselves as more enlightened than the Saudis and possessing a freer press as well as a National Assembly that provides at least the semblance of political participation, the Kuwaitis frequently question Saudi predominance. They also pursue their own foreign policies and maintain diplomatic relations with a number of socialist non-Arab states. The Kuwaitis, for example, are the only "moderate" Gulf state to have normal diplomatic relations with the Soviet Union. Along with the UAE, they are the only Gulf Cooperation Council (GCC) members to have diplomatic relations with Iran. While they are sensitive to Iraqi designs on their territory, which they were forced to contest (with outside help) in 1961, 1973, and 1976, they also recognize the fact that Iran's military power has to be reckoned with, and that there is relatively little the Saudis can do for them. For this reason, although Saudi Arabia is their most important regional ally and their diplomacy is generally coordinated with Saudi Arabia, they are more aloof from U.S. policies. These policies, they believe, place too much emphasis on the Soviets and give too little attention to regional priorities.

Oman is more favorable in its attitude toward U.S. policies, in part because of its geographical isolation from the other Gulf states and in part because of its negligible Palestinian and Shiite population. Most of Oman's relatively small number of expatriates, who do not amount to more than 20% of its 800,000 inhabitants, are from the subcontinent. Oman was the only Gulf state to support Egyptian President Anwar Sadat's peace initiative and the Camp David accords, to distance itself from the decisions of the Baghdad Summit, to grant the U.S. access to facilities, and to invite a joint military exercise on its territory. Hence until recently, when the Gulf states began to give increasing attention to their security concerns, Oman (which had been fighting the Dhofar rebellion since the mid-1960s), was relatively isolated in its relationships with its neighbors.

This brief review of the relationships between the smaller states of the northern Arabian Peninsula littoral and Saudi Arabia suggests that, in spite of longstanding historical quarrels, there is a natural alliance between them. The alliance, which transcends some extremely bitter territorial and boundary disputes, is based on a belief in common ancestry and reinforced by threats from without. In conjunction with events of the last decade, common bonds have contributed to a common concern that beyond a desire for economic integration,[40] some form of political/

---

40. See Roger Nye, "Political and Economic integration in the Arab states of the Gulf," *Journal of South Asian and Middle Eastern Studies* 2:1 (1978), pp. 3-21, who cites eight examples of regional cooperation for economic ends. Political integration, since it involves a loss of national sovereignty and since the benefits are less visible, has (until recently) less overt commitment.

military integration is necessary for collective security.[41]     The concern for political and military integration has been reinforced by a series of recent events: the Israeli bombing of Iraq's nuclear reactor; Iran's bombing on three different occasions of Kuwaiti oil installations; the tripartite agreement signed in August 1981 by Libya, the PDRY, and Ethiopia which formalized their rivalry with Iraq, Saudi Arabia, and Jordan; Iranian support for the December 1981 coup attempt in Bahrain and a subsequent coup attempt in Qatar; the Iranian counteroffensive against Iraq; and the bombing of the American Embassay in Kuwait in December 1983. These events, progressively, have helped to bridge differences among Gulf states. In May 1981 Saudi Arabia, Kuwait, the UAE, Bahrain, Qatar, and Oman (conveniently excluding both Iran and Iraq because of the war between them), were able to form the Gulf Cooperation Council (GCC). Subsequently, the states of the GCC were able to agree on basic principles of collective security and take concrete steps to implement those principles.[42] In October 1983 the GCC conducted its first joint military exercises in the United Arab Emirates western desert—a development whose importance was underscored by Iranian threats to close the Strait of Hormuz. While joint military exercises were more symbolic than functional, the United States should encourage this trend and support it in every way possible.[43]

The Saudis, apparently, have also been giving serious attention to an Omani proposal for a united defense strategy in which member states would group their naval vessels under a joint command and integrate,

---

42. For Saudi Arabia's commitment to pay the construction costs of the causeway between Bahrain and the mainland, which has been interpreted as underscoring the Saudi pledge to defend Bahrain, see the *Wall Street Journal,* July 9, 1981. Saudi Arabia has in fact reached security cooperation agreements with Bahrain, the UAE, and Qatar. *Christian Science Monitor,* November 12 and 13, 1981; February 5, 9, 12, and March 1, 1982; and the *Wall Street Journal,* January 14, 1982. The failure to form a formal defense alliance has been due in part to resistance from Kuwait, which for obvious reasons wants to retain its non-

41. See "Gulf Security Document," *The Middle East,* January 1981, pp. 16-17; and John Duke Anthony, "The Gulf Cooperation Council," a paper presented to the Annual Convention of the Middle East Studies Association of North America, Seattle, Washington, November 5, 1981.
aligned position. There have been talks of a $1 billion arms industry and a Gulf intervention force. Geoffrey Weston, *International Herald Tribune,* June 22, 1983; and *Christian Science Monitor,* December 14, 1983.

43. *International Herald Tribune,* September 24-25, and November 7, 1983. While the symbolic role should not be discounted, the functional role cannot be totally ignored either. As one American official in the Gulf put it, "until recently, the GCC RDF consisted of 27 Rolls Royces filled with bedu."

as well as strengthen, their existing defense systems.[44] To the extent that these developments enhance Gulf security and allow the Gulf states, with outside assistance, to serve as a countervailing force within the region, and to the extent that concerns about regional threats and great power intrusion in the Gulf cement the GCC's increased cohesion, the United States can play a less obtrusive role in Gulf security affairs. This would benefit both Saudi and regional security.

In the meantime, although the U.S. and the Arab states of the Gulf continue to share strong mutual interests, the Gulf states are as anxious about their relationships with the United States as they have been in any period since the imposition of the oil embargo ten years ago. These anxieties derive from several general considerations:

— a conviction that the United States lacks the nerve to exert enough pressure on Israel to achieve a "reasonable" peace settlement;

— a concern that the separate peace between Israel and Egypt, and the war in Lebanon that it made possible, has polarized the Arab world even further, and provided radical regimes such as Syria with enormous potential to destabilize the Gulf mosaic;

— a fear that Soviet influence in the Middle East and South Asia is growing and that the Gulf, without any effective U.S. shield, will be prey to the rapidly growing forces of Communism and radicalism;

— a contrary, but equally prevalent, fear that the United States, overreacting to a perceived Soviet threat, may seek to project its military power into the Gulf, thereby destabilizing conservative regimes and creating the likelihood of great power conflict;

— a perception that United States foreign policy lacks direction and that, as a result, the United States is becoming less reliable as a defender of the Free World; and last, but not least,

— a concern that Iran is bent on exporting its revolution across the Gulf.

In this context, the rapid succession of Soviet "successes" in the Horn of Africa, the People's Democratic Republic of Yemen, and Afghanistan, has dismayed the Gulf states. These destabilizing events, coupled with the revolution in Iran, the subsequent war between Iran and Iraq, and the revolutionary fervor of Iran, have dramatically heightened Gulf fears over vulnerability to attack or subversion. The Gulf states view American capabilities as immense. The perceived impotence and inaction of the United States, therefore, is ascribed to a failure of will, not to a real lack of mobility and power. As a result, the Gulf states are ambivalent about the United States role in their part of

---

44. John Yemma, *Christian Science Monitor,* October 26, 1982.

the world. They believe that however limited American will may be, the United States is the only power capable of deterring Soviet inroads into the region. As a result, they look to the United States for fundamental protection, although they want to keep the U.S. out of the Gulf and "over the horizon" because a United States presence could bring the Soviets in as well.

In the interim, the Arab Gulf states are growing more confident of their influence in international forums—at least in economic matters— and are beginning to establish closer economic, political, and military ties with each other. The key for the United States is to ensure Gulf security by maintaining a balance among the region's three centers of power, to restrain Oman's dangerous enthusiasm for American involvement in the region, and to respect the Saudis' instinct for survival. To push the Saudis beyond what that instinct tells them is acceptable can only result in failure and in damage to the interests that the United States and Saudi Arabia have in common.[45] To increase dramatically the U.S. presence in the region beyond what is necessary for the prepositioning of project stocks and development of the Saudi infrastructure, and to raise dramatically the profile of U.S. forces in the Gulf, could have serious repercussions.

---

45. As several ambassadors in the Gulf states observed to me in the Spring of 1983, we must be careful not to push the Gulf states too far, too fast. While the forces for stability appear to be able to cope with the centrifugal forces of instability, a coalescence of external forces, and particularly U.S.-Saudi relations, could shake the foundations of the House of Saud. See John Shaw and David Long, *Saudi Arabian Modernization: The Impact of Change on Stability* (Washington, D.C.: Georgetown, 1982).

# PART IV

# THE NORTHERN TIER

The countries along the "Northern Tier" of the Middle East and Southwest Asia play an important role in regional and great power politics. As a consequence, their relationships with the Gulf states constitute an important consideration in any U.S. strategy toward the region. While Turkey, Iran, Afghanistan and Pakistan all may be said to form part of a strategic buffer zone that historically has been a bone of contention between East and West, each of these states has a role to play in other regional groupings as well. Iran, which is also a Gulf state, has been examined in the context of Gulf politics. While characterized as a Gulf state, however, Iran has an importance that transcends its position on the Gulf littoral. As a result, readers should be wary of the arbitrary geographical categories that explication requires and keep Iran's role as a buffer between East and West, discussed in Chapter 7, firmly in mind.

Part IV will take a careful look at the nature of the relationships between two areas not normally associated with the Persian Gulf but which nonetheless are crucial to U.S. policy in the region. Chapter 9 will explore Turkey's interests in the Middle East and its increasingly important potential role in the security of the Persian Gulf and Southwest Asia; it will also attempt to address questions raised about the priority of its European and Middle Eastern roles. Chapter 10 will examine U.S. policy toward Southwest Asia. While keeping in mind the relationships between East and West that shape the politics of the subcontinent, discussion of U.S. options will focus on regional imperatives that in turn constrain the influence of the great powers and will suggest how one might think about the interplay between regional and geopolitical forces.

# 9

## Turkey and the Gulf

While Turkey's role in the defense of Europe and Asia Minor continues to be the focal point of its security concerns, its potential role in the security of the Persian Gulf and Southwest Asia has become increasingly significant to the broader security interests of its Western allies. While analysis of the latter role provides insight into the useful part that Turkey can play in supporting mutual strategic concerns, understanding Turkey's attitudes toward both roles is a prerequisite to any discussion of Turkish and American policies because it underscores the constraints that bound Turkish and, hence, American options in the region.

Emerging from a major domestic crisis which has yet to be surmounted and which many Turks feel the Soviets helped to exacerbate, Turkey's generals perceive a lack of European understanding for their country's domestic difficulties. At the same time they sense a greater receptivity in the Middle East to better relations with Turkey. Turkey's economy, meanwhile, fits comfortably with the economies of the Gulf—the Gulf states have the oil Turkey wants and need the manpower as well as agricultural and manufactured products Turkey has. As a result, Turkey has shifted its trade relations increasingly from Europe to the Middle East. With their national embrace of Western values somewhat more restrained than in the past, a number of Turks, responding to existential need and reacting to the limitations of Turkey's nationalist, secular political culture, have found increasing meaning in Islam.[1]

These trends have been reinforced by the military regime's sensitivity to what it feels is the West's poorly informed criticism of its rule. The harsh measures the military government has had to exercise in combatting the problems that led Turkey to the brink of civil war, Turks believe, were justified by circumstance and supported by a national referendum. As a result, General Evren has been critical of what he has referred to as "Byzantine intrigues" to expel Turkey from

---

1. For a more detailed treatment of some of the arguments put forward in this section, see Bruce 'Kuniholm, "Turkey and NATO: Past, Present, and Future," *Orbis* 27:2 (1983), pp. 421-45.

the Council of Europe, to restrict Turkish imports, and to criticize its human rights record. Turkey could do without the West, he observed in May 1983, if the West continues to make things difficult.[2] Where could Turkey turn? One direction was indicated a year earlier when Evren declared that Turkey was a European country and, at the same time, a Middle Eastern country.[3] If the Turks were now qualifying earlier aspirations to be accepted as members of the European community, economic developments and existential concerns, far more than differences within the NATO alliance and sensitivity to criticism, suggest why.

## GROWING ECONOMIC TIES

From 1980 to 1982, while the percentage of Turkey's exports to the European Economic Community dropped from 42.7% to 30.5% of total exports, the percentage that went to the Middle East and North Africa more than doubled (from 22.3% to 45% of the total).[4] In 1982 alone, Turkey's construction contracts in the Middle East and North Africa amounted to over $15 billion, including about $8 billion with Libya, $5.1 billion with Saudi Arabia, and $1.15 billion with Iraq. By the end of 1982 there were also approximately 250,000 Turkish workers in the region, primarily in Libya (100,000) and Saudi Arabia (54,000).[5]

Turkey's economic relations with the Gulf states are increasingly important. In early 1982, Iran and Turkey signed a major barter arrangement in which they exchanged agricultural products and manufactured goods for crude oil. By the end of 1982 Iran was Turkey's major export market. In April 1983, the two countries signed a protocol that called for an increase in the volume of trade from close to $1.6 billion in 1982 to $2.5 billion by the end of 1983.[6] Turkey's relations with Iraq are also significant, particularly for Iraq. The 1000 kilometer pipeline through Turkey, in operation since 1977, is Iraq's only means of exporting oil while the Shatt Al-Arab and the pipeline through Syria both are closed.

---

2. *International Herald Tribune,* May 16, 1983. For earlier indications of Turkey's desires to develop a "multidimensional, balanced foreign policy," see the *New York Times,* Nov. 28, 1982, and *Christian Science Monitor,* December 22, 1982.

3. Paul Henze, "On the Rebound," *Wilson Quarterly,* Special Issue 1982, p. 125.

4. *Turkey,* OECD Economic Survey (Paris: OECD, April 1983), p. 28.

5. Mushtak Parker, "Turkey: Special Report," *Arabia: The Islamic World Review,* February 1983, pp. 37-42.

6. Jonathan Randall, *Washington Post,* April 13, 1981; Mary Anne Weaver, *Christian Science Monitor,* December 6, 1982; the *Turkish Daily News,* April 22, 1983; *Turkey,* OECD Economic Survey, April 1983, p. 28.

The pipeline's 650,000 barrel per day capacity, increased 10% by the use of chemicals, is in the process of being increased further by added compressors, and by April 1984, according to one recent estimate, should reach 1.4 MBD. In October 1983, Iraq and Turkey also agreed to build a pipeline to transport three million tons of liquid petroleum gas annually through Turkish territory to Yumurtalik on the Mediterranean. In addition to oil and gas, trade also plays an important part in Turkey's relations with Iran and Iraq. One analyst estimated that in 1982 approximately six million tons of goods crossed over from Turkey into Iraq and Iran, approximately three million tons to each country. That figure is only two million tons less than all the lend lease goods that went to the U.S.S.R. through the Persian Corridor between 1941 and 1945. The volume of Turkey's trade with Iraq, meanwhile, is second to only that with Germany.[7]

## SOCIO-RELIGIOUS TIES

Turkey's increasingly close association with the Middle East and the greater visibility of Islam in Turkey have raised questions about the role that Islam will play in Turkey's political future. Several scholars have argued that one should not exaggerate religion's role in Turkish politics nor overstate its potential for alienating Turkey from the West. It is not the *force* of religiosity or the intensification of belief that has increased in Turkey, one argues, but the *scope* of religiosity or the range of social contexts within which religious considerations are relevant. The recent turmoil in Turkey, he believes, is not a sign of Islamic resurgence, but rather a spinoff of the polarization between leftist and rightist ideologies. Such ideologies were made possible by the successful institutionalization of political democracy and have taken the place of religious protest. The most important dimension of Islam's recent visibility in Turkey, he adds, is that it meets an inner need for meaning not satisfied by the political culture; in this capacity, it serves as an important source of moral authority and cohesion for urban migrants and "transitionals." To the extent that President Evren encourages this role, while attempting to restore conditions for a viable democracy in Turkey, religion should be seen neither as a substitute for nor as a threat to the nationalist-oriented, secular political order, but as a source

---

7. *The Wall Street Journal,* Nov. 4, 1982; Duygu Bazoglu Sezer, "Turkey's Security Policies," *Adelphi Papers,* No. 164, Spring 1981, p. 37; the *Kuwait Times,* March 7, 1983; *Christian Science Monitor,* April 5, 1983; Earl Foell, *Christian Science Monitor,* October 17, 1983; *Washington Post,* October 21, 1983; and Bruce Kuniholm, *The Origins of the Cold War in the Near East: Great Power Conflict and Diplomacy in Iran, Turkey, and Greece* (Princeton: Princeton University Press, 1980), p. 146.

of support for it. In this context, the anti-Western impulse in the revival of Islam, while it may reinforce Turkey's disenchantment with the West, does not necessarily dictate such a course.[8]

## TURKEY'S ROLE IN THE DEFENSE OF THE GULF REGION

If one were to rank the strategic importance of the Middle East and Soutwest Asia's "Northern Tier" countries, such factors as geography, political cohesion, military capability and sheer numbers would give Turkey priority. This was true in the early 1950s when Turkey joined NATO, and it is even more true now that the Iranian revolution has removed Iran from the ranks of U.S. allies and the Soviets have occupied Afghanistan.

Turkey's strategic importance is further evidenced by the fact that the weakness of either of its flanks poses a serious threat to Western security interests. If Thrace is the most vulnerable point on NATO's southern flank,[9] Iran, which is contiguous to the Soviet Union and not allied with any country, is even more vulnerable. A Soviet attack on Iran would be much less risky than an attack against a member of NATO. Occupation of just the northern part of Iran as in World War II would also provide a much greater payoff. The Soviets would gain the capacity to provide air cover as far as the Persian Gulf, making it much easier for them to deny the West access to Gulf oil. As a result, a Soviet attack on Iran, while unlikely, is nonetheless far more likely than one on Thrace. In the event of such an attack, Turkish support for Iranian resistance would be imperative to the success of broader efforts by the West to oppose Soviet ambitions—a fact that was appreciated at the time of Turkey's accession to NATO.

---

8. Conversations with journalists and professors in Turkey, April 1983. Metin Heper, "Islam, Polity and Society in Turkey: A Middle Eastern Perspective," *Middle East Journal* 35:3 (1981), pp. 345-63; Sezer, "Turkey's Security Policies," pp. 9 and 42; Serif Mardin, "Religion and Politics in Modern Turkey," in James Piscatori, ed., *Islam in the Political Process* (Cambridge: Cambridge University Press, 1983), pp. 138-159. Andrew Mango, *Turkey: A Delicately Poised Ally,* The Washington Papers, Vol. III (Beverly Hills, Cal.: Sage, 1975), p. 63, has observed that within the common framework of national self-assertion, different groupings within Turkey place different values on different foreign connections. The center looks to the West, the left to the "socialist countries," and the extreme right to the Muslim world. Mango notes that the key issue for Turkish opinion, however, is the willingness of foreign powers to accommodate Turkish national interests.

9. Lyman Lemnitzer, "The Strategic Problem of NATO's Northern and Southern Flanks," Orbis 13:1 (1969), p. 103; Ihsan Gurkan, *NATO, Turkey, and the Southern Flank: A Mideastern Perspective* (New York: National Strategy Information Center, 1980), pp. 13, and 48.

Turkey's role in deterring Soviet adventurism in Iran and its potential role in protecting the West's access to oil in the Persian Gulf was highlighted in October 1982 by a US-Turkish co-locator operating base agreement.[10] If funding problems can be solved, this agreement will result in the modernization of ten Turkish airfields and the building of one or two new ones at Mus and Batman in Eastern Turkey. With a length and width sufficient to accommodate long range bombers and cargo planes, these airfields would enhance Turkey's deterrent role and perhaps help exercise a dissuasive influence on any aggressive Soviet intentions in the area. They would put modern NATO fighter bombers within striking distance of the Transcaucasus, and the Rapid Deployment Force (RDF) within 700 miles of Abadan. That would be far closer to the head of the Persian Gulf than any of the facilities to which the U.S. Central Command (CENTCOM) now has access.

Even if these bases are designed primarily for NATO contingencies and their use is subject to Turkish approval, their potential value in the event of a serious crisis means that whether or not they are actually used, they will serve as an important deterrent both to Soviet adventurism in Iran and to Soviet ambitions in the Persian Gulf. Geoffrey Kemp, currently on the National Security Council staff, and many others have argued that NATO must redraw the maps of its strategic theaters to indicate the growing linkages between them. NATO should also remove the artificial distinctions between its borders and the Middle East for purposes of wartime contingencies.[11] That it will do so formally is unlikely. Germany and France consistently oppose such arrangements for constitutional and domestic political reasons. Informally, however, and for planning purposes, NATO has begun to examine out of area contingencies in order to overcome deficiencies in its capacity to react to emergencies, particularly in the Persian Gulf.[12]

---

10. Conversations with officials in the Departments of State and Defense; *Washington Post,* October 16, and November 1, 1982. Construction funds for the Mus and Batman bases in Eastern Turkey—under the co-locator operating bases agreement—are not programmed until FY1984; funding in that year is expected to be $69.2 million, of a programmed total of $135 million.
11. Geoffrey Kemp, "Defense Innovation and Geopolitics: From the Persian Gulf to Outer Space," in *National Security in the 1980's: From Weakness to Strength* (San Francisco, Cal.: Institute for Contemporary Studies, 1980), W. Scott Thompson, ed., p. 72. See also George Harris, "The View from Ankara," *The Wilson Quarterly,* Special Issue (1982), p. 134, and Gurkan, p. 35.
12. Conversations with officials in the Departments of State and Defense. France has a permanent naval presence in the Indian Ocean of 12-18 ships, periodically reinforced by one or two aircraft carriers; it also has 4,500 men stationed at Djibouti. British task forces of six ships also deploy biannually in the

## TURKEY AS LINCHPIN BETWEEN EAST AND WEST

Speculation about Turkey's role in the defense of the Gulf raises questions about its European and Middle Eastern roles and the implications of these roles for U.S. policies in the Gulf. At present, the Turks do not view alternatives to their Western alliance and their special relationship with the United States as promising—at least as long as the Soviet Union remains a potential threat. The Nonaligned Movement (NAM) is too fragmented. Because of the Cyprus question, raised once again on November 15, 1983, when the Turkish Cypriots declared their independence, the NAM is anti-Turkish. It is also unable to provide Turkey with the security or the technical and military assistance that the Turks require.[13]

Thus, while Turkey has an extremely important strategic as well as economic role to play in the Middle East, it sees the best guarantee of its security not in any unstable coalition of weak Middle Eastern or Third World states but in its alliance with the West. Its Middle East role may well become even more important in the next decade, particularly in view of its capacity to deter Soviet adventurism along the Northern Tier and to help ensure Western access to Gulf oil. But this role is likely to develop only in the context of Turkey's relationship with the West. At present, Turkey's ability to become involved in contingency planning is impeded by NATO's failure to remove the artificial barriers between its borders and the Middle East.

---

Indian Ocean. *NATO After Afghanistan,* House Committee on Foreign Affairs, Committee Print (Washington, D.C.: G.P.O., October 27, 1980), pp. 31 ff. For U.S. desires to be free to conduct "out-of-area" operations in the Persian Gulf, see Richard Halloran, *New York Times,* May 16, 1982.

13. Conversation with Turkish academics and officials in the military and the foreign ministry, Istanbul and Ankara, Turkey. For discussion of these issues, see also Sezer, p. 38; Harris, p. 135; George Gruen, "Ambivalence in the Alliance: U.S. Interests in the Middle East and the Evolution of Turkish Foreign Policy," *Orbis* 24:2 (1980), pp. 363-79; Alvin Rubinstein, *Soviet Policy Toward Turkey, Iran, and Afghanistan: The Dynamics of Influence* (New York: Praeger, 1982), pp. 40, 51, 146; Andrew Wilson, "The Aegean Dispute," *Adelphi Papers,* No. 155 (1979/1980), p. 25; the opinions of Mehmet Ali Birand and Zeki Kuneralp, cited in Andrew Mango, "Understanding Turkey," *Middle Eastern Studies,* Vol. 18, No. 2, April 1982, p. 208; Firenc Vali, *Bridge Across the Bosporus: The Foreign Policy of Turkey* (Baltimore: Johns Hopkins University Press, 1971), pp. 157-164. Sezer observes that while association with the U.S. entails risks, eliminating that association will not eliminate other risks and could increase them. The difficult choices confronting Turkey derive from the fact that, like most countries, it is neither totally secure nor totally threatened.

The extent to which U.S.-Turkish interests in the Gulf and South-west Asia are compatible, meanwhile, remains to be seen. Some U.S. officials would like a clearer commitment on the use of bases in Eastern Turkey in the event of a contingency in the Persian Gulf. In return, they are interested in, but not necessarily capable of, supplying the Turks with extensive military assistance as a *quid pro quo.* The Turks are extremely eager to obtain such assistance, but are understandably reluctant to be more forthcoming on the question of access in non-NATO contingencies. To do so would give the United States, in the event of a contingency involving such adversaries as Iran and Iraq, the capacity to damage Turkey's good diplomatic and economic relations with both. Even worse, it could increase the risk of Soviet intervention in Turkey in a non-NATO crisis that would not automatically trigger NATO obligations to protect Turkey. Turks still remember President Johnson's letter to Prime Minister Inonu in June 1964, warning him not to use U.S. supplied military equipment to invade Cyprus and informing Turkey that, if it took a step that resulted in Soviet intervention, its NATO allies might have to reconsider their obligations to Turkey.[14] The arms embargo from 1975-1978 has reinforced Turkish doubts about the reliability of the U.S. as an ally, while differences over Cyprus will continue to pose problems.

As a result, Turkey has attempted to respond as cautiously and constructively as possible to the complex political, economic and social forces evolving in the region. If the Turks have accommodated themselves to new realities, however, there are limits to this accommodation. Just as the Turks are reluctant to do the bidding of the West when it involves a non-NATO contingency, so they are determined not to be intimidated by the threat of greatly increased Soviet capabilities in the region.

Turkey's distrust of the Soviet Union and, consequently, its commitment to an alliance with the West is influenced by history. Russia, whether Christian or Communist, has consistently followed toward Turkey a policy grounded in self-interest and geopolitics.[15] As twelve

---

14. The Johnson letter is reprinted along with Inonu's reply in the *Middle East Journal* 20:3 (1966), pp. 386-93.

15. Another source of Soviet concern about Turkey may be found in the 1979 Soviet census which revealed that 37.2 of 43.8 million Muslims in the U.S.S.R. were of Turkic origin. Cited in Paul Henze, *Goal: Destabilization, Soviet Agitational Propaganda, Instability and Terrorism in NATO South* (Marina del Rey, Cal.: European American Institute for Security Research, December 1981), p. 15. For more details of the problems posed for the Soviet Union by its national minorities, see Helene Carrere d'Encausse, *Decline of an Empire: The Soviet Socialisrt Republics in Revolt,* Martin Sokolinsky and Henry A. La Farge, trans. (New York: Newsweek Books, 1979).

wars between the two countries would indicate, Russian policies have rarely been in Turkey's best interests. Western nations have based their policies on the same considerations as the Russians, but with less damage to Turkey's interests. Since the 1960s, Turkey's alliance with the West has been troubled, but it has also ensured Turkey's survival. Given the predispositions of the states that play a dominant role in the international balance of power and Turkey's historical vulnerability to both East and West, the Turks have tried to walk a delicate line between the competing power blocs.

Were a Soviet threat to diminish markedly, the notion of a neutral non-aligned buffer zone across the Northern Tier states of the Middle East and Southwest Asia would be one that the Turks would find increasingly attractive. This was true, to some extent, during the period of detente; it could be true again if U.S.-Soviet relations took a turn for the better and U.S.-Turkish relations a turn for the worse. Such a development, while unlikely, is nonetheless possible. What it would require is a change in leadership in the Soviet Union, a more constructive Soviet policy toward the states on its southern flank, and a decision to withdraw Soviet troops from Afghanistan. Serious Turkish-NATO differences over both Cyprus and human rights, meanwhile, could encourage the process. Until such changes occur, however, the threat posed by the Soviet Union means that the NATO countries need Turkey and Turkey needs them. As a result, while the Turks may never formally commit themselves to assist the United States in a contingency in the Gulf region, their assistance can never be ruled out either.

This state of affairs may well be in the interests of both parties. To pursue a greater commitment could be extremely costly for the United States and extremely risky for Turkey, since it would make Turkey a prime target in any contingency; nor would such a course, given the caution that the Turks would inevitably exercise, provide much greater deterrence. To discount Turkey's deterrent role, on the other hand, would be to ignore the geopolitical realities of the region and foresake an important component of U.S. and Turkish security interests. As a result, the United States should support Turkey's helpful but nonetheless ambiguous role in the Gulf region while attempting to improve good relations in the context of NATO.

# 10

## Southwest Asia and the Gulf

Any political strategy toward the Persian Gulf is intricately tied to the question of U. S. policies toward Southwest Asia, where intractable regional tensions are shaped and influenced by the broader U.S.-Soviet and Sino-Soviet conflicts. The connection between the two regions will be discussed in the course of examining U.S. policy options toward Pakistan. Before addressing that connection, however, it is necessary first to take a look at the region as a whole and in so doing to keep in mind that the interaction in Southwest Asia between regional and geopolitical forces—which India and Pakistan sometimes invite and the great powers sometimes impose—invariably has disappointed all parties. The result has been a web of relationships which, far more than those between the United States and Turkey, are riddled with ambivalence, ambiguities, and apprehensions. These developments have led one analyst to conclude that however necessary it may be for the United States to involve itself in the subcontinent's political disagreements and security concerns,

> the most promising way to attempt to deal with the subcontinent in the long-run is indirectly, by helping to build better societies. This is emotionally less satisfying than taking a "tough" line—particularly when other counties irritate us at times—but it is more likely to achieve long-term success.[1]

### A REGIONAL POLICY

The notion of building a better society suggests that, instead of emphasizing security relationships with either India or Pakistan, U.S. policy should attempt where possible to separate cold war issues from regional tensions and encourage local initiatives that promote regionalism in the context of nonalignment. Regional receptivity to such ideas, of course, is crucial. According to Jagat Mehta, former Foreign Secretary of India, lessons of the last decade are beginning to register: "The leadership of the erstwhile Hindu Party (Jan Sangh), which for three

---

1. William Barnds, *India, Pakistan, and the Great Powers* (New York: Praeger, 1972), p. 347.

decades has remained unreconciled to partition, now urges good relations with Pakistan. A growing body of non-official opinion in Pakistan feels that, ultimately, national security and progress for Pakistan hinges more on good relations with India than on American arms or exclusively Islamic connections."[2]

Under a regionally-based policy, the United States would avoid pressing any of the countries in the area for "special" security access rights. The United States would use its own resources whenever possible to promote programs which could have a regional impact and enhance regional cooperation and would urge the World Bank and other donors to follow a similar course. It would also try to maintain current projected levels of assistance for India, Bangladesh, Nepal and Sri Lanka, and continue to expand the economic, as opposed to the military, aspects of the new assistance program for Pakistan. While 40 F-16s from the United States will greatly improve Pakistan's ability to reach and attack Indian oil facilities and nuclear power plants, they will not significantly alter India's marked advantage (at least 3:1 and probably greater) in advanced aircraft. MiG-25s, 27s, 29s and 31s from the Soviet Union, Jaguars from Britain, and Mirage 2000s from France, moreover, eventually will increase India's advantage in a competition the Pakistanis cannot hope to win.[3] The $3.2 billion U.S. assistance program to Pakistan, on the other hand, since it is evenly divided between economic assistance and foreign military sales credit guarantees, and since it begins to balance India's large-scale arms purchases from the Soviet Union over the last four years, may help remove Pakistan's incentive to acquire a nuclear weapons capability. At the very least, even if such a capability is developed, the threat of the assistance program's cancellation will impede a decision to conduct a so-called peaceful nuclear explosion (PNE).

---

2. Jagat Singh Mehta, "The Origin of the Cold Wars: Myopia and Misperceptions in the Great Powers and the Subcontinent," Colloquium Paper, Woodrow Wilson Center for International Scholars, Washington, D.C., April 19, 1982. See also Ghulam Mustafa Khar, "Four Choices Facing Front-Line Pakistan," *The Economist* 281 (Oct. 31, 1981), pp. 25-30, who substantiates Mehta's judgment.

3. See "Shared Security Concerns: U.S. Cooperation with Pakistan," Current Policy No. 347, Bureau of Public Affairs (Washington, D.C.: U.S. Department of State, November 12, 1982); *The Military Balance: 1982-1983* (London: International Institute for Strategic Studies, Autumn 1982); and the *International Herald Tribune,* May 21-22, June 5, and July 2-3, 1983. India makes approximately 85% of its weaponry, obtaining most of the remaining 15% (mostly high-tech) from the Soviets at highly concessional terms. The Indians have been seeking to diminish their dependence on the Soviet Union.

Meanwhile, taking advantage of Prime Minister Indira Gandhi's interest in mutual understanding, evidenced by her visit to the United States in July 1982, American officials have been responsive to some of India's concerns. The Reagan administration in 1982 agreed to France's providing nuclear fuel for the U.S.-built Tarapur nuclear reactor near Bombay and in 1983 guaranteed that the reactor would be supplied spare parts by U.S. companies in third countries. At the president's behest, the United States and India have also been discussing a $1 billion arms deal.[4] One policy option suggested by these developments is for the United States to work even more closely with India in order to encourage India's cooperation as the keystone to subcontinental regionalism. Such a role is dictated by India's predominate position in South Asia and was given concrete recognition in March 1983 by Indira Gandhi's leadership of the Nonaligned Movement. Economic and security factors will continue to give India's relationship with the Soviet Union a higher priority than that with the United States, as was evidenced in the Summer of 1983 by an apparent $5 billion Indo-Soviet arms deal.[5] Nonetheless, the United States could build on the gradual but steady improvement in its relations with India by encouraging India's desires not only to expand relations with China and the West but also to reduce its dependence on Moscow, and to establish greater balance in its relations between the U.S. and the U.S.S.R.[6]

As a means of encouraging India in this direction, the United States could support a cooperative grouping of South Asian states which, while working more actively together in the interest of their own security, would be resistant to outside pressures and willing to work with the United States on broad foreign policy issues. This probably would not include any agreement on issues of military access, however, with the possible and limited exception of Pakistan. Moreover, this approach would build on the concerns of each state in the area that international tensions and military competition in the region will lead to great power confrontation. It would also dictate an even-handed role in restraining nuclear competition between India and Pakistan.

Pakistan's acquisition of American F-16's, meanwhile, while fostering a sense of mutual vulnerability could also encourage a sense of

---

4. Bernard Weinraub, *International Herald Tribune,* May 21-22, 1983; "Shultz Tries to Keep U.S.-Indian Ties Durable—But Vague," *Christian Science Monitor,* July 5, 1983.
5. See Don Oberdorfer and William Claiborne, *International Herald Tribune,* July 2-3, 1983.
6. For indication of India's desire to move in this direction, see Walter Andersen, "India in 1982: Domestic Challenges and Foreign Policy Successes," *Asian Survey* 23:2 (1983), pp. 111-122, and n. 4, above.

mutual restraint between India and Pakistan. Under the right circumstances, this development could further political rapprochement among India, China, and Pakistan.[7] It could also promote optimal long-term use of resources on the subcontinent through coordinated and cooperative development efforts by aid consortia and the World Bank, and it would be consistent with support for the more general strategy of a nonaligned buffer zone across the Middle East and Soutwest Asia's northern tier of states.[8]

This approach, however, is not without pitfalls. It is constrained by a number of factors: the present impasse in U.S.-Soviet relations; persistent and deeply held antagonisms between the states of the area; Indian and Pakistani nuclear policies which may seriously compromise American relations with both countries;[9] the risk of Indian resentment at outside efforts to "equate" India with its smaller neighbors; Indian suspicions of China and of Chinese relations with the U.S., Pakistan, and Nepal; and Pakistani fears (reinforced by the Soviet occupation of Afghanistan) of an Indo-Soviet pincer.[10] Such a policy may overesti-

---

7. The best summary of the nuclear problem in South Asia is Richard C. Cronin, "Prospects for Nuclear Proliferation in South Asia," *Middle East Journal* 37:4 (1983), pp. 594-616, who stresses the limited influence available to supplier countries, and who argues that the prospects of proliferation are primarily dependent on the dynamics of India-Pakistan relations. The best hope for containing the problems, he believes, lies in the normalization of India-Pakistan relations. The prospects for normalization, of course, depend on internal as well as on external security. Christopher Van Hollen, "Leaning on Pakistan," *Foreign Policy* No. 38 (1980), pp. 35-50, corectly observes that "if Pakistan is to become genuinely secure, it must be encouraged to liberalize its internal political system and move toward rapprochement with India" (p. 50). For a corroboration of the liberalization argument with respect to the Baluch issue, see Selig Harrison, *In Afghanistan's Shadow: Baluch Nationalism and Soviet Temptations* (Washington, D.C.: Carnegie Endowment for International Affairs, 1981).

8. For discussion of the merits and problems of a Swedenized South and Southwest Asia and a Finlandized Afghanistan, see Jagat Mehta, "Afghanistan: A Neutral Solution," *Foreign Policy* No. 47 (1982), pp. 139-53, and the letters to the editor, *Foreign Policy* No. 49, Winter 1982-83, pp. 186-90.

9. For indications of India's intentions to conduct a second underground test in the Rajasthan desert (the first was conducted in 1974), see *International Herald Tribune,* June 24 and July 16-17, 1983; for one of many discussions of Pakistan's desire to acquire a nuclear potential, see *Christian Science Monitor,* December 1, 1981.

10. For a discussion of Pakistani fears, see Imroze Sagar, "Indo-Soviet Strategic Interests and Collaboration," *Naval War College Review* 34:1 (1981), pp. 13-33; and Parvaiz Iqbal Cheema, "The Afghanistan Crisis and Pakistan's Security Dilemma," *Asian Survey* 33:3 (1983), pp. 227-43.

mate India's capacity and will to play a key role in deterring Soviet hegemony in Afghanistan and could, if poorly managed, lead Pakistan to accelerate rather than delay its acquisition of nuclear weapons. A conjunction of adverse events involving these constraints could undermine the ability of the United States to influence *either* Pakistan or India and chill American relations with the smaller states of the region to the detriment of U.S. security interests. As a result, implementation of the approach described above would depend on an improved dialogue among the United States, India, and Pakistan; and on a willingness by all parties to take the initiatives necessary for their long-term interests.[11]

## THE PAKISTAN OPTION

In the interim, recognizing that the Soviet-Indian relationship is a long-term proposition that will be difficult to alter to any significant degree,[12] the United States could continue its current policy of placing more emphasis on Pakistan. The Pakistan option makes a certain amount of sense within the context of America's Islamic-oriented Gulf interests. Pakistan, like Turkey, has reasonably cordial relations with Iran. Together with Pakistan's willingness to send troops to Saudi Arabia and the Saudis' largess toward Pakistan (approximately $1 billon a year), these relationships lend credence to the notion that U.S. support for Pakistan helps to protect common interests in the Gulf. According to one reliable report there were at least 20,000 Pakistani military personnel in Saudi Arabia in October 1983, including pilots, advisors, instructors, anti-terrorist squads, and intelligence experts. Another contingent of 7,000 reportedly was on its way. Proposals still being examined in Washington and Islamabad include the upgrading of port facilities at Karachi and the development of a new naval facility at Gwadar on the coast of Baluchistan, less than 50 miles from Pakistan's

11. For recent arguments along these lines that suggest the virtues of detaching India from its virtual alliance with the Soviet Union and steering it toward a true neutrality and reconciliation with Pakistan, see Lawrence Ziring, "Indo-Pakistani Relations: Time for a Fresh Start," *Asian Affairs* 8:4 (1981), pp. 199-215; the references in n. 4, above; and Amaury de Riencourt, "India and Pakistan in the Shadow of Afghanistan," *Foreign Affairs* 61:2 (1982/1983), pp. 416-37. For the difficulty of this endeavor, see S. Nihal Singh, "Can the U.S. and India Be Real Friends?" *Asian Survey* 23:9 (1983), pp. 1011-24.

12. In addition to the sources cited in n. 10 and n. 11, above, see Robert L. Horn, "Afghanistan and the Soviet-Indian Influence Relationship," *Asian Survey* 23:3 (1983), pp. 244-60.

border with Iran and only 300 miles across the Gulf of Oman from Muscat.[13]

Emphasis on Pakistan, which *at a minimum* requires a credible economic and military commitment to Pakistan such as the $3.2 billion currently planned, responds to Pakistani as well as regional fears of steadily increasing Indian military power and Indian domination of the subcontinent. It lays the groundwork for a more balanced relationship between India and Pakistan. It also complements the U.S. relationship with Turkey and, because Turkey and Pakistan both have reasonably good relations with Iran, makes it more likely that Iran will be encouraged by its neighbors to remain outside the Soviet orbit. Because of its military orientation, however, an increasingly strong U.S. commitment to Pakistan has a number of liabilities.

Within Pakistan, martial law under the administration of General Muhammad Zia ul-Haq, now in his seventh year as President of Pakistan, has become increasingly unpopular, particularly in the province of Sind. As a consequence, Zia has promised to hold elections to the National Assembly, end martial law, and share power with a prime minister—all by March 1985. Unlike the Turkish generals who held elections in November 1983 when they said they would, Zia has twice postponed and then cancelled scheduled elections. Many Pakistanis, particularly Sindis, are frustrated over the failure to return to civilian rule and angered over corruption within the regime. Resenting Punjabi domination of the armed forces, where Punjabis outnumber Sindis by a ratio of 40:1, and the federal civil service, where Sindis make up only 5% of the total, urban and rural Sindis have given their support to a movement that seeks to end martial law, restore civil rights, and revive democratic institutions. While the Movement for the Restoration of Democracy's campaign of national civil disobedience is restricted for the time being to the Sind (the home of the executed Zulfikar Ali Bhutto, whose Pakistan People's Party is spearheading the movement), it is nonetheless the first major challenge to the military government.

---

13. For discussion of the Saudi-Pakistani relationship, see Claudia Wright, "India and Pakistan Join in the Gulf Game," *Middle East,* June 1981, pp. 31-34; Shirin Tahir-Kheli and William O. Staudenmaier, "The Saudi-Pakistani Military Relationship: Implications for U.S. Policy," *Orbis* 26:1 (1982), pp. 155-71; David O. Smith, "Pakistan and the Middle East Connection," *Military Review* 62:10 (1982), pp. 42-49; and Mary Anne Weaver, *Christian Science Monitor,* October 3, 1983. Tahir-Kheli asserts that there are 250,000 Pakistanis in Saudi Arabia, while other sources in the Gulf states suggest that there are over a million Pakistanis in the Gulf. In 1982, remittances from 2.2 million Pakistanis in foreign countries amounted to $1.5 billion. Marvin Weinbaum and Stephen Cohen, "Pakistan in 1982: Holding On," *Asian Survey* 23:2 (1983), p. 128.

Most observers feel that Zia will weather such opposition as long as it does not spread to the Punjab and as long as his army remains loyal, but violence in the Sind underscores the fragility of his regime.[14] To the extent that Zia postpones a return to democratic rule, excessive U.S. support for Pakistan risks identifying the United States with his policies, alienating those who oppose his military regime, and jeopardizing good relations with whatever regimes that follow.

Excessive support for Pakistan also risks undermining long-term U.S. interests by antagonizing India, whose government continues to be concerned by the fact that over 80% of Pakistan's troops are deployed on the Indian border.[15] Insofar as U.S. support for Pakistan is accompanied by significant aid to Afghanistan, it will also antagonize the Soviet Union. India could compensate by moving closer to the Soviet Union, calling a halt to its gradual rapprochement with China, and beefing up its forces along Pakistan's border. Depending upon the threats that India perceives, a number of worrisome scenarios are immaginable: a preemptive strike against Pakistan's nuclear facilities, a military move against the territories of Azad Kashmir, or, in conjunction with the Soviet Union, and in support of Pushtun, Baluch, and Sindi separatist movements, an attempt to dismember Pakistan. As a result, a strong American commitment to Pakistan should be pursued with caution.

## THE AFGHAN CONNECTION

If a strong U.S. commitment to Pakistan poses problems, however, so does a weak one. The dilemma for the United States in dealing with Pakistan is that without a significant American commitment, Zia, who rejected President Carter's 1980 offer of $400 million as "peanuts,"

---

14. See Javed Ansari, "Pakistan Revisited: Why General Zia's regime Cannot Last Long," *Arabia: The Islamic World Review* No. 22 (1983), pp. 8-13; the *International Herald Tribune,* August 13-14, and 29 (William Stevens), October 1-2 (William Eaton), and September 2, 1983; and Mary Anne Weaver, *Christian Science Monitor,* August 22, 31, and September 2, 1983. As *The Financial Times* (London) editorialized: "The predicament that Mr. Zia faces is how to reconcile the urgent need for stability with the growing demands for pluralism. In the past, pluralism in Pakistan has been virtually synonymous with instability, while stability has been achieved only through dictatorship." Cited in the *International Herald Tribune,* September 2, 1983.
15. During the Carter administration, the Pakistanis rejected a U.S. Proposal that they redeploy their forces from the Indian to Afghan fronts because of their belief that India was the more serious threat. Raju G.C. Thomas, "The Afghanistan Crisis and South Asian Security," *Journal of Strategic Studies* 4:4 (1981), p. 428.

would be unwilling to jeopardize his relations with the Soviet Union. Zia now does jeopardize his position by allowing his country to serve as a supply line for aid to Afghanistan—a prerequisite for any meaningful assistance to the resistance in Afghanistan.[16] If the U.S. cuts back on its assistance to Pakistan, the opportunity to aid Afghanistan is not the only policy option that would be foreclosed. Responding to a combination of Soviet influence and intimidation, Zia might well be tempted to accommodate Soviet desires that Pakistan assume a neutral, nonaligned status—*without* a Soviet withdrawal from Afghanistan, leaving the Soviet Union as the dominant force in regional politics.[17] While American and Western intelligence sources agree that Moscow has not improved its logistical capabilities in Afghanistan for offensive action in the Persian Gulf region, the potential for such improvement is everpresent. The all-weather airbase at Shindand, for example, is only 600 miles from the Strait of Hormuz, and Soviet reconnaisance planes flying from Shindand currently monitor U.S. naval ships in the Indian Ocean.[18] Over time, the implications of a continued Soviet occupation of Afghanistan could be serious—not only for Afghanistan, but for Pakistan, the Gulf states, and the United States as well.

At present, approximately 105,000 Soviet troops occupy Afghanistan. Of the 15.5 million people who once lived there, at least one in five has become a refugee. The Pakistani government estimates that 2.8 million Afghan refugees are presently in Pakistan, with approx-

---

16. Pakistan felt that the $400 million offer was enough to provoke hostility without ensuring security. *New York Times,* July 16, 1980.

17. A number of individuals have noted the popularity in Pakistan—even among the military—of closer ties with the Soviet Union. The real debate developing within Pakistan, Ghulam Mustafa Khar asserts, "is about whether to accept the Soviet or Indian alternatives." Khar, "Four Choices Facing Front-Line Pakistan," p. 27; see also Ali Mehrunnisa, "Soviet-Pakistan Ties Since the Afghan Crisis," *Asian Survey* 23:9 (1983), pp. 1025-42; and Javed Ansari, "Pakistan Revisited," who notes the Pakistan army's need for political rapprochement with the Soviet Union and the People's Party's desire to abandon the Afghan *jihad.* One observer has suggested that the U.S. leaked news of its aid to Afghanistan to prevent Pakistan from being more receptive to Soviet overtures over the Afghan problem. The leverage held by the United States is that Pakistan could lose U.S. assistance if it is too soft. See Mary Anne Weaver, *Christian Science Monitor,* May 10, and Louis Wiznitzer, *Christian Science Monitor,* June 14, 1983.

18. Selig Harrison, "A Breakthrough in Afghanistan?" *Foreign Policy* No. 51, Summer 1983, pp. 8-9; Dimitri Simes, *Christian Science Monitor,* June 13, 1983; Yossef Bodansky, cited in Drew Middleton, *International Herald Tribune,* November 8, 1983; and de Riencourt, "India and China in the Shadow of Afghanistan," p. 432.

imately 500,000 in Baluchistan and the Punjab, and the rest in the North West Frontier Province, living in 320 tent villages. The United Nations High Commission for Refugees, taking into account double registration and exaggeration, estimates the number to be about 2.2 million. In conjunction with another 650,000 refugees in Iran (joining about 850,000 who worked in Iran before 1979), not to mention 1.2 million internal refugees who have now descended on Kabul, and anywhere from 150,000 to 500,000 Afghan dead, numbers alone give a grim account of the intentions behind Soviet policy.[19]

The Soviets have replaced the reserve divisions that made up most of the invading forces, in part to make up for their deficiencies and in part because the size of the Afghan army has shrunk from 80-90,000 in December 1979 to somewhere between 30,000 and 40,000. Even these latter figures are deceiving because the desertion rate in some units is nearly 80%. This desertion rate has been a gain for the resistance movement, which according to some estimates has acquired 80 percent of its weapons from the Soviets. Reports of extensive bombing amounting to the "rubbleization" of villages and "migratory genocide," meanwhile, all seem to suggest a hard-nosed Soviet policy of decentralization. In conjunction with efforts to improve and expand roads, and to build supply depots, airfields and communication facilities, these reports indicate that the Soviets are settling in for a long stay. Some analysts believe that the Soviets desire to leave, but most are skeptical. They argue that the Soviets will get out only on their own terms. What those terms are is not yet clear, but at the very least they include long-term Soviet control over the policies of Afghanistan. Approximately 5-6,000 Soviet troops have been killed in Afghanistan, and another 12-15,000 wounded. Since the Soviets have neither a free press, nor uncensored television crews covering the war, such losses are not unbearable for a country with a population as large as that of the Soviet Union. The kinds of domestic pressures that forced the United States out of Vietnam are simply not relevant to the Soviet involvement in Afghanistan.

---

19. Louis Dupree, "Afghanistan in 1982: Still No Solution," *Asian Survey* 23:2 (1983), pp. 133-42; Alvin Rubinstein, "The Soviet Union and Afghanistan," *Current History* 82 (October 1983), pp. 318-21, 337-38; U.S. Department of State, "Afghan Refugees in Pakistan," *Gist,* Bureau of Public Affairs (Washington, D.C.: U.S. Department of State, September 1982); U.S. Department of State, "Afghanistan: Four Years of Occupation," Special Report No. 112, Bureau of Public Affairs, Washington, D.C., December 1983; and a fascinating series of articles on Afghanistan by William Branigan, *Washington Post,* October 16-22, 1983. The cost of minimal support for the refugees in 1982 was $600 million, of which Pakistan's share was $270 million.

Analogies between the two wars are further misleading because Vietnam presented a far more difficult logistical problem for the United States and did not provide the direct benefits, such as natural gas, that Afghanistan does for the U.S.S.R.[20]

Afghanistan's strength in resisting Soviet military might, it should be noted, is also its weakness. The 60-200 resistance organizations, which claim anywhere from 20-100,000 men, lack organizational structure and cohesion. While decentralization makes a decisive Soviet victory over the Afghans exceedingly difficult—"since they lack a single head they cannot be defeated by a single stroke"—it also precludes the kind and cohesion. While decentralization makes a decisive Soviet victory over the Afghans exceedingly difficult—"since they lack a single head they cannot be defeated by a single stroke"—it also precludes the kind of unified effort and coordination necessary for an Afghan victory.[21] The latter problem has led the Islamic Conference to predicate significant material aid on the unification of the resistance movement— a goal that has not been realized. In the absence of agreement, moderate Islamic elements have even sought to resurrect the deposed monarch Muhammad Zahir Shah in an effort to find a common denominator among the opposing factions; but unity is still elusive and appears to go against the inclination of most groups. Hizb-i-Islami and Jamiyat-i-Islami, perhaps the two largest resistance organizations, have serious differences with each other and among themselves. These differences appear to be endemic to Afghanistan, and are mirrored in the Soviet-supported People's Democratic Party of Afghanistan, whose Khalq and Parcham factions (the first largely Pathans from Ghilzai who speak Pushtun, and the second largely urban-based radicals who speak Dari) occasionally engage in hostilities that have left scores of dead.[22]

---

20. *Ibid.* See also Nancy and Richard Newell, *The Struggle for Afghanistan* (Ithaca: Cornell University Press, 1981), p. 180; Edward Girardet, *Christian Science Monitor,* September 6, 1983; Daniel Southerland, *Christian Science Monitor,* July 7, 1983; Jere Van Dyk, *International Herald Tribune,* October 19, 1983. For reports of Soviet use of chemicals and toxins against the resistance in Afghanistan, see *Chemical Warfare in Southeast Asia and Afghanistan: An Update,* Report from Secretary of State George Shultz, Special Report No. 104 (Washington, D.C.: U.S. Department of State, November 1982). Alvin Rubinstein, *Soviet Policy Toward Turkey, Iran, and Afghanistan: The Dynamics of Influence* (New York: Praeger, 1982), p. 175, observes that in 1979 Afghanistan exported 2.1 billion cubic meters of gas (97% of its total output) to Soviet Central Asia, and probably at an extremely favorable price.

21. Lord Saint Brides, "Afghanistan: The Empire Plays to Win," *Orbis* 24:3 (1980), p. 539.

22. Nancy and Richard Newell, *The Struggle for Afghanistan,* pp. 62, 182-185, 189; Rubinstein, *Soviet Policy Toward Turkey, Iran, and Afghanistan,* p. 165; the

Solutions to the problems in Afghanistan are not promising. Were the Soviets to leave tomorrow, what would happen there—the overthrow of the Soviet-supported Communist regime—is precisely what the Soviets were trying to prevent when they went in in the first place. If the Soviets stay on, whether at the same or a more intensive level of involvement, the resistance will continue at the cost of thousands of Afghan lives, which ultimately may be lost in vain. The dilemma that this poses for the United States when it examines the question of what kind of assistance it should give to the resistance, is complicated further by the fact that whatever efforts are undertaken require careful coordination with Pakistan.   Pakistani interests and policies could be seriously affected by American efforts to assist the Afghans—or by the decision *not* to undertake such assistance. The Soviet Union, if pressed by guerrillas, could conduct military actions against the sanctuaries in Pakistan, which provide support for the guerrillas by means of some 230 passes and trails between Pakistan and Afghanistan. The Soviets could also support Pushtun irredentism and Baluch separatism in an effort to dismember Pakistan.[23] If the Soviets, over time, were to consolidate their hold on Afghanistan, the latter threat would still be present and would be accompanied by an even greater Soviet capacity for intimidation.

Talks begun in Geneva in June 1982 under United Nations auspices have continued throughout 1983 (a third round took place in June 1983) and have identified at least five issues crucial to any solution:

---

*Christian Science Monitor,* August 17 (David Foquet), August 19 (Daniel Southerland), August 22, August 24 and September 6 (Edward Girardet), 1983; and the *International Herald Tribune,* September 8, 1983. Some fundamentalist groups see Muhammad Zahir Shah as little more than a Western-oriented non-entity whose uninspired rule (1933-1973) was known mostly for the king's lavish lifestyle, and who has played no role in the resistance. Tajiks and Hazaras, moreover, object to him on the grounds that he is a Pushtun from the Durrani Tribe. Nonetheless, if he can obtain international recognition for the "United Front for the Liberation of Afghanistan," set up by three groups belonging to the moderate alliance, he could receive some support from fundamentalists.

23. For the Baluch problem, see Selig Harrison, *In Afghanistan's Shadow: Baluch Nationalism and Soviet Temptations.* For the Pushtun or Pukhtun problem, see Andre Singer, *Guardians of the North-West Frontier: The Pathans* (Amsterdam: Time-Life Books, 1982); and Akbar Ahmed, "Afghanistan and Pakistan: The Great Game of the Tribes," *Journal of South Asian and Middle East Studies* 4:4 (1981), pp. 45-62; and *Puktun Economy and Society: Traditional Structure and Economic Development in a Tribal Society* (Boston: Routledge & Kegan Paul, 1980).

— the withdrawal (in phases) of Soviet troops;
— cessation of outside aid (noninterference and nonintervention);
— repatriation (in phases) of Afghan refugees;
— international guarantees that the settlement will be observed; and
— self-determination for the Afghans.

Semantics, of course, present real problems. Implicit in Soviet objectives is a regime that is "friendly" to the Soviet Union. Whether it is possible to have "self-determination" in Afghanistan and, simultaneously, a regime that is "friendly" to the Soviet Union is a moot point. Finland is cited by some authorities as a potential model; that is, a nation in which the Soviets do not attempt to impose a Communist regime, but are given guarantees that the country cannot be used to threaten the U.S.S.R. The British, it may be recalled, had an arrangement somewhat similar to this with Afghanistan from about the middle of the nineteenth century until 1919. An alternative model that is less auspicious, however, is Poland after World War II, where self-determination and a regime "friendly" to the Soviet Union were—at least in Stalin's view—incompatible.[24]

## THE INTERPLAY BETWEEN PROBLEMS AND OPTIONS

While the solution to the Afghan problem rests, ultimately, in Moscow, the context within which such a solution might take place can be affected by the regional orientation of U.S. policies. Nancy and Richard Newell suggest, for example, that "[b]y offering to supply military and medical equipment *at the request* of the Islamic Conference or some other agency that might be established to conduct collective regional defense, the United States could act as a counterforce against Soviet encroachment without intruding its own military forces directly into the region."[25] Such a policy would be compatible with United States support for the Islamic Conference. For this particular policy to be truly effective, however, the United States would have to establish a credible deterrent to Soviet intimidation of Pakistan and make a real effort to remove Islamic concerns by addressing the Palestinian problem.

In the final analysis, a Soviet departure from Afghanistan will require more than U.S. support for the resistance, which the United States can

---

24. For the Finish model, see Mehta, cited in n. 8. See also Louis Wiznitzer, *Christian Science Monitor,* June 14, 1983; William Stevens, *International Herald Tribune,* June 16, 1983; John Darnton, *International Herald Tribune,* June 27, 1983; Robert Macauley, *Christian Science Monitor,* August 16, 1983; and Kuniholm, *The Origins of the Cold War in the Near East,* p. 253.

25. Newell and Newell, *The Struggle for Afghanistan,* p. 211.

express in conjunction with its commitment to Pakistan. Political pressure on the Soviet Union from India will also be necessary and can occur only in a regional context in which India feels secure. For this reason, it is important that the relationship between the two primary policy options in the region—the first an attempt to foster regional cooperation, the second a commitment to bolster Pakistan's standing in the region—be constantly kept in mind. Neither option, by itself, can address all U.S. concerns in the region; flexible application of both options, on the other hand, may create an environment that is conducive to many of the interests that we have in common with the states of the region.

# Conclusion

The political and military strategies outlined above, while only suggestive and requiring both greater precision and further elaboration, nonetheless provide a framework within which to view American security policy in the Persian Gulf region. In the absence of such a framework, which officials in the White House concede the administration lacks,[1] and without agreement within the government about what the framework ought to be, the United States will continue to be in danger of operating on the basis of inadequate assumptions and engaging in short-term tactical maneuvers to extricate itself from situations that have not been forseen in the development of current policies. Without a framework that bounds U.S. options, events themselves will determine administrative actions, and policy initiatives will be left to others.

Development of a political-military strategy for the Persian Gulf and Southwest Asia is among the Reagan Administration's more pressing tasks. Once developed, such a strategy in conjunction with similar strategies for other regions would provide the machinery of government with the guidance needed to plan and coordinate policy initiatives. Outside the government, critics of particular decisions would be forced to address the limitations and inconsistencies inherent in their own perspectives and to consider the broader contexts within which difficult choices are made. Public articulation of a comprehensive framework, at once flexible enough to accommodate change, but rigorous enough to ensure that the relationship among various interests has been carefully considered, would set the terms of a public debate. Such a debate, in turn, would generate a more responsible discussion of how to balance conflicting interests in the face of the various threats to which they are vulnerable; it would establish a clearer sense of priorities; and it would allow for a more informed analysis of proposed increases in the defense budget.[2] Finally, because discussion would underscore the West's

---

1. See the editorial page, *Christian Science Monitor,* December 14, 1983.
2. For a discussion of attacks by conservatives and liberals on the strategy—or absence of strategy—that provides a rationale for the administration's military spending plans, see Richard Halloran in the *New York Times,* March 22, 1982. For a discussion of the administration's response to this criticism, and the FY 1984-1988 Defense Guidance, see the *New York Times,* May 25 and 30, 1982; and the *Washington Post,* May 27, and June 2, 1982. For more recent criticism, see Chapter 4, n. 16.

dependence on vulnerable supplies of Gulf oil, it could help to marshall broader support for a meaningful domestic energy program.[3]

3. In spite of complacency setting in regarding energy use, the International Energy Agency in October 1982 concluded that unless nations did more to reduce their dependence on imported oil, the world could face shortages of up to four million barrels of oil a day by 1990. *Christian Science Monitor,* October 18, 1982. See also the concerns about a third oil shock expressed in Daniel Yergin and Martin Hillenbrand, eds., *Global Insecurity: A Strategy for Energy and Economic Renewal* (Boston: Houghton Mifflin, 1982); and Daniel Yergin, "Third Oil Shock Might be Manageable After All," *International Herald Tribune,* October 17, 1983, who notes that what kept the Iran-Iraq war from having any affect on the world oil market was a large cushion of unused capacity resulting from conservation, recession, fuel switching and new oil production. His concern is that escalation of hostilities in the Gulf could raise the question of yet another oil shock and that complacency, coupled with a return to dependence on the Gulf, could make the consequences of instability in that region even more dangerous for the world economy.

# PART V

## BIBLIOGRAPHY

This bibliography includes important works on the history of the Persian Gulf but emphasizes contemporary English-language citations that are relevant to the problem of formulating a U.S. policy toward the region. Researchers interested in the early history of the Gulf should refer to the bibliographies and other aids that augment the works cited. Those concerned with U.S. policy should update the bibliography by consulting *Middle East Journal, Foreign Affairs, Foreign Policy, Orbis,* and other journals that contain important articles on policy problems in the Middle East. The *Middle East Journal* is a particularly valuable resource because of its excellent book reviews, its thorough bibliography of periodical literature, its current list of recent publications, and its helpful quarterly chronology of recent events.

This bibliography was completed in January 1984. It is designed to be useful and, for this reason, is broken down into sub-sections. While the location of particular citations occasionally may seem arbitrary, the problem is unavoidable if the bibliography is to serve its purpose. Fortunately, the problem can be overcome by a sensitivity to the broader contexts within which particular categories of citations can be found. Researchers will find it beneficial before beginning their investigations to look carefully at the detailed table of contents, which should provide a helpful overview of the interrelationships among some of the categories under investigation.

## TABLE OF CONTENTS

# REFERENCES

*THE PERSIAN GULF AND ARABIAN PENINSULA*

*General*

**1** *Area Handbook for the Persian Gulf States.* Richard Nyrop, *et al.* Washington, D.C.: G.P.O., 1977.

**2** Boxer, C.R. "Anglo-Portuguese Rivalry in the Persian Gulf, 1615-1635." In Edgar Prestage, ed. *Chapters in Anglo-Portuguese Relations.* Watford: Voss & Michael, 1935.

**3** Busch, Briton Cooper. *Britain and the Persian Gulf, 1894-1914.* Berkeley: University of California Press, 1967.

**4** _____. *Britain, India, and the Arabs, 1914-1921.* Berkeley: University of California Press, 1971.

**5** Hawley, Donald. *The Trucial States.* London: Allen & Unwin, 1970.

**6** Hourani, George F. *Arab Seafaring in the Indian Ocean in Ancient and Early Medieval Times.* Princeton: Princeton University Press, 1951.

**7** Kelly, John B. *Britain and the Persian Gulf, 1795-1880.* Oxford: Clarendon Press, 1968.

**8** _____. *Eastern Arabian Frontiers.* New York: Praeger, 1964.

**9** Lorimer, J.G. *Gazetteer of the Persian Gulf, Oman and Central Arabia,* 2 vols. Calcutta: Government of India, 1908-15.

**10** Savory, Roger. "The History of the Persian Gulf: A.D. 600-1800." In Cottrell, Alvin, *et al.*, eds., *The Persian Gulf States: A General Survey,* pp. 14-40.

**11** _____ "The History of the Persian Gulf: The Ancient Period." In Cottrell, Alvin, *et al.*, eds., pp. 3-13.

**12** Wilson, Arnold T. *The Persian Gulf: An Historical Sketch from the Earliest Times to the Beginning of the Twentieth Century.* Oxford: Clarendon Press, 1928.

**13** Yapp, Malcolm E. "The History of the Persian Gulf: British Policy in the Persian Gulf." In Cottrell, Alvin, *et al.*, eds., *The Persian Gulf States: A General Survey,* pp. 70-100.

**14** _____. "The History of the Persian Gulf: The Nineteenth and Twentieth Centuries." In Cottrell, Alvin, *et al.*, eds., *The Persian Gulf States: A General Survey,* pp. 41-70.

Britain's Withdrawal from the Gulf

**15** Darby, Phillip. *British Defense Policy East of Suez, 1947-1968.* London: Oxford University Press, 1973.

**16** *The Gulf: Implications of British Withdrawal.* Special Report Series No. 8. Washington, D.C.: Center for Strategic and International Studies, Georgetown University, Feb. 1969.

**17** Holden, David. *Farewell to Arabia.* London: Faber & Faber, 1966.

**18** \_\_\_\_\_. "The Persian Gulf: After the British Raj." *Foreign Affairs* 49:4 (1971), pp. 721-35.

**19** Kelly, John B. *Arabia, the Gulf and the West: A Critical View of the Arabs and their Oil Policy.* New York: Basic Books, 1980.

The Recent Past

**20** Amirsadeghi, Hossein, ed. *The Security of the Persian Gulf.* New York: St. Martin's Press, 1981.

**21** Anthony, John Duke. *Arab States of the Lower Gulf: People, Politics, Petroleum.* Washington, D.C.: Middle East Institute, 1975.

**22** *The Arab Oil-Producing States of the Gulf: Political and Economic Developments. AEI Foreign Policy and Defense Review* 2:3 & 4. Washington, D.C.: American Enterprise Institute, 1980.

**23** Chubin, Shahram, ed. *Security in the Persian Gulf 1: Domestic Political Factors.* Montclair, N.J.: Allanheld, Osmun, 1981.

**24** \_\_\_\_\_. *Security in the Persian Gulf 4: The Role of the Outside Powers.* Totowa, N.J.: Allanheld, Osmun, 1982.

**25** Cottrell, Alvin J., *et al.*, eds. *The Persian Gulf States: A General Survey.* Baltimore, Md.: Johns Hopkins University Press, 1980.

**26** Dunn, Michael. "The Gulf Organizes for Strength." *Defense and Foreign Affairs* 9:32, (1981).

**27** Gordon, Murray, ed. *Conflict in the Persian Gulf.* New York: Facts on File, 1981.

**28** Haendel, Dan. "The Persian Gulf: Geopolitics Revisited." *International Security Review* 6:1 (1981), pp. 79-92.

**29** Halliday, Fred. *Arabia Without Sultans: A Political Survey of Instability in the Arab World.* New York: Random House, Inc., 1974,1975.

**30** Harris, Phil, *et al. New Communications Order 3: Flow of News in the Gulf.* New York: Unesco Unipub Reprint, 1982.

**31** Hopwood, Derek, ed. *The Arabian Peninsula: Society and Politics.* London: Allen & Unwin, 1972.

**32** Hurewitz, J.C. *The Persian Gulf: After Iran's Revolution.* Headline Series No. 244. New York: Foreign Policy Association, April 1979.

**33** Ibrahim, Saad Eddin. "Superpowers in the Arab World." *Washington Quarterly* 4:3 (1981), pp. 89-96.

**34** Jay, Peter. "Regionalism as Geopolitics." *Foreign Affairs* 58:3 (1980), pp. 485-514.

**35** Khadduri, Majid. *Arab Personalities in Politics.* Washington, D.C.: Middle East Institute, 1981.

**36** Litwak, Robert. *Security in the Persian Gulf 2: Sources of Inter-State Conflict.* Montclair, N.J.: Allanheld, Osmun, 1981.

**37** Long, David. *The Persian Gulf: An Introduction to its Peoples, Politics, and Economics,* Rev. ed. Boulder, Col.: Westview, 1978.

**38** *The Middle East Review, 1983.* Saffron Walden, Essex, England: World of Information, 1982.

**39** Nye, Roger P. "Political and Economic Integration in the Arab States of the Gulf." *Journal of South Asian and Middle Eastern Studies,* 2:1 (1978), pp. 3-21.

**40** Perera, Judith, and Manning, Robert. "Not Seeing Eye to Eye." *Middle East Magazine,* No. 89 (March 1982), pp. 13-15.

**41** Plascov, Avi. *Security in the Persian Gulf 3: Modernization, Political Development and Stability.* Totowa, N.J.: Allanheld, Osmun, 1982.

**42** Raban, Jonathan. *Arabia: A Journey Through the Labyrinth.* New York: Simon & Schuster, 1979.

**43** Ramazani, Rouhollah K. *The Persian Gulf and the Strait of Hormuz.* Alphen aan den Rijn, Netherlands: Sijthoff & Noordhoff, 1979.

**44** Richardson, John P. "Europe and the Arabs: A Developing Relationship." *The Link,* 14:1 (1981).

**45** Taylor, Alan R. *The Arab Balance of Power.* Syracuse: Syracuse University Press, 1982.

**46** Thompson, William R. "Delineating Regional Subsystems: Visit Networks and the Middle Eastern Case." *International Journal of Middle East Studies*, 13:2 (1981), pp. 213-35.

The U.S. and the Persian Gulf

**47** Newsom, David. "America Engulfed." *Foreign Policy*, No. 43 (Summer 1981), pp. 17-32.

**48** Quandt, William. "The Middle East Crises." *Foreign Affairs* 58:3 (1980), pp. 540-62.

**49** Al-Salem, Faisal. "The U.S. and the Gulf: What Do the Arabs Want?" *Journal of South Asian and Middle Eastern Studies*, 4:1 (1982), pp. 8-32.

**50** U.S. Congress. House. Committee on Foreign Affairs. *New Perspectives on the Persian Gulf.* Hearings before the Subcommittee on the Near East and South Asia. Washington, D.C.: G.P.O., 1973.

**51** _____. *U.S. Interests in and Policy Toward the Persian Gulf.* Hearings before the Subcommittee on the Near East. Washington, D.C.: G.P.O., 1972.

**52** _____. *U.S. Security Interests in the Persian Gulf.* Report of a Staff Study Mission to the Persian Gulf, Middle East, and Horn of Africa. Washington, D.C.: G.P.O., March 16, 1981.

**53** U.S. Department of State. Bureau of Public Affairs. *U.S. Policy Toward the Persian Gulf.* Current Policy, No. 160 (Under Secretary for Political Affairs David Newsom). Washington, D.C.: U.S. Department of State, April 11, 1980.

**54** _____. *U.S. Policy Toward the Persian Gulf.* Current Policy, No. 390 (Assistant Secretary for Near East and South Asian Affairs Nicolas Veliotes). Washington, D.C.: U.S. Department of State, May 10, 1982.

**55** Van Hollen, Christopher. "Don't Engulf the Gulf." *Foreign Affairs* 59:5 (1981), pp. 1064-78.

Legal Issues

**56** Amin, Sayed Hassan. *International and Legal Problems of the Gulf.* London: Middle East & North Africa Press, 1981.

**57** Al-Baharna, Husain M. *The Arabian Gulf States: Their Legal and Political Status and their International Problems.* 2nd ed. Beirut: Librarie du Liban, 1975.

**58** Cooperation Council for the Arab States of the Gulf. *Charter of the Cooperation Council for the Arab States of the Gulf.* Riyadh: Bahr Al-Olum Press, n.d.

**59** MacDonald, Charles G. "Iran's Strategic Interests and the Law of the Sea." *The Middle East Journal* 34:2 (1980), pp. 302-22.

**60** _____ . "Regionalism and the Law of the Sea: The Persian Gulf Perspective." *Naval War College Review* 32:5 (1980), pp. 73-81.

*The Smaller Gulf States*

Bahrain

**61** Belgrave, Charles D. *Personal Column.* London: Hutchinson, 1960. Rep. 1972.

**62** Khuri, Fuad. *Tribe and State in Bahrain: The Transformation of Social and Political Authority in an Arab State.* Chicago: University of Chicago Press, 1980.

Kuwait

**63** Freeth, Zahra, and Winstone, H.V.F. *Kuwait: Prospect and Reality.* London: Allen & Unwin, 1972.

**64** El Mallakh, Ragaei. *Kuwait: Trade and Investment.* Boulder, Col.: Westview, 1979.

**65** _____ , and Atta, Jacob K. *The Absorptive capacity of Kuwait: Domestic and International Perspectives.* Lexington, Mass.: Lexington Books, 1982.

**66** al-Sabah, Y.S.F. *The Oil Economy of Kuwait.* London: Kegan Paul, 1980.

The United Arab Emirates

**67** Khalifa, Ali Muhammad. *The United Arab Emirates: Unity in Fragmentation.* Boulder, Col.: Westview, 1979.

**68** El Mallakh, Ragaei. *The Economic Development of the United Arab Emirates.* New York: St. Martin's, 1981.

**69** Zahlan, Rosemarie Said. *The Origins of the United Arab Emirates: A Political and Social History of the Trucial States.* New York: St. Martin's, 1978.

Qatar

**70** El Mallakh, Ragaei. *Qatar: Development of an Oil Economy.* London: Croom Helm, 1979.

**71** Zahlan, Rosemarie Said. *The Creation of Qatar.* New York: Harper & Row, 1979.

*Saudi Arabia*

**72** Dawisha, Adeed. "Internal Values and External Threats: The Making of Saudi Arabia." *Orbis* 23:1 (1979), pp. 129-43.

**73** Helms, Christine Moss. *The Cohesion of Saudi Arabia: Evolution of Political Identity.* London: Croom Helm, 1980.

**74** Hobday, Peter. *Saudi Arabia Today: An Introduction to the Richest Oil Power.* London: Macmillan, 1978.

**75** Holden, David, and Johns, Richard. *The House of Saud: The Rise and Rule of the Most Powerful Dynasty in the Arab World.* New York: Holt, Rinehart & Winston, 1981.

**76** Iseman, Peter. "The Arabian Ethos." *Harper's* 256 (Feb. 1978), pp. 37-56.

**77** Lacey, Robert. *The Kingdom: Arabia and the House of Saud.* New York: Harcourt Brace Jovanovich, 1981.

**78** Long, David. *The Hajj Today: A Survey of the Contemporary Makkah Pilgrimmage.* Albany: State University of New York Press, 1979.

**79** _____. *Saudi Arabia.* Beverley Hills, Cal.: Sage, 1976.

**80** _____, and Shaw, John. *Saudi Arabian Modernization: The Impact of Change on Stability.* Washington Papers, No. 89. Washington, D.C.: Center for Strategic and International Studies, Georgetown University, 1982.

**81** McHale, T.R. "A Prospect of Saudi Arabia." *International Affairs* 56 (Autumn, 1980), pp. 622-47.

**82** El Mallakh, Ragaei. *Saudi Arabia: Rush to Development.* Baltimore: Johns Hopkins University Press, 1982.

**83** _____, and El Mallakh, Dorthea, eds. *Saudi Arabia: Energy, Development, Planning, and Industrialization.* Lexington, Mass.: Lexington Books, 1982.

**84** Niblock, Tim, ed. *State, Society and Economy in Saudi Arabia.* New York: St. Martin's, 1982.

**85** Rentz, George. "The Fahd Peace Plan." *Middle East Insight* 2:2 (1982), pp. 21-24.

**86** "A Survey of Saudi Arabia: Filling a Void." *The Economist* 282 (Feb. 13, 1982), pp. 1-34, 48ff.


Saudi Security and U.S.-Saudi Relations

**87** Bloomfield, Lincoln P., Jr., "Saudi Arabia Faces the 1980s: Saudi Security Problems and American Interests." *Fletcher Forum* 5:2 (1981), pp. 243-77.

**88** Cordesman, Anthony. "Saudi Arabia, AWACS, and America's Search for Strategic Stability in the Near East." *Working Paper* No. 26A. Washington, D.C.: Woodrow Wilson Center for International Scholars, Sept. 1981.

**89** Dawisha, Adeed. "Saudi Arabia's Search for Security." *Adelphi Papers,* No. 158. London: International Institute for Strategic Studies, 1979.

**90** _____. "Saudi Arabia and the Arab-Israeli Conflict: the Ups and Downs of Pragmatic Moderation." *International Journal* 38:4 (1983), pp. 674-89.

**91** Goose, S. "The U.S. Military in Saudi Arabia: Investing in Stability or Disaster?" *Defense Monitor* 10:4 (1981), pp. 1-12.

**92** Haig, Alexander. "Saudi Security, Middle East Peace, and U.S. Interests." U.S. *Department of State Bulletin* 81 (Nov. 1981), pp. 60-63.

**93** Kuniholm, Bruce. "What the Saudis Really Want: A Primer for the Reagan Administration." *Orbis* 25:1 (1981), pp. 107-22.

**94** Long, David. "U.S.-Saudi Relations: A Foundation of Mutual Needs." *American-Arab Affairs,* No. 4 (1983), pp. 12-22.

**95** Preece, Richard. *Saudi Arabia and U.S. Interests: A Background Summary.* Washington, D.C.: Congressional Research Service, Library of Congress, April 12, 1981.

**96** Quandt, William. "Riyadh Between the Superpowers." *Foreign Policy*, No. 44 (1981), pp. 37-56.

**97** _____. *Saudi Arabia in the 1980s.* Washington, D.C.: Brookings Institution, 1981.

**98** _____. "Saudi Arabia Security and Foreign Policy in the 1980s." *Middle East Insight* 2:2 (1982), pp. 25-30.

**99** Twinam, Joseph. "Saudi Arabia and U.S. Security Policy." U.S. *Department of State Bulletin* 81 (Nov. 1981), pp. 63-66.

**100** U.S. Congress. House. *Activities of the United States Army Corps of Engineers in Saudi Arabia.* Hearings before the Committee on Foreign Affairs, Washington, D.C.: G.P.O., June 25, 1979.

**101** _____. *Saudi Arabia and the United States: The New Context in an Evolving Special Relationship.'* Report prepared for the Committee on Foreign Affairs by the Congressional Research Service. Washington, D.C.: G.P.O., August 1981.

**102** U.S. Congress. Senate. *Arms Sales Package to Saudi Arabia.* Parts 1 & 2. Hearings before the Committee on Foreign Relations. Washington, D.C.: G.P.O., October 1981.

**103** _____. *Military and Technical Implications of the Proposed Sale of Air Defense Enhancements to Saudi Arabia.* Report of the Hearings before the Committee on Armed Services. Washington, D.C.: G.P.O., 1981.

*Oman*

**104** Cordesman, Anthony A. "Oman: The Guardian of the Eastern Gulf." *Armed Forces Journal International* 120:10 (1983), pp. 22-31.

**105** Fiennes, Ranulph. *Where Soldiers Fear to Tread.* London: Hodder & Staughton, 1975.

**106** Fullerton, M. "Oman: A Proud Past, Daring Present, and Tentative Future." *International Insight* 1:6 (1981), pp. 29-32.

**107** Interview with Sultan Qaboos bin Said. *Middle East Insight* 2:2 (1982), pp. 10-12.

**108** Nader, George. "Oman's Modernization and Strategic Role." *Middle East Insight* 2:2 (1982), 37-39.

**109** Peterson, John. *Oman in the Twentieth Century.* London: Croom Helm, 1978.

**110** El-Rihaishy, Ahmed Nassir. "Oman's Objectives and Policies in the 1980's." *Middle East Insight* 2:2 (1982), pp. 40-48.

**111** Skeet, Ian. *Muscat and Oman: The End of an Era.* London: Faber & Faber, 1974.

**112** Townsend, John. *Oman: The Making of the Modern State.* London: Croom Helm, 1977.

*The Yemen*

**113** *Area Handbook for the Yemens.* Richard Nyrop, et al. Washington, D.C.: G.P.O., 1977.

**114** Bidwell, Robin. *The Two Yemens.* Boulder, Col.: Westview, 1963.

**115** Bujra, Abdalla S. *The Politics of Stratification: A Study of Political Change in a South Arabian Town.* Oxford: Clarendon Press, 1971.

**116** Gavin, R.J. *Aden Under British Rule, 1839-1967.* London: Hurst, 1975.

**117** Ingrams, Harold. *The Yemens: Imams, Rulers, and Revolutions.* London: John Murray, 1963.

**118** Johnston, Charles. *The View from Steamer Point: Three Crucial Years in South Arabia.* New York: Praeger, 1964.

**119** O'Ballance, Edgar. *The War in the Yemen.* Hamden, Conn.: Archon, 1971.

**120** Peterson, John. *Yemen: The Search for a Modern State.* Baltimore: Johns Hopkins University Press, 1982.

**121** Ruszkiewiez, John. "How the U.S. Lost its Footing in the Shifting Sands of the Persian Gulf — A Case History of the Yemen Arab Republic." *Armed Forces Journal International* 118:1 (1980), pp. 62-72.

**122** Stookey, Robert W. *South Yemen: A Marxist Republic in Arabia.* Boulder, Col.: Westview, 1982.

**123** ———. *Yemen: The Politics of the Yemen Arab Republic.* Boulder, Col.: Westview, 1978.

**124** Trevaskis, Kennedy. *Shades of Amber: A South Arabian Episode.* London: Hutchinson, 1968.

**125** Wenner, Manfred. *Modern Yemen, 1918-1967.* Baltimore: Johns Hopkins University Press, 1968.

## ISLAM, ARABISM, AND POLITICS

*Islam*

Review Articles

**126** Esposito, John. "Islam and Politics, Review Article," *Middle East Journal* 36:3 (1982), pp. 415-20.

**127** Geertz, Clifford. "Conjuring with Islam." *New York Review of Books* 24:9 (May 27, 1982), pp. 25-28.

**128** Voll, John. "Interpreting Islam, Review Article," *Middle East Journal* 37:1 (1983), pp. 93-96.

General

**129** Cudsi, Alexander S., and Dessouki, Ali E. Hillal, eds. *Islam and Power in the Contemporary Muslim World.* Baltimore: Johns Hopkins University Press, 1981.

**130** Donohue, John, and Esposito, John. *Islam in Transition: Muslim Perspectives.* New York: Oxford University Press, 1982.

**131** Esposito, John, ed. *Islam and Development: Religion and Sociopolitical Change.* Syracuse, N.Y.: Syracuse University Press, 1980.

**132** Faksh, Mahmud A. "Basic Characteristics of an Islamic State." *Journal of South Asian and Middle Eastern Studies* 5:2 (1981), pp. 3-16.

**133** ____. "Theories of State in Islamic Political Thought." *Journal of South Asian and Middle Eastern Studies* 6:3 (1983), pp. 62-79.

**134** Farghal, Mahmoud. "Islamic Ideology: Essence and Dimensions." *American-Arab Affairs* No. 4 (Spring 1983), pp. 100-107.

**135** Haddad, Yvonne. *Contemporary Islam and the Challenge of History.* Albany: State University of New York Press, 1982.

**136** Kramer, Martin. "The Ideal of an Islamic Order." *Washington Quarterly* 3:1 (1980), pp. 3-13.

**137** Lawrence, Bruce. "Islam and the Third World." *Duke University Letters.* [Durham, N.C.], No. 34 (April 14, 1982).

**138** Lippman, Thomas. *Understanding Islam: An Introduction to the Muslim World.* New York: New American Library, 1982.

**139** Mortimer, Edward. *Faith & Power: The Politics of Islam.* New York: Random House, 1982.

**140** Piscatori, James P. ed. *Islam in the Political Process.* Cambridge: Cambridge University Press, 1983.

**141** Pullapilly, Cyriac, ed. *Islam in the Contemporary World.* Notre Dame, Ind.: University of Notre Dame Press, 1980.

**142** Shariati, Ali. *On the Sociology of Islam: Lectures,* Hamid Algar, trans. Berkeley, Cal.: Mizan Press, 1979.

**143** Stoddard, Philip, *et al. Change and the Muslim World.* Syracuse, N.Y.: Syracuse University Press, 1981.

**144** Tibi, Bassam. "The Renewed Role of Islam in the Political and Social Development of the Middle East." *Middle East Journal* 37: 1 (1983), pp. 3-13.

**145** Yadegari, Mohammad. "Ideological Change in the Muslim World." *Journal of South Asian and Middle Eastern Studies* 6:1 (1982), pp. 3-7.

Resurgence/Reassertion/Revival

**146** Ayoob, Mohammed, ed. *The Politics of Islamic Reassertion.* New York: St. Martin's, 1981.

**147** Dekmejian, R. Hrair. "The Anatomy of Islamic Revival: Legitimacy Crisis, Ethnic Conflict and the Search for Islamic Alternatives." *Middle East Journal* 34:1 (1980), pp. 1-12.

**148** Dessouki, Ali E. Hillal, ed. *Islamic Resurgence in the Arab World.* New York: Praeger, 1982.

**149** Griffith, William E. "The Revival of Islamic Fundamentalism." *International Security* 4:1 (1979), pp. 132-138.

**150** Jansen, Godfrey H. *Militant Islam.* New York: Harper & Row, 1980.

**151** Pipes, Daniel. "The World is Political!! The Islamic Revival of the Seventies." *Orbis* 24:1 (1980), pp. 9-41.

**152** Segre, Dan V., and Szyliowicz, Joseph S. "The Islamic Revival." *Washington Quarterly* 4:2 (1981), pp. 126-37.

**153** Taylor, Alan. "The Political Psychology of Islamic Resurgence in the Middle East." *American-Arab Affairs,* No. 4 (Spring 1983), pp. 120-31.

In Particular Countries and Regions

**154** Akhavi, Shahrough. *Religion and Contemporary Politics in Iran: Clergy State Relations in the Pahlavi Period.* Albany: State University of New York Press, 1980.

**155** Aly, Abd al-Monein Said, and Wenner, Manfred W. "Modern Islamic Reform Movements: The Muslim Brotherhood in Contemporary Egypt." *Middle East Journal* 36:3 (1982), pp. 336-61.

**156** Batatu, Hanna. "Iraq's Underground Shi'a Movements: Characteristics, Causes and Prospects." *Middle East Journal* 35:4 (1981), pp. 578-94.

**157** Bill, James A. "Power and Religion in Revolutionary Iran." *Middle East Journal,* 36:1 (1982), pp. 22-47.

**158** Dupree, Louis. "Militant Islam and Traditional Warfare in Islamic South Asia." AUFS Report. Hanover, N.H.: American Universities Field Staff, 1980.

**159** Fischer, Michael M. *Iran: From Religious Dispute to Revolution.* Cambridge, Mass.: Harvard University Press, 1980.

**160** Heper, Metin. "Islam, Polity and Society in Turkey: A Middle Eastern Perspective." *Middle East Journal* 35:2 (1981), 345-363.

**161** Humphreys, R. Stephen. "Islam and Political Values in Saudi Arabia, Egypt and Syria." *Middle East Journal* 33:1 (1979), pp. 1-19.

**162** Richards, John F. "The Islamic Frontier in the East: Expansion into South Asia." *South Asia,* No. 4 (October 1974), pp. 91-109.

**163** Toprak, Binnaz. *Islam and Political Development in Turkey.* Leiden: Brill, 1981.

**164** Whittier, Charles. *Islam in Iran: The Shi'ite Faith, Its History and Teaching.* Report No. 79-78 Gov. Washington, D.C.: Congressional Research Service, Library of Congress, Sept. 11, 1979.

**165** Wright, Theodore P. "Indian Muslims and the Middle East." *Journal of South Asian and Middle Eastern Studies* 6:1 (1982), pp. 48-56.

And the West (including the Debate over Orientalism).

**166** Ghareeb, Edmund. *Split Vision: The Portrayal of Arabs in the American Media.* Washington, D.C.: American-Arab Affairs Council, 1983.

**167** Haddad, Yvonne. "The Islamic Alternative," *The Link* 15:4 (1982), pp. 1-14.

**168** Lewis, Bernard. *The Muslim Discovery of Europe.* New York: Norton, 1982.

**169** _____ . "The Question of Orientalism." *New York Review of Books* 29 (June 24, 1982), pp. 49-56.

**170** Mortimer, Edward. "Islam and the Western Journalist." *Middle East Journal* 35:4 (1981), pp. 492-505.

**171** Mumford, Jay C. "Islamic Responses to Western Contact." *Naval War College Review* 33:6 (1980), pp. 63-81.

**172** Naipul, V.S. *Among the Believers: An Islamic Journey.* New York: Knopf, 1981.

**173** Said, Edward W. *Covering Islam: How the Media and the Experts Determine How We See the Rest of the World.* New York: Pantheon, 1981.

**174** _____ . *Orientalism.* New York: Random House, 1978.

**175** _____ , and Lewis, Bernard. "Orientalism: An Exchange." *New York Review of Books* 29 (August 12, 1982), pp. 44-48.

**176** Shari'ati, Ali. *Marxism and Other Western Fallacise: An Islamic Critique*, R. Campbell, trans. Berkeley, Cal.: Mizan Press, 1980.

*Arabism and Arab Politics*

**177** Ajami, Fouad. *The Arab Predicament: Arab Political Thought and Practice Since 1967.* Cambridge: Cambridge University Press, 1981.

**178** _____ . "The Arab Road." *Foreign Policy*, No. 47 (1982), pp. 3-25.

**179** _____ . "The End of Pan-Arabism." *Foreign Affairs* 57:2 (1978/79), pp. 355-373.

**180** Bill, James A., and Leiden, Carl. *Politics in the Middle East.* Boston, Mass.: Little, Brown,1984.

**181** Glidden, Harold W. "The Arab World." *American Journal of Psychiatry* 128:8 (1972), pp. 98-102.

**182** Hudson, Michael C. *Arab Politics: The Search for Legitimacy.* New Haven, Conn.: Yale University Press, 1977.

**183** Iseman, Peter. "The Arabian Ethos." *Harper's* 256 (Feb. 1978), pp. 37-56.

**184** Khoury, Nabeel A. "The Pragmatic Trend in Inter-Arab Politics." *Middle East Journal* 36:3 (1982), pp. 374-387.

**186** Reiser, Stewart. "Pan-Arabism Revisited." *Middle East Journal* 37:2 (1983), pp. 218-233.

**185** Maddy-Weitzman, Bruce. "The Fragmentation of Arab Politics: Inter-Arab Affairs Since the Afghanistan Invasion." *Orbis* 25:2 (1981), pp. 389-407.

**187** Tibi, Bassam. *Arab Nationalism: A Critical Inquiry.* Marion Farouk-Sluglett and Peter Sluglett, eds. and trans. New York: St. Martin's, 1981.

**188** Voll, John. "Islamic Dimensions in Arab Politics Since World War II." *American-Arab Affairs,* No. 4 (1983), pp. 108-19.

## THE NORTHERN TIER COUNTRIES

*Iran*

The Recent Past

**189** Abrahamian, Ervand. *Iran Between Two Revolutions.* Princeton, N.J.: Princeton University Press, 1982.

**190** Avery, Peter. *Modern Iran.* New York: Praeger, 1965.

**191** Bonine, Michael, and Keddie, Nikki, eds. *Modern Iran: The Dialectics of Continuity and Change.* Albany: State University of New York Press, 1981

**192** Chubin, Shahram, and Zabih, Sepehr. *The Foreign Relations of Iran: A Developing State in a Zone of Great-Power Conflict.* Berkeley: University of California Press, 1974.

**193** Fatemi, Khosrow. "Leadership by Distrust: The Shah's Modus Operandi, *Middle East Journal* 36:1 (1982), pp. 48-61.

**194** Graham, Robert. *Iran: The Illusion of Power.* New York: St. Martin's, 1979.

**195** Halliday, Fred. *Iran: Dictatorship and Development.* New York: Penguin, 1979.

**196** Keddie, Nikki, and Yann, Richard. *Roots of Revolution: An Interpretive History of Modern Iran.* New Haven, Conn.: Yale University Press, 1981.

**197** Pahlavi, Mohammad Reza. *Answer to History.* New York: Stein & Day, 1980.

**198** Ramazani, Rouhollah. *Iran's Foreign Policy, 1941-1973: A Study of Foreign Policy in Modernizing Nations.* Charlottesville: University Press of Virginia, 1975.

**199** Saikal, Amin. *The Rise and Fall of the Shah.* Princeton, N.J.: Princeton University Press, 1980.

**200** Zabih, Sepehr. *The Mossadegh Era: Roots of the Iranian Revolution.* Chicago, Ill.: Lake View Press, 1982.

Islam

**201** Ahmad, Eqbal, ed. *The Iranian Revolution. Race and Class* 21:1 (1979). Special issue.

**202** Akhavi, Shahrough. *Religion and Politics in Contemporary Iran: Clergy-State Relations in the Pahlavi Period.* Albany: State University of New York, 1980.

**203** Bill, James. "Power and Religion in Revolutionary Iran." *Middle East Journal* 36:1 (1982), pp. 22-47.

**204** Enayat, Hamid. "Iran: Khumayni's Concept of the 'Guardianiship of the Jurisconsult.' " In James Piscatori, ed. *Islam in the Political Process.* Cambridge: Cambridge University Press, 1983.

**205** Fischer, Michael M. J. *Iran: From Religious Dispute to Revolution.* Cambridge, Mass.: Harvard University Press, 1980.

**206** Keddie, Nikki, ed. *Religion and Politics in Iran: Shi'ism from Quietism to Revolution.* New Haven. Conn.: Yale University Press, 1983.

**207** Khomeini, Imam. *Islam and Revolution: Writings and Declarations of Imam Khomeini.* Hamid Algar, trans. Berkeley, Cal.: Mizan Press, 1981.

**208** Whittier, Charles. *Islam in Iran: The Shi'ite Faith, Its History and Teaching.* Report No. 79-78 Gov. Washington, D.C.: Congressional Research Service, Library of Congress, Sept. 11, 1979.

The United States and Iran

**209** Brzezinski, Zbigniew. "The Failed Mission: The Inside Account of the Attempt to Free the Hostages in Iran." *New York Times Magazine,* April 18, 1982, pp. 28 ff.

**210** Cottam, Richard. "American Policy and the Iranian Crisis." *Iranian Studies* 13:1-4 (1980), pp. 279-305.

**211** Harter, John. "Mr. Foreign Service on Mossadegh and Wristonization: Interview with Loy Henderson." *Foreign Service Journal* 57:10 (1980), pp. 16-20.

**212** Heikal, Mohamed. *Iran: The Untold Story, An Insiders Account of America's Iranian Adventure and its Consequences for the Future.* New York: Pantheon, 1981.

**213** Herz, Martin F. "Contacts with the Opposition." *Foreign Service Journal* 57:1 (1980), pp. 11 ff.

**214** Jordan, Hamilton. *Crisis: The Last Years of the Carter Presidency.* London: Michael Joseph, 1982.

**215** Keddie, Nikki. "The Iranian Revolution and U.S. Policy." *SAIS Review*, No. 3 (1981-82), pp. 13-26.

**216** Kuniholm, Bruce. *The Origins of the Cold War in the Near East: Great Power Conflict and Diplomacy in Iran, Turkey, and Greece.* Princeton, N.J.: Princeton University Press, 1980.

**217** Ledeen, Michael, and Lewis, William. "Carter and the Fall of the Shah: The Inside Story." *Wilson Quarterly* 3:2 (1980), pp. 3-40.

**218** _____. *Debacle: The American Failure in Iran.* New York: Knopf, 1981.

**219** Melbourne, Roy. "America and Iran in Perspective: 1953 and 1980." *Foreign Service Journal* 57:4 (1980), pp. 10-17.

**220** Ramazani, Rouhollah. *The United States and Iran: Patterns of Influence.* New York: Praeger, 1982.

**221** _____. "Who Lost America?" *Middle East Journal* 36:1 (1982), pp. 5-21.

**222** Roosevelt, Kermit. *Countercoup: The Struggle for the Control of Iran.* New York: McGraw-Hill, 1979.

**223** Rubin, Barry. "Iran, the Ayatollah, and U.S. Options." *Washington Quarterly* 6:3 (1983), pp. 142-55.

**224** _____. *Paved with Good Intentions: The American Experience and Iran.* New York: Oxford University Press, 1980.

**225** Salinger, Pierre. *America Held Hostage: The Secret Negotiations.* Garden City, N.Y.: Doubleday, 1981.

**226** Stempel, John, *Inside the Iranian Revolution.* Bloomington: Indiana University Press, 1981.

**227** Sullivan, William H. "Dateline Iran: The Road not Taken." *Foreign Policy*, No. 40 (1980), pp. 175-86.

**228** _____. *Mission to Iran.* New York: Norton, 1981.

**229** U.S. Congress. House. Committee on Foreign Affairs. *The Iran Hostage Crisis: A Chronology of Daily Developments.* A report prepared by the Congressional Research Service. Washington, D.C.: G.P.O., March 1981.

**230** U.S. Congress. Senate. Committee on Foreign Relations. *U.S. Military Sales to Iran.* A Staff Report to the Committee on Foreign Assistance. Washington, D.C.: G.P.O., July 1976.

The Revolution

**231** Bakhash, Shaul. "The Iranian Revolution." *New York Review of Books* 27 (June 26, 1980), pp. 22-34.

**232** _____. "Who Lost Iran?" *New York Review of Books* 28 (May 14, 1981), pp. 17-22.

**233** Bayat, Mangol. "The Iranian Revolution of 1978-79: Fundamentalist or Modern?" *Middle East Journal* 37:1 (1983), pp. 30-42.

**234** Bill, James. "Iran and the Crisis of '78." *Foreign Affairs* 57:2 (1978/79), pp. 323-42.

**235** Hetherington, Norriss S. "Industrialization and Revolution in Iran: Forced Progress or Unmet Expectations?" *Middle East Journal* 36:3 (1982), pp. 362-73.

**236** Hooglund, Eric J. "The Iranian Revolution." *Middle East Journal* 34:4 (1980), pp. 485-89.

**237** _____. *Land and Revolution in Iran, 1960-1980.* Modern Middle East Series, No. 7. Austin: University of Texas Press, 1980.

**238** Keddie, Nikki. "Iranian Revolutions in Comparative Perspective." *The American Historical Review* 88:3 (1983), pp. 579-98.

**239** Micklos, Jack C. *The Iranian Revolution and Modernization: Way Stations to Anarchy.* National Security Essay Series 83-2. Washington, D.C.: National Defense University Press, 1983.

**240** Ramazani, Rouhollah K. "Iran's Revolution: Patterns, Problems, and Prospects." *International Affairs* 56:3 (1980), pp. 443-57.

**241** Sciolino, Elaine. "Iran's Durable Revolution." *Foreign Affairs* 61:4 (1983), pp. 893-920.

**242** U.S. Foreign Broadcast Information Service. Joint Publications Research Service Special Edition. *National Voice of Iran: November 1978-November 1979.* Arlington, Va.: Joint Publications Research Service, Dec. 10, 1979.

Current Developments

**243** Bill, James. "The Politics of Extremism in Iran." *Current History* 81 (January 1982), pp. 9 ff.

**244** Chubin, Shahram. "Leftist Forces in Iran." *Problems of Communism* 29:4 (1980), pp. 1-25.

**245** Cooley, John. "Iran, the Palestinians and the Gulf." *Foreign Affairs* 57:5 (1979), pp. 1017-34.

**246** Dawisha, Adeed. "Iran's Mullahs and the Arab Masses." *Washington Quarterly* 6:3 (1983), pp. 162-68.

**247** Fenton, Thomas. "Iran." *Washington Quarterly* 6:2 (1983), pp. 186-89.

**248** "How the Mullahs Line Up." *Middle East,* June 1982, pp. 25-28.

**249** "Iran Since the Revolution." *MERIP Reports* 13:3 (1983). Entire issue.

**250** *The Iranian Revolution and the Islamic Republic: Proceedings of a Conference.* Nikki Keddie and Eric Hooglund, eds. The Middle East Institute and the Woodrow Wilson Center for International Scholars, Washington. D.C., 1982.

**251** "Khomeini and the Opposition." *MERIP Reports,* No. 104 (March-April 1982). Entire issue.

**252** Olson, William. "The Succession Crisis in Iran." *Washington Quarterly* 6:3 (1983), pp. 156-61.

**253** "Reflections on the Quarter." *Orbis* 24:4 (1981), pp. 711-18.

**254** Rouleau, Eric. "Khomeini's Iran." *Foreign Affairs* 59:1 (1980), pp. 1-21.

**255** Zabih, Sepehr. *Iran Since the Revolution.* Baltimore, Md.: Johns Hopkins University Press, 1982.


*The Iran-Iraq War*

**256** Cordesman Anthony. "Lessons of the Iran-Iraq War: The First Round." *Armed Forces Journal International* 119:8 (1982), pp. 32-47.

**257** _____. "Lessons of the Iran-Iraq War: Part Two, Tactics, Technology, and Training." *Armed Forces Journal International* 119:10 (1982), pp. 68-85.

**258** _____. "The Iraq-Iran War: Attrition Now, Chaos Later." *Armed Forces Journal International* 120:9 (1983), pp. 36 ff.

**259** Dessouki, Ali E. Hillal, ed. *The Iran-Iraq War: Issues of Conflict and Prospects for Settlement.* Policy Memorandum No. 40. Princeton, N.J.: Center for International Studies, August 1981.

**260** Dowdy, William L. "Naval Warfare in the Gulf: Iraq versus Iran." *U.S. Naval Institute Proceedings* 107:6 (1981), pp. 114-17.

**261** Ghareeb, Edmund. "The Forgotten War." *American-Arab Affairs,* No. 5 (1983), pp. 59-75.

**262** Grummon, Stephen R. *The Iran-Iraq War: Islam Embattled.* Washington, D.C.: Praeger, 1982.

**263** Hickman, William F. *Ravaged and Reborn: The Iranian Army 1982.* Washington, D.C.: Brookings, 1982.

**264** Helms, Christine Moss. "The Iraqi Dilemma: Political Objectives versus Military Strategy." *American-Arab Affairs,* No. 5 (1983), pp. 76-85.

**265** Ismael, Tareq. *Iraq and Iran: Roots of Conflict.* Syracuse, N.Y.: Syracuse University Press, 1982.

**266** Jawdat, Nameer Ali. "Reflections on the Gulf War." *American Arab Affairs,* No. 5 (1983), pp. 86-98.

**267** O'Ballance, Edgar. "The Iraqi-Iranian War: The First Round." *Parameters* 11:1 (1981), pp. 54-59.

**268** Owens, Frank E. and Mukkerjee, Ronendra. "Iran and Iraq: Lessons of the 'Postscript War.'" *Army* 33:8 (1983), pp. 31-36.

**269** Staudenmaier, William. "Military Policy and Strategy in the Gulf War." *Parameters* 12:2 (1982), pp. 25-35.

**270** Tahir-Kheli, Shirin, and Ayubi, Shaheen. *The Iran-Iraq War: New Weapons, Old Conflicts.* New York: Praeger, 1983.

**271** U.S. Foreign Broadcast Information Service. Special Memorandum, *Teheran Radio Arabic-Language Broadcasts.* Springfield, Va., Jan. 7, 1980.

**272** Wright, Claudia. "Implications of the Iraq-Iran War." *Foreign Affairs* 59:2 (1980/1981), pp. 286-302.

*Iraq*

**273** Batatu, Hanna. *The Old Social Classes and the Revolutionary Movements of Iraq: A Study of Iraq's Old Landed and Commercial Classes and of its Communists, Ba'thists, and Free Officers.* Princeton, N.J.: Princeton University Press, 1979.

**274** Dann, Uriel. *Iraq under Qassem: A Political History, 1958-1963.* New York: Praeger, 1969.

**275** Khadduri, Majid. *Independent Iraq, 1952-1958: A Study in Iraqi Politics,* 2nd ed. London: Oxford University Press, 1960.

**276** _____. *Republican Iraq: A Study in Iraqi Politics since the Revolution of 1958.* London: Oxford University Press, 1969.

**277** _____. *Socialist Iraq: A Study in Iraqi Politics since 1968.* Washington, D.C.: Middle East Institute, 1978.

**278** Penrose, Edith and E.F. *Iraq: International Relations and National Development.* Boulder, Col.: Westview, 1978.

*Islam*

**279** Batatu, Hanna. "Iraq's Underground Shi'a Movements: Characteristics, Causes, and Prospects." *Middle East Journal* 35:4 (1981), pp. 578-94.

**280** Hudson, Michael. "The Islamic Factor in Syrian and Iraqi Politics." In James Piscatori, ed., *Islam in the Political Process,* pp. 73-97. Cambridge: Cambridge University Press, 1983.

The Israeli Bombing of Osiraq (see also NUCLEAR PROLIFERATION)

**281** Feldman, Shai. "The Bombing of Osiraq—Revisited." *International Security* 7:2 (1982), pp. 114-142.

**282** U.S. Congress. Senate. "The Israeli Air Strike." Hearings before the Committee on Foreign Relations. Washington, D.C.: G.P.O., June 1981.

Current Developments

**283** Dawisha, Adeed I. "Iraq: The West's Opportunity." *Foreign Policy*, No. 41 (1980-81), pp. 134-53.

**284** Iskander, Amir. *Saddam Hussein: The Fighter, the Thinker, and the Man.* Hassan Selim trans. Paris: Hachette Realites, 1980.

**285** Kashkett, Steven. "Iraq and the Pursuit of Nonalignment." *Orbis* 26:2 (1982), pp. 477-94.

**286** Kelidar, Abbas. "Iraq: The Search for Stability." *Conflict Studies*, No. 59. London: Institute for the Study of Conflict, 1975.

**287** Lamb, David. "Iraq." *Washington Quarterly* 6:2 (1983), pp. 183-86.

**288** Marr, Phebe A. "The Political Elite of Iraq." In George Lenczowski, ed. *Political Elites in the Middle East.* Washington, D.C.: American Enterprise Institute, 1975.

**289** Turner, Arthur C. "Iraq: Pragmatic Radicalism in the Fertile Crescent." *Current History* 18 (January 1982), pp. 14 ff.

**290** Wright, Claudia. "Iraq — New Power in the Middle East." *Foreign Affairs* 58:2 (1979/80), pp. 257-77.

*Ethnic Minorities*

**291** Aghajanian, Akbar. "Ethnic Inequality in Iran: An Overview," *International Journal of Middle East Studies* 15:2 (1983), pp. 211-24.

Baluch

**292** Harrison, Selig S. "Baluch Nationalism and Superpower Rivalry." *International Security* 5:3 (1980/81), pp. 152-63.

**293** _____. *In Afghanistan's Shadow: Baluch Nationalism and Soviet Temptations.* Washington, D.C.: Carnegie Endowment for International Peace, 1981.

Kurds

**294** Chaliand, Gerard, ed. *People Without a Country: The Kurds and Kurdistan*, Michael Pallis, trans. London: Zed Press, 1980.

**295** Ghareeb, Edmund. *The Kurdish Question in Iraq.* Syracuse, N.Y.: Syracuse University Press, 1981.

**296** Husseini, Shaikh Izzedin. "A Dictatorship under the Name of Islam." *MERIP Reports*, No. 113 (1983), pp. 9-10.

**297** Kutschera, Chris. *Le Mouvement Nationale Kurde.* Paris: Flammarion, 1979.

**298** _____. "The Kurdish Factor in the Gulf War." *Military Review* 61:6 (1981), pp. 13-20.

**299** O'Ballance, Edgar. *The Kurdish Revolt, 1961-1970.* Hamden, Conn.: Archon, 1973.

**300** Sim, Richard. "Kurdistan: The Search for Recognition." *Conflict Studies,* No. 124. London: Institute for the Study of Conflict, 1981.

Others (for Armenians, see Turkey)

**301** Ahmed, Akbar. *Pukhtun Economy and Society: Traditional Structure and Economic Development in a Tribal Society.* Boston: Routledge & Kegan Paul, 1980.

**302** _____. "Afghanistan and Pakistan: The Great Game of the Tribes," *Journal of South Asian and Middle Eastern Studies* 3:4 (1980), pp. 23-41.

**303** Farmayan, H. "Turkoman Identity and Presence in Iran." *Journal of South Asian and Middle Eastern Studies,* Vol. IV, No. 4, Summer 1981, pp. 45-62.

**304** Garthwaite, Gene R. *Khans and Shahs: The Bakhtiari in Iran.* Cambridge: Cambridge University Press, 1983.

**305** Singer, Andre. *Guardians of the North-West Frontier: The Pathans.* Amsterdam: Time-Life Books, 1982.

**306** Volkan, Vamik. *Cyprus—War and Adaptation: A Psycho-Analytic History of Two Ethnic Groups in Conflict.* Charlottesville: University Press of Virginia, 1979.


*Turkey*

**307** Dodd, C.H. *Politics and Government in Turkey.* Berkeley: University of California Press, 1969.

**308** Johnson, Maxwell O. "The Role of the Military in Turkish Politics." *Air University Review* 33:2 (1982), pp. 49-63.

**309** Karpat, Kemal. *Turkey's Politics: The Transition to a Multi-Party System.* Princeton, N.J.: Princeton University Press, 1959.

**310** Lewis, Bernard. *The Emergence of Modern Turkey.* London: Oxford University Press, 1961.

**311** \_\_\_\_\_. "The Ottoman Empire and its Aftermath," *Journal of Contemporary History* 15:1 (1980), pp. 27-36.

**312** Lewis, Geoffrey. *Turkey.* 3rd. ed. London: Ernest Benn, 1965.

**313** Mango, Andrew. *Turkey: A Delicately Poised Ally.* The Washington Papers 3:28. Beverly Hills, Cal.: Sage, 1975.

**314** Robinson, Richard D. *The First Turkish Republic: A Case Study in National Development.* Cambridge: Harvard University Press, 1963.

**315** Shaw. Stanford, and Shaw, Ezel. *Reform, Revolution, and Republic: The Rise of Modern Turkey, 1808-1975.* Cambridge: Cambridge University Press, 1977.

**316** *Turkey: A Country Study,* 3rd ed. Richard Nyrop et al., eds. Washington, D.C.: G.P.O., 1980.

Islam

**317** Heper, Metin. "Islam, Polity and Society in Turkey: A Middle Eastern Perspective." *Middle East Journal* 35:3 (1981), pp. 345-63.

**318** Mortimer, Edward. "Turkey — Muslim Nation, 'Secular' State." In *Faith & Power: The Politics of Islam.* New York: Random House, 1982.

**319** Mardin, Serif. "Religion and Politics in Modern Turkey." In James Piscatori, ed., *Islam in the Political Process,* pp. 138-159. Cambridge: Cambridge University Press, 1983.

**320** Toprak, Binnaz. *Islam and Political Development in Turkey.* Leiden: Brill, 1981.

Foreign Relations

(General)

**321** Harris, George. "The View from Ankara." *The Wilson Quarterly* 6:5 (1982), pp. 126-35. Special issue.

**322** Karpat, Kemal H. et al. *Turkey's Foreign Policy in Transition, 1950-1974.* Leiden: Brill, 1975.

**323** Sezer, Duygu Bazoglu. "Turkey's Security Policies." *Adelphi Papers,* No. 164. London: International Institute for Strategic Studies, Spring 1981.

**324** Vali, Ferenc. *Bridge Across the Bosporus: The Foreign Policy of Turkey.* Baltimore, Md.: Johns Hopkins University Press, 1971.

(The NATO Alliance)

**325** Gurkan, Ihsan. *NATO, Turkey, and the Southern Flank: A Mideastern Perspective.* Agenda Paper No. 11. New York: National Strategy Information Center, 1980.

**326** Kuniholm, Bruce. "Turkey and NATO: Past, Present and Future." *Orbis* 26:2 (1983), pp. 421-445.

**327** Lemnitzer, Lyman L. "The Strategic Problems of NATO's Northern and Southern Flanks." *Orbis* 13:1 (1969), pp. 100-110.

**328** U.S. Congress. House. *NATO After Afghanistan.* Committee on Foreign Affairs. Washington, D.C.: G.P.O., Oct. 27, 1980.

**329** U.S. Congress. Senate. *Perspectives on NATO's Southern Flank.* A Report to the Committee on Foreign Relations. Washington, D.C.: G.P.O., 1980.

**330** Whetten, Lawrence. "Turkey and NATO's Second Front." *Strategic Review* 9:3 (1981), pp. 57-64.

(U.S.-Turkish Relations)

**331** Gruen, George E. "Ambivalence in the Alliance: U.S. Interests in the Middle East and the Evolution of Turkish Foreign Policy." *Orbis* 24:2 (1980), pp. 363-79.

**332** Hafner, Donald. "Bureaucratic Politics and 'Those Frigging Missiles': JFK, Cuba, and US Missiles in Turkey." *Orbis* 21:2 (1977), pp. 307-32.

**333** Harris, George. *Troubled Alliance: Turkish-American Problems in Historical Perspective, 1945-1971.* Washington, D.C.: American Enterprise Institute, 1972.

**334** Kuniholm, Bruce. *The Origins of the Cold War in the Near East: Great Power Conflict and Diplomacy in Iran, Turkey, and Greece.* Princeton, N.J.: Princeton University Press, 1980.

**335** Laipson, Ellen. *U.S. Aid to Turkey: Congressional Considerations.* Washington, D.C.: Congressional Research Service, Library of Congress, May 28, 1982.

**336** U.S. Congress. House. *Congressional-Executive Relations and the Turkish Arms Embargo.* Congress and Foreign Policy Series, No. 3. Washington, D.C.: G.P.O., June 1981.

**337** _____. *Supplemental Aid Requests for Fiscal Years 1979 and 1980 for Turkey and Oman.* Hearings before the Committee on Foreign Affairs. Washington, D.C.: G.P.O., 1979.

**338** _____. *Turkey's Problems and Prospects: Implications for U.S. Interests.* Report Prepared for the Committee on Foreign Affairs by the Congressional Research Service. Washington, D.C.: G.P.O., 1980.

**339** _____. *United States Military Installations and Objectives in the Mediterranean.* Report prepared for the Committee on International Relations by the Congressional Research Service. Washington, D.C.: G.P.O., 1977.

**340** _____. *United States-Turkey Defense and Economic Cooperation Agreement 1980.* Hearing before the Committee on Foreign Affairs. Washington, D.C.: G.P.O., 1980.

**341** U.S. Congress. Senate. *United States Foreign Policy Objectives and Overseas Military Installations.* Report prepared for the Committee on Foreign Relations by the Congressional Research Service. Washington, D.C.: G.P.O., April 1979.

(Greek-Turkish Problems, including Cyprus)

**342** Lord Caradon. *Cyprus—Past and Future; a personal Perspective.* The Sixth Stephen J. Brademas, Sr., Lecture. Brookline, Mass.:Hellenic Press, 1981.

**343** Denktash, Rauf. *The Cyprus Triangle.* Winchester, Mass.: Allen & Unwin, 1982.

**344** Heinl, Robert. "The Turkish-Greek Conflict: U.S. Intelligence Suffers Most." *Sea Power* 21(Feb. 1978), pp. 9-11.

**345** Laipson, Ellen. *U.S. Interests in the Eastern Mediterranean: Turkey, Greece, and Cyprus.* Report No. 83-73F. Washington, D.C.: Congressional Research Service, Library of Congress, April 19, 1983.

**346** Rusinow, Dennison I. *The Cyprus Deadlock: Forever or Another Day?* American Universities Field Staff Reports, 1981/No. 11 Europe. Hanover, N.H.: American Universities Field Staff, 1981.

**347** Salih, Halil Ibrahim. *Cyprus: The Impact of Diverse Nationalism on a State.* University: University of Alabama Press, 1978.

**348** U.S. Congress. Senate. *Turkey, Greece, and NATO: The Strained Alliance.* A Staff Report to the Committee on Foreign Relations. Washington, D.C.: G.P.O., 1980.

**349** Veremis, Thanos. "Greek Security: Issues and Politics." *Adelphi Papers*, No. 179. London: International Institute of Strategic Studies, 1982.

**350** Wilson, Andrew. "The Aegean Dispute." *Adelphi Papers*, No. 155. London: International Institute of Strategic Studies, 1979/1980.

(The Middle East)

**351** Baytok, Taner. "Recent Developments in the Middle East and Southwest Asia: Impacts on Western Security." *NATO Review*, No. 4 (Aug. 1981), pp. 10-13.

**352** Henze, Paul. "Turkey, the Alliance and the Middle East: Problems and Opportunities in Historical Perspective." *Working Paper*, No. 36. Washington, D.C.: Woodrow Wilson Center for International Scholars, 1981.

**353** Karaosmanoglu, Ali L. "Turkey's Security and the Middle East." *Foreign Affairs* 62:1 (1983), pp. 157-75.

(The Armenian Question; for Kurds, see Ethnic Minorities)

**354** Foreign Policy Institute. *The Armenian Issue in Nine Questions and Answers*. Ankara: Foreign Policy Institute, 1982.

**355** Ravitch, Norman. "The Armenian Catastrophe: Of History, Murder & Sin." *Encounter* 57:6 (1981), pp. 69-84.

(Extremism and Terrorism)

**356** Harris, George S. "The Left in Turkey." *Problems of Communism* 29:4 (1980), pp. 26-41.

**357** Henze, Paul. *Goal Destabilization, Soviet Agitational Propaganda, Instability and Terrorism in NATO South*. Marina del Rey, Cal.: European American Institute for Security Research, 1981.

**358** Landau. Jacob. "The Nationalist Action Party in Turkey." *Journal of Contemporary History* 17:4 (1982), pp. 587-606.

**359** _____. *Pan-Turkism in Turkey: A Study of Irredentism*. Hamden, Conn.: Archon, 1981.

**360** _____. *Radical Politics in Modern Turkey*. Leiden: Brill, 1974.

**361** U.S. Congress. Senate. *Terrorism: The Turkish Experience.* Hearing before the Subcommittee on Security and Terrorism of the Committee on the Judiciary. Washington, D.C.: G.P.O., June 25, 1981.

**362** U.S. Foreign Broadcast Information Service. Joint Publications Research Service Special Edition. *"Our Radio" and "Voice of Turkish Communist Party" (VOTCP): January 1978-December 1979.* Arlington, Va.: Joint Publications Research Service, Dec. 19, 1979.

**363** Mehmet, Ozay. "Turkey in Crisis: Some Contradictions in the Kemalist Development Strategy," *International Journal of Middle East Studies* 15:1 (1983), pp. 47-66.

(Economic Issues and Trends)

**364** Ozbudun, Ergun, and Ulusan, Aydin, eds. *The Political Economy of Income Distribution in Turkey.* New York: Holmes & Meier, 1980.

**365** *Turkey.* OECD Economic Surveys, 1981-1982. Paris: OECD, April 1982.

**366** _____ OECD Economic Surveys, 1982-1983. Paris: OECD, April 1983.

**367** "Turkey: A Survey." *The Economist* 280 (Sept. 12, 1981), p. 56ff.

(Current Developments)

**368** Brown, James. "Turkey's Policy in Flux." *Current History* 81 (January 1982), pp. 26 ff.

**369** Butler, Francis P. "Reassessing Turkey: A Faithful Ally Disillusioned and in Trouble." *Parameters* 10:1 (1980), pp. 24-32.

**370** *The Constitution of the Republic of Turkey.* Ankara: Directorate General of Press and Information, 1982.

**371** Endruweit, B. "Turkey's Option for Alignment and Non-Alignment: A Sociological Perspective." *Orient* 22:2 (1981), 257-73.

**372** Ersan, Tosum. "Turkey's Battered Democracy." *Index on Censorship,* No. 1 (1982), pp. 11 ff.

**373** Henze, Paul. "On the Rebound." *Wilson Quarterly* 6:5 (1982), pp. 109-125. Special Issue.

**374** Kutschera, Chris. "The Price of Security." *The Middle East,* September 1981, pp. 32-33.

**375** Ludington, Nicholas S., and Spain, James W. "Dateline Turkey: The Case for Patience." *Foreign Policy*, No. 50 (1983), pp. 150-168.

**376** Mackenzie, Kenneth. "Turkey Under the Generals." *Conflict Studies*, No. 126. London: International Institute for Strategic Studies, 1981.

**377** Mango, Andrew. "Understanding Turkey." *Middle Eastern Studies* 18:2 (1982), pp. 194-213.

**378** Parker, Mushtak. "Turkey: Special Report." *Arabia: The Islamic World Review*, No. 18 (1983), pp. 33-51.

**379** Rustow, Dankwart A. "Turkey's Travails." *Foreign Affairs* 58:1 (1979), pp. 82-102.

**380** "Turkey: The Generals Take Over." *MERIP Reports*, No. 93 (1981). Entire issue.

**381** Turner, Michael. "Politics and the Future of Turkish Democracy." *Turkish Studies Association Bulletin* 5:2 (1981), pp. 1-4.

SOUTHWEST ASIA

*Afghanistan*

**382** Dupree, Louis. *Afghanistan*. Princeton, N.J.: Princeton University Press, 1973, 1978, 1980.

The Soviet Invasion and Occupation

**383** Bradsher, Henry S. *Afghanistan and the Soviet Union*. Durham, N.C.: Duke University Press, 1983.

**384** Chaliand, Gerard. *Report From Afghanistan*. Tamar Jacoby, trans. New York: Viking, 1981.

**385** Dupree, Louis. *Afghanistan: 1980, The World Turned Upside Down*. AUFS Report. Hanover, N.H.: American Universities Field Staff, 1980.

**386** _____. *Red Flag Over the Hindu Kush*. Part I: Leftist Movements in Afghanistan (LD-2-'79); Part II: The Accidental Coup, or Taraki in Blunderland (LD-3-'79); Part III: Rhetoric and Reforms, or Promises! Promises! (LD-2-'80); Part IV: Foreign Policy and the Economy (LD-3-'80); Part V: Repressions, or Security Through Terror, Purges I-IV (LD-3-'80); Part VI: Repressions, or Security Through Terror, Purges IV-VI (LD-5-'80). Hanover, N.H.: American Universities Field Staff, 1979, 1980.

**387** Griffiths, John C. *Afghanistan: Key to a Continent.* Boulder, Col.: Westview, 1981.

**388** Hammond, Thomas T. *Red Flag Over Afghanistan: The Communist Coup, the Soviet Invasion, and their Consequences.* Boulder, Col.: Westview, 1983.

**389** Male, Beverley. *Revolutionary Afghanistan: A Reappraisal.* New York: St. Martin's, 1982.

**390** Mortimer, Edward. "The Faraway War." *New York Review of Books* 30 (Dec. 22, 1983), pp. 3-10.

**391** Monks, Alfred L. *The Soviet Intervention in Afghanistan.* Washington, D.C.: American Enterprise Institute, 1981.

**392** Newell, Nancy and Richard. *The Struggle for Afghanistan.* Ithaca, N.Y.: Cornell University Press, 1981.

Soviet Views, Strategy, and Tactics

**393** "Afghanistan and the Strategy of Empire." *Grand Strategy: Countercurrents* 1:1 (1981), pp. 1-4.

**394** Brides, Lord Saint. "Afghanistan: The Empire Plays to Win." *Orbis* 24:3 (1980), pp. 533-40.

**395** Collins, Joseph J. "Afghanistan: The Empire Strikes Out." *Parameters* 12:1 (1982), pp. 32-41.

**396** _____. "The Soviet Invasion of Afghanistan: Methods, Motives, and Ramifications." *Naval War College Review* 33:6 (1980), pp. 53-61.

**397** Fukuyama, Francis. "The Future of the Soviet Role in Afghanistan: A Trip Report." *Rand Note* N-1579-RC. Santa Monica, Cal.: Rand Corp., Sept. 1980.

**398** Hart, Douglas M. "Low-intensity Conflict in Afghanistan: The Soviet View." *Survival* 24:2 (1982), pp. 61-66.

**399** Malhuret, Clause. "Report from Afghanistan." *Foreign Affairs* 62:2 (1983/84), pp. 426-435.

**400** Muradov, Gulam. "National-Democratic Revolution in Afghanistan: A Soviet View." *Journal of South Asian and Middle Eastern Studies* 6:1 (1982), pp. 57-74.

**401** Rubinstein, Alvin. "Afghanistan: Embraced by the Bear." *Orbis* 26:1 (1982), pp. 135-53.

**402** _____. "The Last Years of Peaceful Coexistence: Soviet- Afghan Relations." *The Middle East Journal* 36:2 (1982), pp. 165-83.

Afghanistan Under Soviet Occupation

**403** Branigan, William. *Washington Post*, October 16-22, 1983. A seven-part series.

**404** Girardet, Edward. "With the Resistance in Afghanistan." *Christian Science Monitor*, June 22 and 28; July 2, 7, 19, and 26, 1982.

**405** Kamrany, Nake. "Afghanistan Under Soviet Occupation." *Current History* 81 (May 1982), pp. 219 ff.

**406** Khalilzad, Zalmay. "Soviet-Occupied Afghanistan." *Problems of Communism* 29:6 (1980), pp. 23-40.

**407** A Nearby Observer. "The Afghan-Soviet War: Stalemate or Evolution?" *Middle East Journal* 36:2 (1982), pp. 151-64.

**408** U.S. Department of State. *Afghanistan: 18 Months of Occupation.* Special Report No. 86. Washington, D.C.: G.P.O., Aug. 1981.

**409** _____. *Afghanistan: 2 Years of Occupation.* Special Report No. 91. Washington, D.C.: G.P.O., Dec. 1981.

**410** _____. *Afghanistan: 3 Years of Occupation.* Special Report No. 106. Washington, D.C.: G.P.O., Dec. 1982.

**411** _____. *Afghanistan: Four Years of Occupation.* Special Report No. 112. Washington, D.C.: G.P.O., Dec. 1983.

**412** _____. *Chemical Warfare in Southeast Asia and Afghanistan.* Special Report No. 98. Washington, D.C.: G.P.O., March 22, 1982.

**413** Wafdar, K. "Afghanistan in 1981: The Struggle Intensifies." *Asian Security* 22:2 (1982), pp. 147-54.

Regional Views (see also various countries)

**414** Jha, S. "Nepal's Reaction to the Soviet Military Presence in Afghanistan." *India Quarterly* 37:1 (1981), pp. 59-71.

**415** Thomas, Raju G.C. "The Afghan Crisis and South Asian Security." *Journal of Strategic Studies* 4:4 (1981), pp. 415-34.

Solutions?

**416** Dupree, Louis. "Afghanistan in 1982: Still No Solution." *Asian Survey* 23:2 (1983), pp. 133-42.

**417** Harrison, Selig S. "Dateline Afghanistan: Exit Through Finland? *Foreign Policy*, No. 41 (1980-81), pp. 163-87.

**418** _____ "A Breakthrough in Afghanistan?" *Foreign Policy*, No. 51 (1983), pp. 3-26.

**419** Mehta, Jagat S. "Afghanistan: A Neutral Solution." *Foreign Policy*, No. 47 (1982), pp. 139-53.

**420** _____. *Solution in Afghanistan: From Swedenization to Finlandization.* Occasional Paper No. 158, Kennan Institute for Advanced Russian Studies. Washington, D.C.: Woodrow Wilson Center for International Scholars, 1982.

**421** U.S. Congress. House. *An Assessment of the Afghanistan Sanctions: Implications for Trade and Diplomacy in the 1980's.* Report prepared for the Subcommittee on Europe and the Middle East of the Committee on Foreign Affairs by Congressional Research Service. Washington, D.C.: G.P.O., April 1981.

*Pakistan*

**422** Ahmed, Akbar S. "Order and Conflict in Muslim Society: A Case Study from Pakistan." *Middle East Journal* 36:2 (1982), pp. 184-204.

**423** Ansari, Javed. "Pakistan Revisited: Why General Zia's Regime Cannot Last Long." *Arabia: The Islamic World Review*, No. 22 (1983), pp. 8-13.

**424** Braibanti, Ralph, *et al.*, eds. *Pakistan: The Long View.* Durham, N.C.: Duke University Press, 1977.

**425** Burki, Shahid Javed. *Pakistan Under Bhutto, 1971-1977.* New York: St. Martin's, 1980.

**426** Cohen, Stephen, and Weinbaum, Marvin G. "Pakistan in 1981: Staying On." *Asian Security* 22:2 (1982), pp. 136-46.

**427** Korson, J. Henry. "Islamization and Social Policy in Pakistan." *Journal of South Asian and Middle Eastern Studies* 6:2 (1982), pp. 71-90.

**428** Kraft, Joseph. "Letter from Pakistan." *New Yorker*, August 10, 1981, pp. 53-75.

**429** Malik, Lynda. "Measuring Consensus in Pakistan." *Journal of South Asian and Middle Eastern Studies* 6:1 (1982), pp. 33-47.

**430** Sayeed, Khalid. *Politics in Pakistan: The Nature and Direction of Change.* New York: Praeger, 1980.

**431** Syed, Anwar H. "The Idea of a Pakistani Nationhood." *Polity* 12:4 (1980), pp. 575-97.

**432** _____. *Pakistan: Islam, Politics, and National Solidarity.* New York: Praeger, 1982.

**433** Weinbaum, Marvin, and Cohen, Stephen. "Pakistan in 1982: Holding On." *Asian Survey* 23:2 (1983), pp. 123-32.

**434** Ziring, Lawrence. "Political Dilemmas and Instability in South and Southwest Asia." *Asian Affairs: An American Review,* Spring 1983, pp. 37-47.

**435** _____. *Pakistan: The Enigma of Political Development.* Boulder, Col.: Westview, 1980.

Foreign Policy

**436** Askari-Rizvi, Hasan. "Pakistan: Ideology and Foreign Policy." *Asian Affairs: An American Review,* Spring 1983, pp. 48-59.

**437** Chaudri, M. "Pakistan and Regional Security: A Pakistani View." *India Quarterly* 36:2 (1980), pp. 179-92.

**438** Cheema, Pervaiz Iqbal. "The Afghanistan Crisis and Pakistan's Security Dilemma." *Asian Survey* 23:3 (1983), pp. 227-43.

**439** Khan, Sultan Muhammed. "Pakistani Geopolitics: The Diplomatic Perspective." *International Security* 5:1 (1980), pp. 26-36.

**440** Khar, Ghulam Mustafa. "Four Choices Facing Front-Line Pakistan." *Economist* 281 (Oct. 31, 1981), pp. 25-30.

**441** Kumar, S. "Pakistan and Regional Security — A Comment." *India Quarterly* 36:3-4 (1980), pp. 383-86.

Great Power Relations ( see also The Soviet Union under GEOPOLITICAL FACTORS)

**442** Barnds, William J. *India, Pakistan, and the Great Powers.* New York: Praeger, 1972.

**443** Brides, Lord Saint. "New Perspectives on the Hindu Kush." *International Security* 5:3 (1980/81), pp. 164-170.

**444** Brown, Norman W. *The United States and India, Pakistan, Bangladesh.* Cambridge, Mass.: Harvard University Press, 1972.

**445** Gelb, Leslie, and Ullman, Richard. "Keeping Cool at the Khyber Pass." *Foreign Policy*, No. 38 (1980), pp. 3-18.

**446** Harrison, Selig S. "Fanning the Flames in South Asia." *Foreign Policy*, No. 45 (1981-82), pp. 84-102.

**447** Mehrunnisa, Ali. "Soviet-Pakistan Ties Since the Afghan Crisis." *Asian Survey* 23:9 (1983), pp. 1025-42.

**448** Richter, William. "Pakistan: A New 'Front-Line' State?" *Current History* 81 (May 1982), pp. 202 ff.

**449** Sen Gupta, Bhabani. *The Fulcrum of Asia: Relations Among China, India, Pakistan and the U.S.S.R.* New York: Pegasus, 1970.

**450** Sherwani, Latif Ahmed. *Pakistan, China and America.* Karachi: Council for Pakistan Studies, 1980.

**451** Tahir-Kheli, Shirin. "Proxies and Allies: The Case of Iran and Pakistan." *Orbis* 24:2 (1980), pp. 339-53.

**452** Wolpert, Stanley. *Roots of Confrontation in South Asia: Afghanistan, Pakistan, India and the Superpowers.* New York: Oxford University Press, 1982.

(India)

**453** Alam, G.M. Shahidul. "Peacekeeping Without Conflict Resolution: The Kashmir Dispute." *The Fletcher Forum* 6:1 (1981), pp. 61-90.

**454** Brajovic, Rode. "The Indo-Pakistani Dialogue." *Review of International Affairs* 32:750 (1981), pp. 26-28.

**455** Brines, Russel. *The Indo-Pakistani Conflict.* London: Pall Mall, 1968.

**456** Gupta, Sisir. *Kashmir: A Study in Indian Pakistani Relations.* Bombay: Asia Publishing House, 1966.

**457** de Riencourt, Amaury. "India and Pakistan in the Shadow of Afghanistan." *Foreign Affairs* 61:2 (1982/1983), pp. 416-37.

**458** Saliq, Siddiq. *Witness to Surrender.* Karachi: Oxford University Press, 1978.

**459** Sen, L.P. *Slender Was the Thread.* Poona: Sangam Press, 1973.

**460** Singh, Sukhwant. *India's Wars Since Independence.* 3 Vols. New Delhi: Vikas, 1980, 1981, and 1982.

**461** Ziring, Lawrence. "Indo-Pakistani Relations: Time for a Fresh Start." *Asian Affairs: An American Review* 84 (1981), pp. 199-215.

(Middle East)

**462** Mohammadally, S. "Pakistan-Iran Relations (1947-1979)." *Pakistan Horizon* 32:4 (1979), pp. 51-63.

**463** Smith, David O. "Pakistan and the Middle East Connection." *Military Review* 62:10 (1982), pp. 42-49.

**464** Tahir-Kheli, Shirin, and Staudenmaier, William O. "The Saudi-Pakistani Military Relationship: Implications for U.S. Policy." *Orbis* 26:1 (1982), pp. 155-171.

**465** Wright, Claudia. "India and Pakistan join in the Gulf Game." *Middle East*, June 1981, pp. 31-34.

(United States)

**466** Jones, Rodney. "Mending Relations with Pakistan." *Washington Quarterly* 4:2 (1981), pp. 17-29.

**467** Tahir-Kheli, Shirin. *The United States and Pakistan: The Evolution of an Influence Relationship.* New York: Praeger, 1982.

**468** U.S. Congress. House. *Proposed U.S. Assistance and Arms Transfers to Pakistan: An Assessment.* Report of a Staff Study Mission to the Committee on Foreign Affairs. Washington, D.C.: G.P.O., 1981.

**469** _____. *Security and Economic Assistance to Pakistan.* Hearings and Markups before the Committee on Foreign Affairs. Washington, D.C.: G.P.O., 1982.

**470** U.S. Congress. Senate. *Aid and the Proposed Arms Sales of F-16's to Pakistan.* Hearings before the Committee on Foreign Relations. Washington, D.C.: G.P.O., 1982.

**471** U.S. Department of State. *Shared Security Interests: U.S. Cooperation with Pakistan.* Current Policy No. 347. Washington, D.C.: Department of State, Nov. 12, 1981.

**472** Van Hollen, Christopher. "Leaning on Pakistan." *Foreign Policy*, No. 38 (1980), pp. 35-50.

**473** _____. "The Tilt Policy Revisited: Nixon-Kissinger Geopolitics and South Asia." *Asian Survey* 20:4 (1980), pp. 339-361.

*India*

**474** Andersen, Walter K. "India in 1981: Stronger Political Authority and Social Tension." *Asian Survey* 22:2 (1982), pp. 119-35.

**475** _____. "India in 1982: Domestic Challenges and Foreign Policy Successes." *Asian Survey* 23:2 (1983), pp. 111-22.

**476** Frankel, Francine. "India's Promise." *Foreign Policy*, No. 38 (1980), pp. 67-79.

**477** Hardgrave, Robert. "India Enters the 1980's." *Current History* 81 (May 1982), pp. 197 ff.

**478** Honsa, Carol. "India: Mosaic of Contradictions." *Christian Science Monitor*, Sept. 7, 8, 9, 10, 1982.

**479** Kaufman, Michael. "Mrs. Gandhi Grooms Another Son." *New York Times Magazine*, June 13, 1982, pp. 40 ff.

**480** Mehta, Ved. "Letter from New Delhi." *New Yorker*, August 3, 1981, pp. 38-58.

**481** Sahgal, Nayantara. *Indira Gandhi: Her Road to Power.* New York: F. Ungar, 1982.

Foreign Policy (see also Great Power Relationships under Pakistan)

**482** Andersen, Walter K. "India in Asia: Walking on a Tightrope." *Asian Survey* 19:12 (Dec. 1979), pp. 1241-53.

**483** Cohen, Stephen. "Toward a Great State in Asia." In Onkar Marwah and Jonathan Pollack, eds. *Military Power and Policy in Asian States: China, India, Japan.* Boulder, Col.: Westview, 1980.

**484** Khalilzad, Zalmay. "The Strategic Significance of South Asia." *Current History* 8: (May 1982), pp. 193 ff.

**485** Rose, Lee, and Kumar, Satish. "South Asia: A Regional Perspective." In Werner Feld and Gavin Boyd, eds., *Comparative Regional Systems: West and East Europe, North American, the Middle East and Developing Countries.* New York: Pergamon Press, 1980.

**486** Thomas, Raju. "Aircraft for the Indian Air Force: The Context and Implications of the Jaguar Decision." *Orbis* 24:1 (1980), pp. 85-101.

**487** Vasudevan, P. "The Afghan Crisis and Super Power Strategies: Implications for India's Foreign Policy." *India Quarterly* 36:3-4 (1980), pp. 285-95.

(Soviet Union)

**488** Ghosh, Partha, and Panda, Rajaran. "Domestic Support for Mrs. Ghandi's Afghan Policy: The Soviet Factor in Indian Politics." *Asian Survey* 23:3 (1983), pp. 261-79.

**489** Sagar, Imroze. "Indo-Soviet Strategic Interests and Collaboration." *Naval War College Review* 34:1 (1981), pp. 13-33.

(United States)

**490** Myers, Ramon, ed. *A U.S. Foreign Policy for Asia: The 1980s and Beyond.* Stanford, Cal.: Hoover Institution Press, 1982.

**491** Nagarajan, K.V. "Indo-U.S. Relations in the 1980's." *The Washington Quarterly* 3:1 (1980), pp. 67-75.

**492** Palmer, Norman. "Indo-American Relations: The Politics of Encounter." *Orbis* 23:2 (1979), pp. 403-420.

**493** Singh, S. Nihal. "Can the U.S. and India Be Real Friends?" *Asian Survey* 23:9 (1983), pp. 1011-24.

**494** Thomas, Raju. "Security Relationships in Southern Asia: Differences in Indian and American Perspectives." *Asian Survey* 21:7 (1981), pp. 689-709.

**495** U.S. Congress. House. *The United States, India, and South Asia: Interests and Trends, and Issues for Congressional Concern.* Prepared for the Committee on International Relations by the Congressional Research Service. Washington, D.C.: G.P.O., 1978.

**496** U.S. Congress. Senate. *United States-Indian Relations.* A Report to the Committee on Foreign Relations. Washington, D.C.: G.P.O., March 1982.

(Middle East)

**497** Franda, Marcus. *India, Iran, and the Gulf.* AUFS Report, 1978/No. 17, Asia. Hanover, N.H.: American Universities Field Staff, 1978.

**498** Mc Donnell, Pat. "India Pushes on Contracts to Pay off Oil." *Middle East*, Feb. 1981, p. 61.

**499** Wright, Claudia. "India and Pakistan Join in the Gulf Game." *The Middle East*, June 1981, pp. 31-34.

Indian Ocean Issues (see also Strategic Choke Points and Related Naval Issues)

**500** Alford, J. "Strategic Developments in the Indian Ocean Area." *Asian Affairs* 12:2 (1981), pp. 141-49.

**501** Bowman, Larry W., and Clark, Ian. *The Indian Ocean in Global Politics.* Boulder, Col.: Westview, 1981.

**502** Dowdy, William L., and Trood, Russel. "The Indian Ocean: An Emerging Geostrategic Region." *International Journal* 383 (1983), pp. 432-58.

**503** Rais, Rasul. "An Appraisal of U.S. Strategy in the Indian Ocean." *Asian Survey* 23:9 (1983), pp. 1043-51.

**504** Sojka, Gary L. "The Missions of the Indian Navy." *Naval War College Review* 36:1 (1983), pp. 2-15.

**505** Stone, N. "An Indian Ocean Fleet — The Case and the Cost." *U.S. Naval Institute Proceedings* 107:7 (1981), pp. 54-57.

**506** Tahtinen, Dale R. *Arms in the Indian Ocean: Interests and Challenges.* Washington, D.C.: American Enterprise Institute, 1977.

**507** U.S. Congress. House. *Means of Measuring Naval Power with Special Reference to U.S. and Soviet Activities in the Indian Ocean.* Prepared for the Committee on Foreign Affairs by the Congressional Research Service. Washington, D.C.: G.P.O., 1974.

**508** Vivekanandan, B. "The Indian Ocean as a Zone of Peace: Problems and Prospects." *Asian Survey* 21:12 (1981), pp. 1237-49.

**509** Wall, Patrick. *The Indian Ocean and the Threat to the West.* London: Stacey International, 1975.

(Nuclear Issues)

**510** Dunn, Lewis. "Half Past India's Bang." *Foreign Policy,* No. 36 (1979), pp. 71-79.

**511** Noorani, A.G. "Indo-U.S. Nuclear Relations." *Asian Survey* 21:4 (1981), pp. 399-416.

**512** U.S. Congress. Senate. *Tarapur Nuclear Fuel Export.* Report of the Committee on Foreign Relations. Washington, D.C.: G.P.O., 1980.

**513** _____. *The Tarapur Nuclear Fuel Export Issue.* Joint Hearings before the Committee on Foreign Relations and the Committee on Governmental Affairs. Washington, D.C.: G.P.O., 1980.

## GEOPOLITICAL FACTORS

*The Northern Tier*

**514** Clayton, Gerald .D. *Britain and the Eastern Question: Missolonghi to Gallipoli.* London: University of London Press, 1971.

**515** Fromkin, David. "The Great Game in Asia." *Foreign Affairs* 58:4 (1980), pp. 936-51.

**516** Ingram, Edward. *The Beginning of the Great Game in Asia, 1828-1834.* Oxford: Clarendon Press, 1979.

**517** Kelly, J.B. "Great Game or Grand Illusion." *Survey* 24:2 (1980), pp. 109-127.

**518** Klass, R.T. "The Great Game Revisited." *National Review*, Oct. 26, 1979, pp. 1366-68.

**519** Kuniholm, Bruce. *The Origins of the Cold War in the Near East: Great Power Conflict and Diplomacy in Iran, Turkey, and Greece.* Princeton, N.J.: Princeton University Press, 1980.

**520** Lenczowski, George. "The Arc of Crisis: Its Central Sector." *Foreign Affairs* 57:4 (1979), pp. 796-820.

**521** Millman, Richard. *Britain and the Eastern Question, 1875-1879.* Oxford: Clarendon Press, 1979.

**522** McNeill, William H. "The Care and Repair of Public Myth." *Foreign Affairs* 61:1 (1982), pp. 1-13.

**523** Ramazani, Rouhollah. *The Northern Tier: Afghanistan, Iran, and Turkey.* New York: Van Nostrand, 1966.

**524** Thomas, Raju G.C. *The Great-Power Triangle and Asian Security.* Lexington, Mass.: Lexington Books, 1983.

**525** Yapp, Malcolm E. *Strategies of British India: Britain, Iran and Afghanistan, 1798-1850.* Oxford: Clarendon Press, 1980.

*The Soviet Union*

The Middle East

**526** Agwami, M. "The Arab-Soviet Tangle—A Review Article." *India Quarterly* 36:2 (1980), pp. 210 ff.

**527** Chubin, Shahram. "Gains for Soviet Policy in the Middle East." *International Security* 6:4 (1982), 122-52.

**528** _____. *Regional Perceptions of the Impact of Soviet Policy in the Middle East.* Prepared for the International Security Studies Program. Washington, D.C.: Woodrow Wilson Center for International Scholars, Sept. 9, 1981.

**529** _____. *Soviet Policy Toward Iran and the Gulf.* Adelphi Papers, No. 157. London: International Institute for Strategic Studies, 1980.

**530** _____. "The Soviet Union and Iran." *Foreign Affairs* 61:4 (1983), 921-49.

**531** Dawisha, Karen. *Moscow's Moves in the Direction of the Gulf—So Near and Yet So Far.* Kennan Institute for Advanced Studies, Occasional Paper No. 122. Washington, D.C.: Woodrow Wilson Center for International Scholars, 1980.

**532** Donaldson, Robert. "The Soviet Union in the Third World." *Current History* 81 (Oct., 1982), pp. 313 ff.

**533** Freedman, Robert O. "Moscow and the Gulf in 1981." *Middle East Insight* 2:2 (1982), pp. 13-20.

**534** Halliday, Fred M. *Soviet Policy in the Arc of Crisis.* Washington, D.C.: Institute for Policy Studies, 1981.

**535** Hensel, Howard M. "Moscow's Perspective on the Fall of the Shah." *Asian Affairs* 14:2 (1983), pp. 148-59.

**536** _____. "Soviet Policy Toward the Rebellion in Dhofar." *Asian Affairs* 13:2 (1982), pp. 183-207.

**537** Kelly, J.B. "The Kremlin and the Gulf." *Encounter* 54:4 (1980), pp. 84-90.

**538** Price, David Lynn. "Moscow and the Persian Gulf." *Problems of Communism* 282 (1979), pp. 1-13.

**539** Ro'i, Yaacov, ed. *The Limits to Power: Soviet Policy in the Middle East.* New York: St. Martin's, 1979.

**540** Rubinstein, Alvin Z. "The Evolution of Soviet Strategy in the Middle East." *Orbis* 24:2 (1980), pp. 323-37.

**541** _____. *Soviet Policy Toward Turkey, Iran, and Afghanistan: The Dynamics of Influence.* New York: Praeger, 1982.

**542** _____. "The Soviet Union and Iran Under Khomeini." *International Affairs* 57:4 (1981), pp. 599-617.

**543** Spulber, Nicolas. "Israel's War in Lebanon: Through the Soviet Looking Glass." *Middle East Review* 15:3&4 (1983), pp. 18-24.

**544** Weir, Andrew, and Bloch, Jonathan. "Moscow's Shadow Play." *Middle East*, Jan. 1982, pp. 24-26.

**545** Yodfat, Aryeh. "The USSR's Attitude to the Gulf War." *Asian Affairs* 13:3 (1982), pp. 281-87.

Islam

**546** Bennigsen, Alexandre, and Broxup, Marie. *The Islamic Threat to the Soviet State.* New York: St, Martin's, 1983.

**547** Crisostomo, Rosemarie. "The Muslims of the Soviet Union." *Current History* 81 (Oct. 1982), pp. 309 ff.

**548** Critchlow, James. "Minarets and Marx." *Washington Quarterly* 3:2 (1980), pp. 48-57.

**549** d'Encausse, Helene Carrere. *Decline of an Empire: The Soviet Socialist Republics in Revolt.* Martin Sokolinsky and Henry A. La Farge, trans. New York: Newsweek Books, 1979.

Asia

**550** Horn, Robert. "Afghanistan and the Soviet-Indian Influence Relationship." *Asian Survey* 23:3 (1983), pp. 244-60.

**551** _____. "The Soviet Union and Sino-Indian Relations." *Orbis* 26:4 (1983), pp. 889-906.

**552** Hudson, George. "Current Soviet Security Policy and the Sino-Soviet Split." *Mershon Center Quarterly Report* 6:2 (1981). Entire issue.

**553** Noorani, A.G. "Soviet Ambitions in South Asia." *International Security* 4:3 (1979/1980), pp. 31-39.

**554** Robinson, Thomas. "The Soviet Union and Asia in 1981." *Asian Survey* 22:1 (1982), pp. 13-32.

**555** Seton-Watson, Hugh. "The Last Empires." *Washington Quarterly* 3:2 (1980), pp. 41-46.

**556** Tahir-Kheli, Shirin. "Soviet Fortunes on the Southern Tier: Afghanistan, Iran, and Pakistan." *Naval War College Review* 34:6 (1981), pp. 3-13.

Military Factors (see also Indian Ocean Issues under India)

**557** Allard, K. "Soviet Airborne Forces and Preemptive Power Projection." *Parameters* 10:4 (1980), pp. 42-51.

**558** Dunn, Keith. "Constraints on the USSR in Southwest Asia: A Military Analysis." *Orbis* 25:3 (1981), pp. 607-29.

**559** _____. "Strategy, the Soviet Union and the 1980s." *Naval War College Review* 24:5 (1981), pp. 15-31.

**560** Epstein, Joshua. "Soviet Vulnerabilities in Iran and the RDF Deterrent." *International Security* 6:2 (1981), pp. 126-158.

**561** Luns, Joseph M.A.H. "Political-Military Implications of Soviet Naval Expansion." *NATO Review*, No. 1 (1982), pp. 1-6.

**562** Ross, Dennis. "Considering Soviet Threats to the Persian Gulf." *International Security* 6:2 (1981), pp. 159-180.

**563** U.S. Department of the Navy. *Soviet Naval Developments.* 2nd ed. Annapolis, Md.: Nautical & Aviation, 1981.

United States

**564** Barnet, Richard J. "U.S.-Soviet Relations: The Need for a Comprehensive Approach." *Foreign Affairs* 57:4 (1979), pp. 779-95.

**565** Jacobsen, Carl. "Soviet-American Policy: New Strategic Uncertainties." *Current History* 81 (Oct. 1982), pp. 305 ff.

**566** Laqueur, Walter. "Reagan and the Russians." *Commentary* 73:1 (1981), pp. 19-26.

**567** Legvold, Robert. "Containment Without Confrontation." *Foreign Policy*, No. 40 (1980), pp. 74-98.

**568** Marantz, Paul. "Changing Soviet Conceptions of East-West Relations." *Current History* 81 (Oct. 1982), pp. 331 ff.

**569** Talbot, Strobe. "Communism: The Specter and the Struggle." *Time* 119 (Jan. 4, 1982), pp. 38-50.

**570** U.S. Congress. House. *East-West Relations in the Aftermath of the Soviet Invasion of Afghanistan.* Hearings before the Committee on Foreign Affairs. Washington, D.C.: G.P.O., 1980.

**571** U.S. International Communications Agency. Office of Research. *Soviet Perceptions of the U.S.: Results of a Surrogate Interview Project.* Washington, D.C.: USICA, 1980.

*China and Japan*

**572** Abidi, A.H.H. *China, Iran, and the Persian Gulf.* Atlantic Highlands, N.J.: Humanities, 1982.

573 Behbehani, Hashim. *China's Foreign Policy in the Arab World, 1955-1975: Three Case Studies.* London: Kegan Paul, 1981.

574 Curtis, Gerald L. "Japanese Security Policies and the United States." *Foreign Affairs* 59:3 (1981) pp. 852-74.

575 Gordon, Bernard. "Asian Angst." *Foreign Policy*, No. 47 (1982), pp. 46-65.

576 "Gulf States Stepping up the Chinese Connection." *Arabia: Islamic World Review*, No. 22 (1983), pp. 48-49.

577 Harris, Lillian C. "China's Islamic Connection." *Asian Affairs: An American Review* 8:5 (1981), pp. 291-303.

578 Maxwell, Neville. *India's China War.* Garden City, N.Y.: Doubleday, 1972.

579 Segal, Gerald. "China and Afghanistan." *Asian Survey* 21:11 (1981), pp. 1158-74.

580 Sherwani, Latif Ahmad. *Pakistan, China and America.* Karachi: Council for Pakistan Studies, 1980.

581 Shichor, Yitzhak. *The Middle East in China's Foreign Policy 1949-1977.* New York: Cambridge University Press, 1979.

582 Stoessel, Walter J., Jr. *Developing Lasting U.S. - China Relations.* Current Policy No. 398. Washington, D.C.: Department of State, June 1, 1982.

583 Vertzberger, Yaacov. "Afghanistan in China's Policy." *Problems of Communism* 31:3 (1982), pp. 1-23.

584 _____ "India's Border Conflict with China: A Perceptual Analysis." *Journal of Contemporary History* 17:4 (1982), pp. 607-31.

585 _____ "The Political Economy of Sino-Pakistani Relations: Trade and Aid, 1963-1982." *Asian Survey* 23:5 (1983), pp. 637-52.

586 White, Tyrene. "U.S. Military Sales and Technology Transfers to China: The Policy Implications." *Mershon Center Quarterly Report* 6:3 (1981), pp. 1-8.

587 Yoshitsu, Michael M. "Iran and Afghanistan in Japanese Perspective." *Asian Survey* 21:5 (1981), pp. 501-15.

NUCLEAR PROLIFERATION (see also various countries)

588 Cronin, Richard P. "Prospects for Nuclear Proliferation in South Asia." *Middle East Journal* 37:4 (1983), pp. 594-616.

**589** Pajak, Roger F. *Nuclear Proliferation in the Middle East: Implications for the Superpowers.* National Security Affairs Monograph Series No. 82-1. Washington, D.C.: National Defense University Press, 1982.

**590** Power, Paul F. "Preventing Nuclear Conflict in the Middle East: The Free Zone Strategy." *Middle East Journal* 37:4 (1983), pp. 617-635.

**591** Quester, George H. "Nuclear Weapons and Israel." *Middle East Journal* 37:4 (1983), pp. 547-564.

**592** Smith, Gerard, and Rathjens, George. "Reassessing Nuclear Nonproliferation Policy." *Foreign Affairs* 59:4 (1981), pp. 875-94.

**593** Snyder, Jed C. "The Road to Osiraq: Baghdad's Quest for the Bomb." *Middle East Journal* 37:4 (1983), pp. 565-593.

**594** U.S. Congress. House. *Nuclear Proliferation: Dealing with Problem Countries.* Hearings before the Committee on Foreign Affairs. Washington, D.C.: G.P.O., 1981.

**595** U.S. Congress. Senate. *Analysis of Six Issues about Nuclear Capabilities of India, Iraq, Libya, and Pakistan.* Prepared for the Committe on Foreign Relations by the Congressional Research Service. Washington, D.C.: G.P.O., 1982.

**596** _____. *The Israeli Air Strike.* Hearings before the Committee on Foreign Relations. Washington, D.C.: G.P.O., 1981.

**597** Waltz, Kenneth N. "The Spread of Nuclear Weapons: More May be Better." *Adelphi Papers,* No. 171. London: International Institute for Strategic Studies, 1981.

**598** Yager, Joseph A., ed. *Nonproliferation and U.S. Foreign Policy.* Washington, D.C.: Brookings Institution, 1980.

## MILITARY ISSUES

*General*

**599** *Congressional Quarterly Weekly Report.* Washington, D.C.: Congressional Quarterly, 1943-.

**600** Congressional Quarterly, Inc. *The Middle East,* 5th ed., Washington, D.C.: Congressional Quarterly, 1981.

**601** _____. *U.S. Defense Policy: Weapons, Strategy and Commitments,* Second ed. Washington, D.C.: Congressional Quarterly, 1980.

*The Military Balance and Arms Transfers*

The Military Balance.

**602** *The Balance of Military Power: An Illustrated Assessment Comparing the Weapons and Capabilities of NATO and the Warsaw Pact.* Miller, D.M.O., et al. New York: St, Martin's, 1981.

**603** *Challenges for U.S. National Security, Assessing the Balance: Defense Spending and Conventional Forces, A Preliminary Report, Part II.* Washington, D.C.: Carnegie Endowment for International Peace, 1981.

**604** Collins, John. *U.S.-Soviet Military Balance: Concepts and Capabilities, 1960-1980.* New York: McGraw-Hill, 1980.

**605** Collins, John, and Severns, Elizabeth Ann. *U.S.-Soviet Military Balance—Book VI, Far East and Middle East Assessments.* Washington, D.C.: Congressional Research Service, July 1980.

**606** Cordesman, Anthony. "The Changing Military Balance in the Gulf and Middle East." *Armed Forces Journal International* 119:1 (1981), pp. 52-60.

**607** _____. *Jordanian Arms and the Middle East Balance.* Washington, D.C.: Middle East Institute, 1983.

**608** Cottrell, Alvin J. *Soviet-U.S. Naval Competition in the Indian Ocean, 1968-1980.* Occasional Paper No. 1980/5, Center for International Security Studies.   Pittsburg: University of Pittsburgh, July 1980.

**609** McNaugher, Thomas. *Balancing Soviet Power in the Gulf.* Working Paper. Washington, D.C.: Brookings Institution, 1982.

**610** Mansur, Abdul Kasim (Anthony Cordesman). "The Military Balance in the Persian Gulf: Who Will Guard the Gulf States from the Guardians?" *Armed Forces Journal International* 118:3 (1980), pp. 44-86.

**611** *The Military Balance 1981-1982.* London: International Institute for Strategic Studies, Sept. 1981.

**612** *The Military Balance 1982-1983.* London: International Institute for Strategic Studies, Autumn 1982.

**613** Thompson, W. Scott. "The Persian Gulf and the Correlation of Forces." *International Security* 7:1 (1982), pp. 155-80.

**614** U.S. Congress. House. *Means of Measuring Naval Power with Special Reference to U.S. and Soviet Activities in the Indian Ocean.* Prepared for the Committee on Foreign Affairs by the Congressional Research Service. Washington, D.C.: G.P.O., 1974.

**615** Watson, Bruce. *Red Navy at Sea: Soviet Naval Operations on the High Seas, 1956-1980.* Boulder, Col.: Westview, 1982.

Arms Transfers

**616** "The Arms Race in the Middle East." *MERIP Reports* 13:2 (1983). Entire issue.

**617** *Arms Sales to Saudi Arabia: AWACS and the F-15 Enhancements.* Issue Brief No. IB81078. Washington, D.C.: Congressional Research Service, Library of Congress, last update April 1, 1982.

**618** *Arms Sales: A Useful Foreign Policy Tool?* Washington, D.C.: American Enterprise Institute, 1982.

**619** "The AWACS Debate." *Survival* 24:1 (1982), pp. 37-42.

**620** Cooper, Bert H. "The F-15 Eagle: Description of Performance and Mission Capabilities." Washington, D.C.: Congressional Research Service, May 21, 1981.

**621** Cordesman, Anthony. "Defense Burden Sharing: A Brief Scorecard on our Major Allies (and ourselves)." *Armed Forces Journal International* 120:2 (1982), pp. 64 ff.

**622** Glassman, Jon D. *Arms for the Arabs: The Soviet Union and War in the Middle East.* Baltimore, Md.: Johns Hopkins University Press, 1975.

**623** Hurewitz, Jacob C. *Middle East Politics: The Military Dimension.* New York: Praeger, 1979.

**624** Jabber, Fuad. *Not by War Alone: Security and Arms Control in the Middle East.* Berkeley: University of California Press, 1980.

**625** Pierre, Andrew J. "Arms Sales: The New Diplomacy." *Foreign Affairs* 60:2 (1981/82), pp. 266-86.

**626** _____. *The Global Politics of Arms Sales.* Princeton, N.J.: Princeton University Press, 1982.

**627** Sampson, Anthony. *The Arms Bazaar: From Lockheed to Lebanon.* New York: Viking, 1977.

**628** "Senate Supports Reagan on AWACS Sale." *Congressional Quarterly Weekly Report* 39 (Oct. 31, 1981), pp. 2095-2100.

**629** Sivard, Ruth Leger. *World Military and Social Expenditures 1981.* Leesburg, Va.: World Priorities, 1981.

**630** Thomas, C. Darald. "Weapons Capabilities, Arms Transfers and Defense Policies in the Middle East." *Middle East Journal* 37:2 (1983), pp. 255-260.

**631** U.S. Arms Control and Disarmament Agency. *World Military Expenditures and Arms Transfers, 1970-1979.* Washington, D.C.: U.S. Arms Control & Disarmament Agency, 1982.

**632** U.S. Congress. Senate. *Arms Sales Package to Saudi Arabia.* Hearings before the Committee on Foreign Relations. Washington, D.C.: G.P.O., 1981.

**633** _____. *Military and Technical Implications of the Proposed Sale of Air Defense Enhancements to Saudi Arabia.* Report of the Hearings, Committee on Armed Services. Washington, D.C.: G.P.O., 1981.

**634** _____. *The Proposed AWACS/F-15 Enhancement Sale to Saudi Arabia.* A Staff Report for the Committee on Foreign Relations. Washington, D.C.: G.P.O., 1981.

**635** U.S. Department of Defense. Security Assistance Agency. *Foreign Military Sales, Foreign Military Construction Sales and Military Assistance Facts as of September 1982.* Washington, D.C.: Data Management Division, Comptroller, Defense Security Assistance Agency, 1983.

**636** U.S. Department of State. *Conventional Arms Transfers in the Third World, 1972-1981.* Washington, D.C.: U.S. Department of State, August 1982.

**637** _____. Bureau of Public Affairs. *Security and Economic Assistance for FY 1984.* Current Policy No. 454 (Secretary of State George Shultz). Washington, D.C.: U.S. Department of State, February 16, 1983.

**638** Wrenn, Harry L. *The Airborne Warning and Control System (AWACS): A Brief Description.* Washington, D.C.: Congressional Research Service, Library of Congress, May 7, 1981.

**639** _____. *The Sidewinder AIM-9L: A Brief Discussion.* Washington, D.C.: Congressional Research Service, Library of Congress, June 3, 1981.

*The Rapid Deployment Force*

**640** Bates, E. Asa. "The Rapid Deployment Force — Fact or Fiction?" *Royal United Services Institute Journal for Defense Studies* 126 (June 1981), pp. 23-33.

**641** Bowden, James A. "The RDJTF and Doctrine." *Military Review* 62:11 (1982), pp. 50-64.

**642** Cittadino, John, and McLesky, Frank. "C$^3$ for the Rapid Deployment Joint Task Force (RDJTF)." *Signal* 36 (Sept. 1981), pp. 31-34.

**643** Collins, John. "Rapid Deployment Forces: Fact Versus Fantasy." *Marine Corps Gazette* 65:2 (1981), pp. 68-69.

**644** *A Discussion of the Rapid Deployment Force with Lieutenant General P.X. Kelley.* AEI Special Analyses. Washington, D.C.: American Enterprise Institute, 1980.

**645** Fabyanic, Thomas A. "Conceptual Planning and the Rapid Deployment Joint Task Force." *Armed Forces & Society* 7 (Spring 1981), pp. 343-65.

**646** *Fact Sheet.* Public Affairs Office, HQ, Rapid Deployment Joint Task Force. Washington, D.C.: RDJTF, revised Nov. 1981, and Aug. 1982.

**647** Grace, J. "Land the Landing Force Where it will do the Most Good: A New Look at an Old Mission." *U.S. Naval Institute Proceedings* 107:5 (1981), pp. 114-31.

**648** Hanks, Robert. "Rapid Deployment in Perspective." *Strategic Review* 9:2 (1981), pp. 17-23.

**649** Hieb, Ross J. "MPS—A Concept of Deployment, Not Employment." *Marine Corps Gazette* 67:8 (1983), pp. 47-56.

**650** Jampoler, Andrew. "America's Vital Interests: Is the New Rapid Deployment Force old Wine in a new Bottle?" *U.S. Naval Institute Proceedings* 107:1 (1981), pp. 29-34.

**651** Johnson, Maxwell. *The Military as an Instrument of U.S. Policy in Southwest Asia: The Rapid Deployment Joint Task Force, 1979-1982.* Boulder, Col.: Westview, 1983.

**652** Johnson, Thomas, and Barret, Raymond. "The Rapid Deployment Joint Task Force." *U.S. Naval Institute Proceedings* 106:11 (1980), pp. 95-98.

**653** Kelley, P.X. "Progress in the RDJTF." *Marine Corps Gazette* 65:6 (1981), pp. 38-44.

**654** \_\_\_\_\_. "Rapid Deployment: A Vital Trump." *Parameters* 11:1 (1981), pp. 50-53.

**655** Kramer, Ken. *The Rapid Deployment Force: Facts, Issues and Questions.* Washington, D.C.: Defense Task Force, March 21, 1980.

**656** Krulak, Victor H. "The Rapid Deployment Force: Criteria and Imperatives." *Strategic Review* 8:2 (1980), pp. 39-44.

**657** Mans, Rowley. "Light Armor in the Rapid Deployment Force." *Armed Forces Journal International* 118:11 (1981), pp. 49-53.

**658** Paine, Christopher. "On the Beach: The Rapid Deployment Force and the Nuclear Arms Race." *MERIP Reports,* No. 111 (1983), pp. 3-11, 30.

**659** "Rapid Deployment Force: Will Europe Help America Help Europe?" *Economist* 285 (December 11-17, 1982), pp. 62-64.

**660** Record, Jeffrey. *The Rapid Deployment Force and U.S. Military Intervention in the Persian Gulf.* Cambridge, Mass.: Institute for Foreign Policy Analysis, 1981.

**661** _____. "The RDF: Is the Pentagon Kidding?" *Washington Quarterly* 4:3 (1981), pp. 41-51.

**662** Toch, Thomas. "Rapid Deployment: A Questionable Trump." *Parameters* 10:3 (1980), pp. 89-91.

**663** U.S. Congress. House. *Military Readiness and the Rapid Deployment Joint Task Force (RDJTF).* Hearings before the Committee on the Budget, 96th Congress, Second Session. Washington, D.C.: G.P.O., 1980.

**664** U.S. Congressional Budget Office. *Rapid Deployment Forces: Policy and Budgetary Implications.* Prepared by John D. Mayer, Jr., for the Senate Committee on Armed Services Subcommittee on Sea Power and Force Projection and the Joint Economic Committee. Washington, D.C.: Congressional Budget Office, Feb. 1983.

**665** Waltz, Kenneth. "A Strategy for the Rapid Deployment Force." *International Security* 5:4 (1981), pp. 49-73.

**666** Wright, Michael. "The Marine Corps Faces the Future." *New York Times Magazine,* June 20, 1982.

Facilities and Access

**667** Kline, Hibberd. "Diego Garcia and the Need for a Continuous American Presence in the Indian Ocean." *Marine Corps Gazette* 59:4 (1975), pp. 29-34.

**668** Moorer, Thomas. "The Search for U.S. Bases in the Indian Ocean: A Last Chance." *Strategic Review* 8:2 (1980), pp. 30-38.

**669** Sowell, Lewis S. *Base Development and the Rapid Deployment Force: A Window to the Future.* National Security Affairs Monograph Series 82-5. Washington, D.C.: National Defense University Press, 1982.

**670** U.S. Congress. House. *Diego Garcia 1975: The Debate over the Base and the Island's Former Inhabitants.* Hearings before the Committee on International Relations. Washington, D.C.: G.P.O., 1975.

**671** _____. *Military Construction Appropriations for 1982, Part 5.* Hearings before a subcommittee of the Committee on Appropriations. Washington, D.C.: G.P.O., 1981.

**672** U.S. Congress. Senate. *United States Foreign Policy Objectives and Overseas Military Installations.* Prepared for the Committee on Foreign Relations by the Congressional Research Service. Washington, D.C.: G.P.O., 1979.

**673** U.S. Congressional Budget Office. *The Marine Corps in the 1980's: Prestocking Proposals, the Rapid Deployment Force and Other Issues.* Washington, D.C.: Congressional Budget Office, May 1980.

**674** _____. *The U.S.-Moroccan Agreement and its Implications for U.S. Rapid Deployment Forces.* Washington, D.C.: Congressional Budget Office, March 1983.

**675** Wooten, James P. *Regional Support Facilities for the Rapid Deployment Force.* Report No. 82-53F. Washington, D.C.: Congressional Research Service, Library of Congress, March 25, 1982.

**676** Zakheim, Dov. "Of Allies and Access." *Washington Quarterly* 4:1 (1981), pp. 87-96.

Sealift and Related Naval Issues

**677** Amoss, W.J. "Sealift and the Reality of American Power." *Sea Power* 24 (March 1981), pp. 70 ff.

**678** Beakey, Dan. *Logistics over the Shore: Do We Need It?* National Security Affairs Monograph Series 82-6. Washington, D.C.: National Defense University Press, 1982.

**679** Kyle, Deborah. "Sealift." *Armed Forces Journal International* 119:11 (1982), pp. 57-60.

**680** Pianka, Thomas. "A U.S. Perspective on Lines of Communication, Straits, and National Security in the Persian Gulf and Indian Ocean." In Enver Koury and Emile Nakhleh, eds., *The Arabian Peninsula, Red Sea and Gulf: Strategic Considerations,* pp. 54-79. Hyattsville, MD.: Institute of Middle Eastern and North African Affairs, 1979.

**690** Quinlan, David. "Naval Forces are Rapid Deployment Forces." *U.S. Naval Institute Proceedings* 107:11 (1981), pp. 32-35.

**691** U.S. Congress. House. *Defense Sealift Capability.* Hearings before the Committee on Merchant Marine and Fisheries. Washington, D.C.: G.P.O., 1980.

**692** U.S. Congress. Senate. *Department of Defense Authorization for Appropriations for Fiscal Year 1982, Part 4: Sea Power and Force Projection.* Washington, D.C.: G.P.O., 1981.

*U.S. Strategy and related Military and Budget Issues*

**693** Abshire, David. "Twenty Years in the Strategic Labyrinth." *Washington Quarterly* 5:1 (1982), pp. 83-105.

**694** Berry, Clifton F. "USAF Doctrine Comes Alive." *Air Force* 66:7 (1983), pp. 34-43.

**695** Campbell, John. "The Middle East: A House of Containment Built on Shifting Sands." *Foreign Affairs* 60:3 (1982), pp. 593-628.

**696** Chubin, Shahram. "U.S. Security Interests in the Persian Gulf in the 1980s." *Daedalus* 109:4 (1980), pp. 31-65.

**697** _____. "The Security Factor in U.S. Middle East Policy." *American-Arab Affairs*, No. 5 (1983), pp. 1-9.

**698** Cordesman, Anthony. "After AWACS: Establishing Western Security Throughout Southwest Asia." *Armed Forces Journal International* 119:4 (1981), pp. 64-70.

**699** _____. "The 'Oil Glut' and the Strategic Importance of the Gulf States." *Armed Forces Journal International* 121:3 (1983), pp. 30-47.

**700** _____. "The U.S. Search for Strategic Stability in the Persian Gulf." *Armed Forces Journal International* 119:1 (1981), pp. 61-84.

**701** Etzold, Thomas. "From Far East to Middle East: Overextension in American Strategy since World War II." *U.S. Naval Institute Proceedings* 107:5 (1981), pp. 66-77.

**702** Fitzgerald, Benedict. "A U.S. Strategy for the Middle East." *Parameters* 11:3 (1981), pp. 54-62.

**703** Fukuyama, F. "Nuclear Shadowboxing: Soviet Intervention in the Middle East." *Orbis* 25:3 (1981), pp. 579-605.

**704** Garfinkle, A. "America and Europe in the Middle East: A New Coordination?" *Orbis* 25:3 (1981), pp. 631-648.

**705** Haendel, Dan. "The Persian Gulf: Geopolitics Revisited." *International Security Review* 6:4 (1981), pp. 79-92.

**706** Jampoler, Andrew. "Reviewing the Conventional Wisdom." *U.S. Naval Institute Proceedings* 109:7 (1983), pp. 22-28.

**707** Johnson, Maxwell. "U.S. Strategic Options in the Persian Gulf." *U.S. Naval Institute Proceedings* 107:2 (1981), pp. 53-59.

**708** Kemp, Geoffrey T.H. "Defense Innovation and Geopolitics: From the Persian Gulf to Outer Space." In W. Scott Thompson, ed., *National Security in the 1980s: From Weakness to Strength*, pp. 69-79. San Francisco, Cal.: Institute for Contemporary Studies, 1980.

**709** Khouri, Fred J. "The Challenge to U.S. Security and Middle East Policy." *American-Arab Affairs*, No. 5 (1983), pp. 10-20.

**710** McNaugher, Thomas. "Balancing Soviet Power in the Persian Gulf." *The Brookings Review* 1:4 (1983), pp. 20-24.

**711** Meyer, Edward C. "The JCS—How Much Reform is Needed?" *Armed Forces Journal International* 119:8 (1982), pp. 82-90.

**712** Meo, Leila, ed. *U.S. Strategy in the Gulf: Intervention Against Liberation*. Belmont, Mass.: Association of Arab-American University Graduates, 1981.

**713** Montgomery, Robin N. "The Questionable Strategy for the Middle East." (Part 1) *National Defense* 65 (May-June 1981), pp. 64-68+; (Part 2) *National Defense* 66 (July-August 1981), pp. 34-38.

**714** Nakhleh, Emile. "The Palestine Conflict and US Strategic Interests in the Persian Gulf." *Parameters* 11:1 (1981), pp. 71-78.

**715** Newsom, David. "Miracle or Mirage: Reflections on U.S. Diplomacy and the Arabs." *Middle East Journal* 35:3 (1981), pp. 299-313.

**716** Noyes, James H. *The Clouded Lens: Persian Gulf Security and U.S. Policy*. Stanford, Cal.: Hoover Institution Press, 1979.

**717** Osgood, Robert. "The Revitalization of Containment." *Foreign Affairs* 60:3 (1982), pp. 465-502.

**718** Pipes, Daniel. "Increasing Security in the Persian Gulf." *Orbis* 26:1 (1982), pp. 30-34.

**719** Ramazani, R.K. "Security in the Persian Gulf." *Foreign Affairs* 57:4 (1979), pp. 821-35.

**720** *Rethinking U.S. Security Policy for the 1980s*. Proceedings of the Seventh Annual National Security Affairs Conference, 21-23 July 1980. Washington, D.C.: National Defense University Press, 1980.

**721** Schemmer, Benjamin. "NATO's Challenge in the Persian Gulf and Middle East." *Armed Forces Journal International* 119:3 (1981), pp. 34-35+.

**722** Stivers, William. "Doves, Hawks and Detente." *Foreign Policy*, No. 45 (1981-82), pp. 126-144.

**723** Stojanovic, R. "Geostrategic Interests of the Two Blocs in the Arabian Gulf." *Review of International Affairs* 32:2 (1980), pp. 135-46.

**724** Tahir-Kheli, Shirin, and Staudenmaier, William O. "The Saudi-Pakistani Military Relationship: Implications for U.S. Policy." *Orbis* 26:1 (1982), pp. 155-71.

**725** *The 1980s: Decade of Confrontation?* Proceedings of the Eighth Annual National Security Affairs Conference, 13-15 July 1981. Washington, D.C.: National Defense University Press, 1981.

**726** U.S. Congress. House. *U.S. Security Interests in the Persian Gulf.* Committee on Foreign Affairs. Washington, D.C.: G.P.O., March 16, 1981.

**727** U.S. Congress. Senate. *Persian Gulf Situation.* Hearing before the Committee on Foreign Relations. Washington, D.C.: G.P.O., 1981.

**728** _____. *U.S. Security Interests and Policies in Southwest Asia.* Hearings before the Committee on Foreign Relations. Washington, D.C.: G.P.O., 1980.

**729** U.S. Department of State. Bureau of Public Affairs. *U.S. Security Framework.* Current Policy No. 221 (Under Secretary of State for Security Assistance Matthew Nimetz). Washington, D.C.: G.P.O., Sept. 16, 1980.

**730** Van Cleave, William R. "Strategy and the Navy's 1983-87 Program: Skepticism is Warranted." *Armed Forces Journal International* 119:8 (1982), pp. 49-51.

**731** Vlahos, Michael. "Maritime Strategy Versus Continental Commitment?" *Orbis* 26:3 (1982), pp. 583-89.

**732** Wohlstetter, Albert. "Meeting the Threat at the Persian Gulf." *Survey* 24:2 (1980), pp. 128-88.

**733** Zartman, I. William. "The Power of American Purposes." *Middle East Journal* 35:2 (1981), pp. 163-177.

The Debate over a Continental or Maritime Strategy

**734** Dunn, Keith A., and William O. Staudenmaier. "Strategy for Survival." *Foreign Policy*, No. 52 (1983), pp. 22-42.

**735** Komer, Robert. "Maritime Strategy vs. Coalition Defense." *Foreign Affairs* 60:5 (1982), pp. 1124-44.

**736** _____. "Security Challenges in the '80s." *Armed Forces Journal International* 119:3 (1981), pp. 64 ff.

**737** _____. Letters to the Editor. *Foreign Affairs* 61:2 (1982/83), pp. 453-54, 456.

**738** Lehman, John. Letter to the Editor. *Foreign Affairs* 61:2 (1982/83), pp. 455-456.

**739** Turner, Stansfield, and Thibault, George. "Preparing for the Unexpected: The Need for a New Military Strategy." *Foreign Affairs* 61:1 (1982), pp. 122-35.

**740** _____. Letter to the Editor. *Foreign Affairs* 61:2 (1982/83), pp. 454-55.

**741** West, Francis J. "NATO II: Common Boundaries for Common Interests." *Naval War College Review* 34:1 (1981), pp. 59-67.

Problems of Military Intervention

**742** Collins, John; Mark, Clyde; and Severns, Elizabeth Ann. *Petroleum Imports from the Persian Gulf: Use of U.S. Armed Forces to Ensure Supplies.* Issue Brief No. IB9046. Washington, D.C.: Congressional Research Service, updated Dec. 1981.

**743** Dunn, Keith A. "Soviet Constraints in Southwest Asia: A Military Analysis." *Strategic Issues Research Memorandum,* AC81066, pp. 1-28. Carlisle Barracks, Pa.: Strategic Studies Institute, U.S. Army War College, December 7, 1981.

**744** Hackett, Sir John. "Protecting Oil Supplies: The Military Requirements." In "Third World Conflict and International Security (Part I)," *Adelphi Papers,* No. 166, pp. 41-51. London: International Institute for Strategic Studies, 1980.

**745** Ignotus, Miles [Edward Luttwak]. "Seizing Arab Oil." *Harper's* 250 (March 1975), pp. 45-62.

**746** Lawrence, Robert G. "Arab Perspectives of U.S. Security Policy in Southwest Asia." *American-Arab Affairs,* No. 5 (1983), pp. 27-38.

**747** Tucker, Robert. "American Power and the Persian Gulf." *Commentary* 70:5 (1980), pp. 25-41.

**748** _____ "Oil and American Power—Six Years Later." *Commentary* 68:3 (1979), pp. 35-42.

**749** \_\_\_\_\_. "Oil and American Power—Three Years Later." *Commentary* 63:1 (1977), pp. 29-36.

**750** \_\_\_\_\_. "Oil: The Issue of American Intervention." *Commentary* 59:1 (1975), pp. 21-31.

**751** \_\_\_\_\_ "Further Reflections on Oil and Force." *Commentary* 59:3 (1975), pp. 45-56.

**752** U.S. Congress. House. *Oil Fields as Military Objectives: A Feasibility Study.* Prepared for the Committee on International Relations by the Congressional Research Service. Washington, D.C.: G.P.O., 1975.

The Eilts-Kelly Debate

**753** Eilts, Hermann. "A Rejoinder to J.B. Kelly." *International Security* 5:4 (1981), pp. 195-203.

**754** \_\_\_\_\_. "Security Considerations in the Persian Gulf." *International Security* 5:2 (1980), pp. 79-113.

**755** Kelly, J.B. *Arabia, the Gulf and the West: A Critical View of the Arabs and their Oil Policy.* New York: Basic Books, 1980.

**756** \_\_\_\_\_. "A Response to Hermann Eilts' 'Security Considerations in the Persian Gulf'." *International Security* 5:4 (1981), pp. 186-195.

**757** Mansur, Abdul Kasim   [Anthony Cordesman]. "The American Threat to Saudi Arabia." *Armed Forces Journal International* 118:1 (1980), pp. 47-60.

**758** Tucker, Robert. "Appeasement & the AWACS." *Commentary* 72:6 (1981), pp. 25-30.

**759** \_\_\_\_\_. "The Middle East: Carterism Without Carter?" *Commentary* 72:3 (1981), pp. 27-36.

Strategic Choke Points and Related Naval Issues (see also Indian Ocean Issues under India)

**760** Dowdy, William L., and Trood, Russel. "The Indian Ocean: An Emerging Geostrategic Region." *International Journal* 38:3 (1983), pp. 432-458.

**761** Hanks, Robert. *The Unnoticed Challenge: Soviet Maritime Strategy and the Global Choke Points.* Cambridge, Mass.: Institute for Policy Analysis, 1980.

**762** Hessman, James D. "Sea Power and the Central Front." *Air Force* 66:7 (1983), pp. 52-58.

763 Johnson, Thomas, and Barret, Raymond. "Mining the Strait of Hormuz." *U.S. Naval Institute Proceedings* 107:12 (1981), pp. 83-85.

764 Jordan, Kevin. "Naval Diplomacy in the Persian Gulf." *U.S. Naval Institute Proceedings* 107:11 (1981), pp. 26-31.

765 Khoury, Enver M. *The Arabian Peninsula, Red Sea, and Gulf: Strategic Considerations.* Hyattsville, Md.: Institute of Middle Eastern & North African Affairs, 1979.

766 Kyle, Deborah. "Mine Warfare." *Armed Forces Journal International* 119:8 (1982), pp. 70-72.

767 Lapidoth-Eschelbacher, Ruth. *The Red Sea and the Gulf of Aden.* The Hague: M. Nijhoff, 1982.

768 Leifer, Michael. "The Security of Sea-lanes in South-East Asia." *Survival* 25:1 (1983), pp. 16-24.

769 O'Keefe, James, and Hallenbeck, David. "Protecting the Carrier Against Torpedo Attack." *Naval War College Review* 35:1 (1982), pp. 50-53.

770 Rais, Russel B. "An Appraisal of U.S. Strategy in the Indian Ocean." *Asian Survey* 23:9 (1983), pp. 1043-51.

771 Ramazani, Rouhollah. *The Persian Gulf and the Strait of Hormuz.* Alphen aan den Rijn, The Netherlands: Sijthoff & Noordhoff, 1979.

772 Roberts, S. "Western European and NATO Navies." *U.S. Naval Institute Proceedings* 107:3 (1981), pp. 28-34.

773 U.S. Department of the Navy. *Soviet Naval Deployments,* 2nd. ed. Annapolis, Md.: Nautical and Aviation, 1981.

774 Vertzberger, Yaacov. "The Malacca-Singapore Straits: The Suez of South-East Asia." *Conflict Studies,* No. 140. London: International Institute for Strategic Studies, 1982.

775 Walsh, Thomas L. "Bab-el-Mandab: The Gateway of Tears for the U.S.?" *Armed Forces Journal International* 118:1 (1980), pp. 74-76.

776 Westwood, James T. "The Soviet Union and the Southern Sea Route." *Naval War College Review* 35:1 (1982), pp. 54-67.

777 Wildemann, L. "Naval Presence and Strategy in the Inner Crescent." *Journal of South Asia and Middle East Studies* 3:3 (1980), pp. 15-32.

778 Wise, J. "Access to the Indian Ocean." *Military Review* 60:11 (1980), pp. 63-71.

779 Zakheim, Dov. "Towards a Western Approach to the Indian Ocean." *Survival* 22:1 (1980), pp. 7-14.

Airpower

780 Alford, Jonathan. "Strategic Developments in the Indian Ocean Area." *Asian Affairs* 12:2 (1981), pp. 141-149.

781 Allard, Kenneth. "Soviet Airborne Forces and Preemptive Power Projection." *Parameters* 10:4 (1980), pp. 42-51.

782 Milton, T.R. "Tactical Air Power in the Gulf." *Islamic Defense Review* 6:2 (1981), pp. 15-17.

783 Schemmer, Benjamin. "Budget Cutters are Only Ones Likely to Win Battle over C-5B/747F/C-17 Airlift Alternatives." *Armed Forces Journal International* 119:11 (1982), pp. 38-44.

784 Vajs, Kristin M. "AWACS: Airborne Warning and Control System." Washington, D.C.: Congressional Research Service, Library of Congress, June 12, 1981.

Related Budget Issues

785 Abellera, James, *et al. The FY 1982-1986 Defense Program: Issues and Trends. AEI Foreign Policy and Defense Review*, Vol. 3, Nos. 4 and 5, Washington, D.C., 1981. Entire issue.

786 Congressional Research Service. *The Persian Gulf: Are We Committed? At What Cost?—A Dialogue with the Reagan Administration.* Prepared for the Use of the Joint Economic Committee, 97th Congress. Washington, D.C.: Congressional Research Service, Library of Congress, October 1981.

787 Etzold, T. "From Far East to Middle East: Overextension in American Strategy since World War II." *U.S. Naval Institute Proceedings* 107:5 (1981), pp. 66-77.

788 Stone, Norman. "An Indian Ocean Fleet — The Case and the Cost." *U.S. Naval Institute Proceedings* 107:7 (1981), pp. 54-57.

789 U.S. Congress. House. *Department of Defense Appropriations for 1982, Part 4.* Hearings before a subcommittee of the Committee on Appropriations. Washington, D.C.: G.P.O., 1981.

790 _____. *Department of Defense Authorization Act, 1982.* Report to the Committee on Armed Services. Washington, D.C.: G.P.O., 1981.

**791** _____. *Report of Secretary of Defense Caspar Weinberger to the Congress on the FY 1983 Budget, FY 1984 Authorization Request and FY 1983-1987 Defense Programs.* Washington, D.C.: G.P.O., Feb. 8, 1982.

**792** _____. *Report of Secretary of Defense Caspar Weinberger to the Congress on the FY 1984 Budget, FY 1985 Authorization Request and FY 1984-1988 Defense Programs.* Washington, D.C.: G.P.O., Feb. 1, 1983.

ECONOMIC ISSUES

*Energy and Oil*

The Politics and Geopolitics of Oil

**793** Blair, John M. *The Control of Oil.* New York: Pantheon, 1976.

**794** Brown, William R. "The Oil Weapon." *Middle East Journal* 36:3 (1982), pp. 301-18.

**795** Deese, D. "Oil, War and Grand Strategy." *Orbis* 25:3 (1981), pp. 525-55.

**796** Pfaltzgraff, Robert L., Jr. *Energy Issues and Alliance Relationships: The United States, Western Europe and Japan.* Cambridge, Mass.: Institute for Foreign Policy Analysis, 1980.

**797** Schneider, Steven. *The Oil Price Revolution.* Baltimore, Md.: Johns Hopkins University Press, 1983.

**798** Shwadran, Benjamin. *The Middle East, Oil, and the Great Powers.* 3rd ed. New York: Wiley, 1973.

**799** U.S. Congress. House. *The Middle East and Europe: Energy, Autonomy, and Development.* Report of a Congressional Study Mission submitted to the Committee on Foreign Affairs. Washington, D.C.: G.P.O., 1982.

**800** U.S. Congress. Senate. *Geopolitics of Oil.* Hearings before the Committee on Energy and Natural Resources. Washington, D.C.: G.P.O., 1980.

**801** _____. *The Geopolitics of Oil.* Staff Report for the Committee on Energy and Natural Resources. Washington, D.C.: G.P.O., 1980.

**802** U.S. Congress. Senate and House. *Economic Consequences of the Revolution in Iran.* A Compendium of Papers submitted to the Joint Economic Committee. Washington, D.C.: G.P.O., 1980.

## U.S. Energy Policy

**803** "Energy and National Security Comments." Energy and National Security Project. Columbus, Ohio: Ohio State University, Spring 1980.

**804** *Energy Policy.* Washington, D.C.: Congressional Quarterly, April 1979.

**805** Goldstein, Donald. *Energy and National Security: Proceedings of a Special Conference.* Washington, D.C.: National Defense University, 1981.

**806** Levy, Walter J. "The Years that the Locust Hath Eaten: Oil Policy and OPEC Development Prospects." *Foreign Affairs* 57:2 (1978/79), pp. 287-305.

**807** _____. *Oil Strategy and Politics.* Melvin A. Conant, ed. Boulder, Col.: Westview, 1982.

**808** *The Middle East: U.S. Policy, Israel, Oil and the Arabs,* 5th ed. Washington, D.C.: Congressional Quarterly, 1981.

**809** Nau, Henry R. "Securing Energy." *Washington Quarterly* 4:3 (1981), pp. 107-21.

**810** Nye, Joseph S., Jr. "Energy Nightmares." *Foreign Policy,* No. 40 (1980), pp. 74-98.

**811** _____. "We Tried Harder (And Did More)." *Foreign Policy,* No. 36 (1979), pp. 101-04.

**812** Parker, Larry, et al. *Energy and the 97th Congress: Overview.* Issue Brief No. IB81112. Washington, D.C.: Congressional Research Service, Library of Congress, last updated, March 9, 1982.

**813** _____. *The President's Energy Program: Changing the Federal Role in Energy Policy.* Washington, D.C.: Congressional Research Service, Library of Congress, April 16, 1981.

**814** _____. *The Unfolding of the Reagan Energy Program: The First Year.* Report No. 81-266ENR. Washington, D.C.: Congressional Research Service, Dec. 17, 1981.

**815** Rosenbaum, Walter A. *Energy, Politics and Public Policy.* Washington, D.C.: Congressional Quarterly Press, 1981.

**816** Stobaugh, Robert, and Yergin, Daniel. "After the Second Shock: Pragmatic Energy Strategies." *Foreign Affairs* 57:4 (1979), pp. 836-71.

**817** _____. "Energy: An Emergency Telescoped." *Foreign Affairs* 58:3 (1980), pp. 563-95.

**818** _____. *Energy Future: Report of the Energy Project at the Harvard Business School.* New York: Random House, 1979.

**819** Teller, Edward. "Conflict in the Middle East: Time for an American Energy Contingency Plan." *Parameters* 10:4 (1980), pp. 16-19.

**820** U.S. Department of Energy. *Securing America's Energy Future: The National Energy Plan.* Washington, D.C.: G.P.O., July 1981.

**821** U.S. Library of Congress. Congressional Research Service. *Energy Policy: Selected References, 1979-1981.* Washington, D.C.: Congressional Research Service, Library of Congress, 1981.

**822** Yergin, Daniel. "Awaiting the Next Oil Crisis." *New York Times Magazine,* July 11, 1982.

(Future estimates)

**823** Campbell, Robert. "Dwindling Energy." *Washington Quarterly* 3:2 (1980), pp. 58-66.

**824** Randol, William, et al. *Rethinking World Oil Supply/Demand: A Testing Time for OPEC.* New York: Salomon Brothers, Sept. 1980.

**825** U.S. Central Intelligence Agency. National Foreign Assessment Center. *The World Oil Market in the Years Ahead: A Research Paper.* Washington, D.C.: National Foreign Assessment Center, Central Intelligence Agency, 1979.

**826** _____. *Prospects for Soviet Oil Production.* CIA Energy Report 77-10270. Washington, D.C.: Central Intelligency Agency, April 1977.

**827** U.S. Congress. Office of Technology Assessment. *Technology & Soviet Energy Availability: A Summary.* Washington, D.C.: G.P.O., Nov. 1981.

(The Strategic Petroleum Reserve)

**828** Davis, Ruth. "National Strategic Petroleum Reserve." *Science* 213 (Aug. 7, 1981), pp. 618-22.

**829** Krapels, Edward N. *Oil Crisis Management; Strategic Stockpiling for International Security.* Baltimore, Md.: Johns Hopkins University Press, 1980.

**830** U.S. Congress. House. *An Evaluation of the Strategic Petroleum Reserve.* Report prepared for the Committee on Interstate and Foreign Commerce by the Congressional Budget Office. Washington, D.C.: G.P.O., 1980.

**831** _____. *Strategic Petroleum Reserve: Oil Supply and Construct Problems.* Hearings before the Committee on Interstate and Foreign Commerce. Washington, D.C.: G.P.O., 1980.

**832** U.S. Congress. Senate. *Strategic Petroleum Reserve Amendments Act of 1981.* Report of the Committee on Energy and Natural Resources. Washington, D.C.: G.P.O., 1981.

**833** _____. *Strategic Petroleum Reserve Program.* Hearings before the Committee on Energy and Natural Resources. Washington, D.C.: G.P.O., 1981.

**834** U.S. Department of Energy. *Strategic Petroleum Reserve Annual Report.* 1979, 1980, 1981, 1982. Washington, D.C.: U.S. Department of Energy, 1979-1982.

**835** U.S. Federal Energy Administration. *Strategic Petroleum Reserve Plan.* Washington, D.C.: G.P.O., 1976.

**836** _____. *The Strategic Petroleum Reserve: Selected References, 1978-1981.* Washington, D.C.: G.P.O., July 6, 1981.

(U.S.-Soviet Energy Issues & the Yamal [Gas] Pipeline)

**837** Blau, Thomas, and Kirchheimer, Joseph. "European Dependence and Soviet Leverage: the Yamal Pipeline." *Survival* 23:5 (1981), pp. 209-14.

**838** Goldman, Marshall. "The Soviet Energy Pipeline." *Current History* 81 (Oct. 1982), pp. 309 ff.

**839** Gustafson, Thane. "Energy and the Soviet Bloc." *International Security* 6:3 (1981/1982), pp. 65-89.

**840** Karr, Miriam, and Robinson, Roger W., Jr. "Soviet Gas: Risk or Reward." *Washington Quarterly* 4:4 (1981), pp. 3-11.

**841** Klinghoffer, A. "U.S. Foreign Policy and the Soviet Energy Predicament." *Orbis* 25:3 (1981), pp. 557-78.

**842** "Soviet Energy Options and United States Interests." *Mershon Center Quarterly Report* 5:4 (1980). Entire report.

**843** U.S. Department of State. *Soviet-West European Natural Gas Pipeline.* Current Policy No. 331. Washington, D.C.: U.S. Department of State, Oct. 14, 1981.

OPEC and the Gulf Oil Economies (See also particular countries under Persian Gulf)

**844** El Mallakh, Ragaei. *The Economic Development of the United Arab Emirates.* New York: St. Martin's, 1981.

**845** \_\_\_\_\_. *OPEC: Twenty Years and Beyond.* Boulder, Col.: Westview, 1982.

**846** \_\_\_\_\_. *Qatar: Development of an Oil Economy.* London: Croom Helm, 1979.

**847** El Mallakh, Ragaei, and El Mallakh, Dorthea, eds. *Saudi Arabia: Energy, Development Planning, and Industrialization.* Lexington, Mass.: Lexington Books, 1982.

**848** al-Sabah, Y.S.F. *The Oil Economy of Kuwait.* London: Kegan Paul, 1980.

**849** Singer, S. Fred. "An End to OPEC? Bet on the Market." *Foreign Policy,* No. 45 (1981-82), pp. 115-121.

**850** \_\_\_\_\_. "Saudi Arabia's Oil Crisis." *Policy Review,* No. 21 (1982), pp. 87-100.

**851** Stamas, Stephen. "An End to OPEC? More is Needed." *Foreign Policy,* No. 45 (1981-82), pp. 121-125.

**852** Stern, Jonathan P. "Gulf Oil Strategy." *Washington Quarterly* 3:2 (1980), pp. 67-72.

**853** Swearingen, Will D. "Sources of Conflict Over Oil in the Persian/Arabian Gulf." *Middle East Journal* 35:2 (1981), pp. 315-30.

**854** Tetreault, Mary Ann. *The Organization of Arab Petroleum Exporting Countries: History, Policies, and Prospects.* Westport, Conn.: Greenwood, 1981.

*Development, Trade, International Finance, and Foreign Aid.*

## Development

**855** Alessa, Shamlan. *The Manpower Problem in Kuwait.* London: Kegan Paul, 1981.

**856** Birks, J.S., and Sinclair, C.A. *Arab Manpower: The Crisis of Development.* New York: St. Martin's, 1980.

**857** Braibanti, Ralph. "New Perspectives of Development: Some Reflections." *Duke University Letters* [Durham, N.C.], No. 32, March 17, 1982.

**858** Khouja, M.W., and Sadler, P.G. *The Economy of Kuwait — Development and Role in International Finance.* London: Macmillan, 1979.

**859** Al-Kuwari, Ali Khalifa. *Oil Revenues in the Gulf Emirates: Patterns of Allocation and Impact on Economic Development.* Boulder, Col.: Westview, 1978.

**860** El Mallakh, Ragaei. *Saudi Arabia: Rush to Development.* Baltimore, Md.: Johns Hopkins University Press, 1982.

**861** El Mallakh, Ragaei, and Atta, Jacob K. *The Absorptive Capacity of Kuwait: Domestic and International Perspectives.* Lexington, Mass.: Lexington Books, 1981.

**862** Niblock, Tim, ed. *Social and Economic Development in the Arab Gulf.* London: Croom Helm, 1980.

**863** Sayigh, Yusif A. *The Economies of the Arab World: Developments since 1945: The Determinants of Arab Economic Development.* London: Croom Helm, 1978.

**864** Turner, Louis, and Bedore, James. *Middle East Industrialization: A Study of Saudi and Iranian Downstream Investments.* New York: Praeger, 1979.

**865** Ziwar-Daftari, May, ed. *Issues and Development: The Arab Gulf States.* London: MD Research and Services, 1980.

Trade

**866** Carswell, Robert. "Economic Sanctions and the Iran Experience." *Foreign Affairs* 60:2 (1981/82), pp. 247-65.

**867** Cooperation Council for the Arab States of the Gulf. *The Unified Economic Agreement.* Riyadh: Bahr Al-Olum Press, n.d.

**868** *Direction of Trade Statistics, Yearbook 1982.* Washington, D.C.: International Monetary Fund, 1982, and monthly publications, 1983.

**869** El Mallakh, Ragaei. *Kuwait: Trade and Investment.* Boulder, Col.: Westview, 1979.

**870** Turck, Nancy. "The Arab Boycott of Israel." *Foreign Affairs* 55:3 (1977), pp. 472-93.

International Finance

**871** Dodell, Sue E. "United States Banks and the Arab Boycott of Israel." *Columbia Journal of International Law* 17:1 (1978), pp. 119-43.

**872** Lissakers, Karin. "Money and Manipulation." *Foreign Policy*, No. 44 (1981), pp. 107-26.

**873** Reed, Stanley. "Sheik Investing: What Arab Billions are Buying in the U.S." *Barron's* 61 (Sept. 13, 1982), pp. 8 ff.

**874** Sampson, Anthony. *The Money Lenders: Bankers and a World in Turmoil.* New York: Viking, 1981.

**875** *World Bank Annual Report 1982.* Washington, D.C.: World Bank, 1982.

**876** *World Development Report 1981.* Washington, D.C.: World Bank, August 1981.

**877** "World Economic Outlook: A Survey by the Staff of the International Monetary Fund." *Occasional Paper 9.* Washington, D.C.: International Monetary Fund, April 1982.

Foreign Aid

**878** Amuzegar, Jahangir. "Oil Wealth: A Very Mixed Blessing." *Foreign Affairs* 60:4 (1982), pp. 814-35.

**879** Nowels, Larry Q. *Foreign Aid: Budget and Policy Issues for FY82.* Issue Brief No. IB81098. Washington, D.C.: Congressional Research Service, last updated April 1, 1982.

**880** Shihata, Ibrahim. *The Other Face of OPEC: Financial Assistance to the Third World.* London: Longman, 1982.

**881** Streit, Peggy. "Straight Answers on Foreign Aid." *Agenda* 3:6 (1980), pp. 22-23.

**882** U.S. Agency for International Development. *Congressional Presentation: Fiscal Year 1983.* Washington, D.C.: G.P.O., 1982.

**883** _____. *Congressional Presentation, Fiscal Year 1983, Annex IV, Near East.* Washington, D.C.: G.P.O., 1982.

U.S. POLICY TOWARD THE PERSIAN GULF (see also THE PERSIAN GULF and U.S. STRATEGY)

**884** Aron, Raymond. "Ideology in Search of Policy." *Foreign Affairs* 60:3 (1982), pp. 503-24.

**885** Binder, Leonard. "U.S. Policy in the Middle East: Exploring New Opportunities." *Current History* 82 (January 1983), pp. 1-4, 37-40.

**886** _____ "U.S. Policy in the Middle East: Toward a Pax Saudiana." *Current History* 81 (January 1982), pp. 1-4, 40-42, 48.

**887** Bradley, C. Paul. *Recent United States Policy in the Persian Gulf (1971-82).* Grantham, N.H.: Thompson & Rutter, 1982.

**888** Campbell, John. "The Middle East: A House of Containment Built on Shifting Sands." *Foreign Affairs* 60:3 (1982), pp. 593-628.

**889** Crabb, Jr., Cecil V. *The Doctrines of American Foreign Policy: Their Meaning, Role, and Future.* Baton Rouge: Louisiana State University Press, 1982.

**890** Hess, Stephen. "The Golden Triangle: The Press at the White House, State, and Defense." *The Brookings Review* 1:4 (1983), pp. 14-19.

**891** Long, David. "The United States and the Persian Gulf." *Current History* 81 (January 1979), pp. 27-30, 37-38.

**892** *The 1980s: Decade of Confrontation?* Proceedings of the Eighth Annual National Security Affairs Conference, 13-15 July 1981. Washington, D.C.: National Defense University Press, 1981.

**893** Ramazani, Rouhollah K. "America and the Gulf — Beyond Peace and Security." *Middle East Insight* 2:2 (1982), pp. 2-9.

*Memoirs and Analyses by Recent Participants*

**894** Brown, Harold D. *Thinking About National Security: Defense and Foreign Policy in a Dangerous World.* Boulder, Colo.: Westview, 1983.

**895** Brzezinski, Zbigniew. *Power and Principle: Memoirs of the National Security Adviser, 1977-1981.* New York: Farrar, Straus, Giroux, 1983.

**896** *Conversations with Harold Saunders: U.S. Policy for the Middle East in the 1980s.* Washington, D.C.: American Enterprise Institute, 1982.

**897** Carter, Jimmy. *Keeping Faith: Memoirs of a President.* New York: Bantam, 1982.

**898** Hoffman, Stanley, and Vance, Cyrus. "Building the Peace: U.S. Foreign Policy for the Next Decade." Washington, D.C.: Center for National Policy, 1982.

**899** Jordan, Hamilton. *Crisis: The Last Years of the Carter Presidency.* London: Michael Joseph, 1982.

**900** Kissinger, Henry. *White House Years.* Boston: Little, Brown, 1979.

**901** _____. *Years of Upheaval.* Boston: Little, Brown, 1982.

**902** Nixon, Richard. *The Memoirs of Richard Nixon.* New York: Grosset & Dunlap, 1978.

**903** Quandt, William B. *Decade of Decisions: American Policy Toward the Arab-Israeli Conflict, 1967-1976.* Berkeley: University of California Press, 1977.

**904** Saunders, Harold H. *The Middle East Problem in the 1980s.* Washington, D.C.: American Enterprise Institute, 1981.

**905** Vance, Cyrus. *Hard Choices: Critical Years in American Foreign Policy.* New York: Simon & Schuster, 1983.

## BIBLIOGRAPHIES AND OTHER AIDS

*Middle East and North Africa*

**906** Atiyeh, George N., comp. *The Contemporary Middle East, 1948-1973: A Selective and Annotated Bibliography.* Boston: G.K. Hall, 1975.

**907** "Bibliography of Periodical Literature." *Middle East Journal.* Washington, D.C.: Middle East Institute, 1947-.

**908** Fatemi, Ali M.S.; Kokoropoulos, Panos; and Amirie, Abbas. *Political Economy of the Middle East: A Computerized Guide to the Literature.* Akron, Ohio: University of Akron, 1970.

**909** Hopwood, Derek, and Grimwood-Jones, Diana, eds. *Middle East and Islam: A Bibliographic Introduction.* Middle East Libraries Committee. Bibliotheca Asiatica, No. 9. Zug, Switzerland: Inter. Documentation, 1972.

**910** Littlefield, D.W. *The Islamic Near East and North Africa: An Annotated Guide to Books in English for Non-Specialists.* Littleton. Col.: Libraries Unlimited, 1977.

**911** Schulz, Ann. *International and Regional Politics in the Middle East and North Africa: A Guide to Information Sources.* Detroit, Michigan: Gale, 1977.

**912** Sweet, Louise E. ed. *The Central Middle East: A Handbook of Anthropology and Published Research on the Nile Valley, the Arab Levant, Southern Mesopotamia, the Arabian Peninsula, and Israel.* New Haven, Conn.: Human Relations Area Files Press, 1971.

**913** U.S. Department of Army. *Middle East: The Strategic Hub: A Bibliographic Survey of the Literature.* Rev. ed. Washington, D.C.: G.P.O., 1978.

The Arab World

**914** Centre d'Etudes pour le Monde Arabe Moderne. *Arab Culture and Society in Change.* Beirut: Universite de St. Joseph, CEMAM Dar el-Mashreq Publishers, 1973.

Israel

**915** Alexander, Yonah. *Israel: Selected, Annotated, and Illustrated Bibliography.* Gilbertsville, N.Y.: Buday, 1968.

## The Arab-Israeli Conflict

**916** "The Arab-Israeli Conflict in Periodical Literature." *Journal of Palestine Studies.* Vol. 1-. Beirut: Institute of Palestine Studies; Kuwait: University of Kuwait, 1971-.

**917** Hussaini, Hatem I. *The Arab-Israeli Conflict: An Annotated Bibliography.* Detroit, Michigan: Association of Arab-American University Graduates, 1975.

**918** Khalidi, Walid, and Khadduri, Jill, eds. *Palestine and the Arab-Israeli Conflict: An Annotated Bibliography.* Beirut: Institute for Palestine Studies, 1974.

## Turkey

**919** Bodurgil, Abraham, comp. *Turkey, Politics and Government: A Bibliography, 1938-1975.* Washington, D.C.: Library of Congress, 1978.

**920** Tamkoc, Metin. *A Bibliography on the Foreign Relations of the Republic of Turkey, 1919-1967: And Brief Biographies of Turkish Statesmen.* Publication 2. Ankara: Middle East Technical University, Faculty of Administrative Sciences, 1968.

## Islam

**921** Gibb, H.A.R., and Kramers, J.H., eds. *Shorter Encyclopaedia of Islam.* Ithaca, N.Y.: Cornell University Press, 1953.

**922** Pearson, J.D., comp. *Index Islamicus, 1906-1955: A Catalogue of Articles on Islamic Subjects in Periodicals and other Collective Publications.* Supplements: I, 1956-60; II, 1961-5; III, 1966-70; IV, 1971-5. London: Mansell, 1958.

**923** *Quarterly Index Islamicus.* London: Mansell, 1977-.

## South Asia

**924** Patterson, Maureen L., in collaboration with William Alspaugh. *South Asian Civilizations: A Bibliographic Synthesis.* Chicago: University of Chicago Press, 1981.

**925** Schwartzberg, Joseph E., ed. *A Historical Atlas of South Asia.* Chicago, Ill.: University of Chicago Press, 1978.

## Other

## Military

**926** *Air University Library Index to Military Periodicals.* Maxwell Air Force Base, Alabama: Air University Library, 1949-.

**927** Albrecht, Ulrich, et al. *A Short Research Guide on Arms and Armed Forces.* New York: Facts on File, 1978, 1980.

Geography

**928** Beaumont, Peter, et al. *The Middle East: A Geographical Study.* New York: Wiley, 1976.

**929** Fisher, William B. *The Middle East: A Physical, Social, and Regional Geography.* 6th ed. London: Methuen, 1971.

Research

**931** Dorr, Steven R. *Scholar's Guide to Washington, D.C. for Middle Eastern Studies.* Washington, D.C.: Smithsonian Institution Press, 1981.

**932** *Mideast File.* Learned Information, Anderson House, Stokes Road, Medford, N.J. 08055.

**933** *Mideast Press Report.* Claremont Research & Publications, 160 Claremont Ave., New York, N.Y. 10027.

**934** Rahim, Enayetu. *Scholar's Guide to Washington, D.C. for South Asian Studies.* Washington, D.C.: Smithsonian Institution Press, 1981.

**935** Simon, Reeva S. *The Modern Middle East: A Guide to Research Tools in the Social Sciences.* Boulder, Col.: Westview, 1978.

# AUTHOR INDEX

Ingrams, Harold, 117
Institute of Palestine Studies, 916
International Institute for
    Strategic Studies, 611-612
International Monetary Fund,
    868, 877
Iseman, Peter, 76, 183
Iskander, Amir, 284
Ismael, Tareq, 265

Jabber, Fuad, 624
Jacobsen, Carl, 565
Jampoler, Andrew, 650, 706
Jansen, Godfrey H., 150
Jawdat, Nameer Ali, 266
Jay, Peter, 34
Jha, S., 414
John, Richard, 75
Johnson, Maxwell O., 308, 651,
    707
Johnson, Thomas, 652, 763
Johnston, Charles, 118
Jones, Rodney, 466
Jordan, Hamilton, 214, 899
Jordan, Kevin, 764

Kamrany, Nake, 405
Karaosmanoglu, Ali L., 353
Karpat, Kemal, 309, 322
Karr, Miriam, 840
Kashkett, Steven, 285
Kaufman, Michael, 479
Keddie, Nikki, 191, 196, 206,
    215, 238, 250
Kelidar, Abbas, 286
Kelley, P.X., 644, 653-654
Kelly, John B., 7-8, 19, 517, 537,
    755-756
Kemp, Geoffrey, 708
Khadduri, Jill, 918
Khadduri, Majid, 35, 275-277
Khalidi, Walid, 918
Khalifa, Ali Muhammad, 67
Khalilzad, Zalmay, 406, 484

Khan, Sultan Muhammed, 439
Khar, Ghulam Mustafa, 440
Khomeini, Rouhollah, 207
Khouja, M.W., 858
Khouri, Fred J., 709
Khoury, Enver M., 765
Khoury, Nabeel A., 184
Khuri, Fuad, 62
Kirchheimer, Joseph, 837
Kissinger, Henry, 900-901
Klass, R.T., 518
Kline, Hibberd, 667
Klinghoffer, A., 841
Komer, Robert, 735-737
Korson, J. Henry, 427
Kraft, Joseph, 428
Kramer, Ken, 655
Kramer, Martin, 136
Kramers, J.H., 922
Krapels, Edward N., 829
Krulak, Victor H., 656
Kumar, Satish, 441, 485
Kuniholm, Bruce, 93, 216, 326,
    334, 519
Kutschera, Chris, 297-298, 374
Al-Kuwari, Ali Khalifa, 859
Kyle, Deborah, 679, 766

Lacey, Robert, 77
Ladeen, Michael, 217-218
Laipson, Ellen, 335, 345
Lamb, David, 287
Landau, Jacob, 358-360
Lapidoth-Eschelbacher, Ruth,
    767
Laqueur, Walter, 566
Lawrence, Bruce, 137
Lawrence, Robert, 746
Legvold, Robert, 567
Lehman, John, 738
Leiden, Carl, 180
Leifer, Michael, 768
Lemnitzer, Lyman L., 327
Lenczowski, George, 520

U.S. Congress. House.
Committee on Foreign Affairs,
50-52, 100-101, 229, 328, 336-
338, 340, 421, 468-470, 507,
570, 594, 614, 726, 799
U.S. Congress. House.
Committee on International
Relations, 339, 495, 670, 752
U.S. Congress. House.
Committee on Interstate and
Foreign Commerce, 830-831
U.S. Congress. House.
Committee on Merchant
Marine and Fisheries, 691
U.S. Congress. Senate.
Committee on Armed
Services, 103, 633, 692
U.S. Congress. Senate.
Committee on Energy and
Natural Resources, 800-801,
832-833
U.S. Congress. Senate.
Committee on Foreign
Relations, 102, 230, 282, 329,
341, 348, 496, 512-513, 595-
596, 632, 634, 672, 727-728
U.S. Congress. Senate.
Committee on the Judiciary,
361
U.S. Congress. Senate and House.
Joint Economic Committee,
802
U.S. Congressional Budget Office,
664, 673-674
U.S. Department of the Army,
913
U.S. Department of Defense,
635, 673-674
U.S. Department of Energy, 820,
834
U.S. Department of the Navy,
563, 773
U.S. Department of State, 53-54,
408-412, 471, 636-637, 729,
843

U.S. Federal Energy
Administration, 835-836
U.S. Foreign Broadcast
Information Service, 242, 271,
362
U.S. International
Communications Agency, 571
U.S. Library of Congress.
Congressional Research
Service, 617, 786, 821
U.S. Office of Technology
Assessment, 827

Vajs, Kristin M., 784
Vali, Ferenc, 324
Vance, Cyrus, 898, 905
Van Cleave, William R., 730
Van Hollen, Christopher, 55, 472-
473
Vasudevan, P., 487
Veremis, Thanos, 349
Vertzberger, Yaacov, 583-585,
774
Vivekanandan, B., 508
Vlahos, Michael, 731
Volkan, Vamik, 306
Voll, John, 128, 188

Wafdar, K., 413
Wall, Patrick, 509
Walsh, Thomas L., 775
Waltz, Kenneth N., 597, 665
Watson, Bruce, 615
Weinbaum, Marvin G., 426, 433
Weir, Andrew, 544
Wenner, Manfred, 125, 155
West, Francis J., 741
Westwood, James T., 776
Whetten, Lawrence, 330
White, Tyrene, 586
Whittier, Charles, 164, 208
Wildemann, L., 777
Wilson, Andrew, 350
Wilson, Arnold, 12
Winstone, H.V.F., 63